IAN FLEMING
AND OPERATION *GOLDEN EYE*

IAN FLEMING AND OPERATION
GOLDEN EYE

Spies, Scoundrels, and Envoys
keeping Spain out of World War II

MARK SIMMONS

CASEMATE
Oxford & Philadelphia

Published in the Great Britain and United States of America in 2018 by
CASEMATE PUBLISHERS
The Old Music Hall, 106–108 Cowley Road, Oxford OX4 1JE, UK
and
1950 Lawrence Road, Havertown, PA 19083, USA

Hardcover Edition: ISBN 978-1-61200-685-7
Digital Edition: ISBN 978-1-61200-686-4

A CIP record for this book is available from the British Library

Printed and bound in the United Kingdom by TJ International

Typeset in India by Versatile PreMedia Services. www.versatilepremedia.com

For a complete list of Casemate titles, please contact:

CASEMATE PUBLISHERS (US)
Telephone (610) 853-9131
Fax (610) 853-9146
Email: casemate@casematepublishers.com
www.casematepublishers.com

CASEMATE PUBLISHERS (UK)
Telephone (01865) 241249
Email: casemate-uk@casematepublishers.co.uk
www.casematepublishers.co.uk

Contents

'Hence to fight and conquer in all your battles is not supreme excellence; supreme excellence consists in breaking the enemy's resistance without fighting. Thus the highest form of generalship is to frustrate the enemy's plans and the next best is to prevent the enemy's alliances ...'
Sun Tzu, Art of War

'If I had a big proposition to handle and could have my pick of helpers I'd plump for the Intelligence Department of the British Admiralty.'
John Buchan, Greenmantle

To the memory of John Gardner 1926–2007, former Royal Marine Commando, writer.

Foreword and Acknowledgements

This book tells the story of Operation *Golden Eye* which I have used also to encompass all the operations and schemes to keep Spain and Portugal out of World War II. It is not a biography of Ian Fleming. John Pearson and Andrew Lycett have both already written admirable biographies – rather it is the story of a wide range of characters from several countries that played their part on the Iberian Peninsula.

In the official British records Operation *Golden Eye* is often used in the two-word form, sometimes one. For clarity I have used the two-word form to denote 'Operation *Golden Eye*' and the single word Goldeneye for Ian Fleming's home on Jamaica. The 1995 James Bond film GoldenEye is named after a satellite in the story.

My interest in the role of Spain in World War II was kindled by a visit to Gibraltar in 1975. Then serving in the Royal Marines Commandos I set foot on the Crown Colony, one of the last 'pink bits', for the first time from the Royal Fleet Auxiliary Landing Ship *Sir Galahad.* Seven years later that ship would be sunk by the Argentine Air Force in San Carlos Waters off the Falkland Islands with great loss of life. In 1975, *Sir Galahad* was part of a large NATO fleet gathering for the exercise *Deep Express*, to show the West's ability to support Turkey against any threat from the Soviet Union.

With several oppos (RM slang for friends) I ventured up to the top of the Rock. Royal Navy ships often run Rock Races, where volunteers run to the summit at 1350ft via the winding roads from the dockyard. On this occasion there was no race so we took the more sedate cable car. The eastern face of the rock at the viewing platform is pretty sheer. Venturing south toward O'Hara's Battery away to the west across Gibraltar Bay is the sprawl of Algeciras. From here you begin to appreciate just how small Gibraltar is with an area of just 2.6 miles. I wondered why Germany had not taken Gibraltar during World War II, especially considering Spain was a Fascist state.

Had the Axis powers taken the Rock in 1940 it would have made the story of World War II vastly different. Would Britain have been able to hold Malta or even the Suez Canal? Even the ultimate defeat of the Axis must be open to question. Further south from O'Hara's Battery was Lord Airey's Battery. I was then ignorant of the story of Operation *Tracer* or that close by, there were six men concealed in the event of invasion. It was all still top secret then.

Around six or seven years before that first visit to Gibraltar I had devoured Ian Fleming's James Bond books reading them one after the other and the first film I saw was *From Russia with Love.* After Sean Connery stopped playing 007 I confess to losing interest.

When I began writing seriously in the 1980s often I would come across Ian Fleming in my research, but this time in his earlier wartime role with naval intelligence. This book covers his involvement with the Iberian Peninsula during World War II. There were two books which inspired me to write about Spain's neutrality. Charles B. Burdick's *Germany's Military Strategy and Spain in World War II,* an old US College library book, opened my eyes to just how committed the Germans had been to planning various invasions of Spain and Portugal. These included Operation *Felix* in 1940, *Isabella-Felix* in 1941, *Ilona* in 1942, and *Gisela* in 1943. There were also variations within them depending on the level of Spanish cooperation. The second book was Craig Cabell's *Ian Fleming's Secret War* where he expressed the opinion that Operation *Golden Eye* really needed a 'book in its own right.' I thought that was a good idea. However, once I had begun it became apparent that there were many other schemes from the Allies which influenced Franco to keep Spain neutral, which I set out to cover under the umbrella of Operation *Golden Eye.*

I am most grateful to the staff at Bletchley Park, the Churchill Archives Centre Cambridge, the Imperial War Museum London, the Royal Marines Historical Society, the Public Records Office at Kew and the Royal Navy Museum.

Overseas museums and libraries have been equally helpful: the Central Intelligence Agency Library, Lillian Goldman Law Library, United States Library of Congress, United States National Archives and Records Administration and the Bundesarchiv-German Federal Archives.

For help and ideas with the manuscript I thank Tom Bonnington my editor at Casemate for his excellent suggestions, Michael Leventhal, Group Captain L. E. (Robbie) Robins CBE AE, DL, and John Sherress. Thanks too to my magazine editors who were always helpful and free with their time, Iain Ballantyne, John Mussell, and Flint Whitlock. Thank you to Tristan Hillgarth for permission to use his father's photograph.

The memories of eyewitnesses to the events have proved a veritable gold mine: Jack Beevor, Ivar Bryce, Winston Churchill, Count Galeazzo Ciano, David & Sybil Eccles, Robert Harling, Sir Samuel Hoare Viscount Templewood, Ewen Montagu, Kim Philby, Franz von Papen, Walter Schellenberg.

Also the works of the following have been invaluable: Christopher Andrew, Andrew Bassett, Patrick Beesley, Michael Bloch, Anthony Cave Brown, Commander Marc Antonio Bragadin, Jimmy Burns, Ian Colvin, Fergus Fleming, Duff Hart-Davis, Anthony Horowitz, Keith Jeffery, David Kahn, Neill Lochery, Andrew Lycett, Ben Macintyre, J. C. Masterman, Donald McLachlan, Russell Miller, David Nutting, Matthew Parker, John Pearson, Paul Preston, Hugh Thomas, Nicholas Rankin, Philip Vickers, John H. Waller, Richard Wigg and Nigel West.

Finally, as always, my wife, Margaret, gave her wholehearted support in the nuts and bolts of building a book, with proof reading, index-compiling, work on the maps, and finding her way through the labyrinth of strange and unfamiliar names, and my creative misspelling of them. Thanks to all. Any mistakes or errors are mine alone.

Dramatis Personae

The Allies

Burns, Thomas Ferrier — Press attaché to the British Embassy Madrid 1940–1944.

Donovan, William Joseph 'Wild Bill' — Head of the US OSS precursor to the CIA, former soldier and diplomat.

Eccles, David McAdam — Worked for British Ministry of Economic Warfare. Economic adviser to ambassadors at Lisbon and Madrid 1940–1942.

Fleming, Commander Ian Lancaster — RNVR assistant to the Director of Naval Intelligence 1939–1945. Author and creator of James Bond.

Godfrey, Admiral John — Director of Naval Intelligence 1939–1942.

Greenleaves, Henry. L. — British agent NID and consul official Tangier.

Harling, Robert Henry — RNVR served in 30AU. Writer and publisher.

Hillgarth, Captain Alan Hugh — Naval attaché Madrid Embassy 1939–1943. Writer.

Hoare, Sir Samuel John — British ambassador to Spain 1939–1945. Soldier, diplomat and politician.

Martin, Major William RM — The Man who Never Was. Fictional character used to deceive Germans in Operation *Mincemeat*.

Menzies, Sir Stewart Graham — British head of SIS/MI6, also known as 'C'.

Montagu, Captain Ewen Edward — Head of NID section 17M. Lawyer and judge.

Philby, Harold Adrian 'Kim' — Served in SIS/MI6 responsible for Spain in World War II. Soviet double agent defected in 1963.

Popov, Duško	Yugoslav British double agent codename 'Tricycle'. Abwehr codename 'Ivan'.
Thoroton, Lieutenant Colonel Charles Julian RM	Charles the Bold, head of NID in Spain during World War I.

The Axis

Bazna, Elyesa	Albanian/Turkish valet at the British Embassy in Ankara. Spied for the Germans under the code name 'Cicero.'
Canaris, Admiral Wilhelm	Director of the Abwehr German Military Intelligence service 1935–1944.
Ciano, Count Gian Galeazzo	Foreign Minister of Fascist Italy 1936–1943. Son-in-law of Benito Mussolini.
Darlan, Admiral Louis Xavier Francois	French admiral who served in the Pro-German Vichy regime as Minister of National Defence.
Himmler, Heinrich	Reichsfuhrer SS, main architect of the Holocaust, Nazi Minister of the Interior.
Piekenbrock, Colonel Hans	Head of the Abwehr section Abt 1 for counter-espionage often accompanied Admiral Canaris on trips to Spain.
Raeder, Grand Admiral Erich	Main German proponent of a Western Mediterranean strategy, including the capture of Gibraltar.
Ribbentrop, Joachim	German Foreign Minister organised the Hendaye meeting between Hitler and Franco.
Schellenberg, Walter Friedrich	German intelligence officer with the SD, later head of the RSHA.
Von Stohrer, Eberhard	Career German diplomat served as German ambassador in Madrid 1939–1943.

The Spanish and Portuguese

Beigbeder, Juan Luis	Minister of Foreign Affairs 1939–1940.
Espirito, Santo, Ricardo	Portuguese businessman and banker.
Franco, General Françisco Bahamonde	Dictator of Spain, the 'Caudillo', 1936–1975.

Grandes, General Agustin Munoz	Commanded the Blue Division, later Spanish Minister of Defence.
Jordan, General Francisco Gomez	Spanish Minister of Foreign Affairs 1942–1944.
Lourenco, Captain Agostinho	Head of the PVDE Portuguese secret police.
March, Juan Alberto	Smuggler, businessman, wealthiest man in Spain.
Salazar, Antonio de Oliveira	Prime Minister of Portugal 1932–1968, in effect dictator.
Serrano Suñer, Ramón	Spanish Interior Minister 1938–1942 and Minister of Foreign Affairs 1940–1942. President of the Falange, brother-in-law of Franco.

Glossary and Acronyms

Abwehr	German military secret service, meaning 'defence' in German.
30AU	30 Assault Unit Royal Marines, also known as 30 Commando.
BNI	British Naval Intelligence.
'C'	Head of British Secret Intelligence Service (SIS) MI6.
CIA	Central Intelligence Agency, replaced OSS, USA.
DEV	División Española de Voluntarios, Blue Division.
DNI	Director of Naval Intelligence, British.
Enigma	German code machine system.
Estado Novo	'New State' Portuguese right-wing political party.
FET	Falange Española Tradicionalista, Fascist party of Spain.
FO	Foreign Office, British.
GCHQ	Government Communications Headquarters, Bletchley Park.
Gestapo	*Geheime Staatspolizei*, German secret state police.
GRU	Soviet military intelligence
JIC	Joint Intelligence Committee, British.
KO	*Kriegs-Organisation* stations Abwehr.
KTB	German National defence branch.
MoI	Ministry of Information, British.
MI5	Military Intelligence section 5. British counter-intelligence service.
MI6	Military Intelligence section 6. British espionage service, often known as SIS.
17M	Signals section NID.
MEW	Ministry Economic Warfare, British.
NID	Naval Intelligence Division, British.
NKGB	The People's Commissariat for State Security, Russian 1941–46.
NKVD	Narodnyi Komissariat Vnutrennikh Del, Soviet secret police.
NSA	National Security Agency, USA.

OKW	*Oberkommando der Wehrmacht*, German Armed Forces High Command.
OSS	Office of Strategic Services, replaced by CIA, USA.
PVDE	Portuguese Secret Police.
RM	Royal Marines.
RNVR	Royal Navy Volunteer Reserve.
RSHA	*Reichssicherheitshauptamt*, supreme state security department. Set up in 1939 to supervise the Gestapo and SD.
Section D	SIS sabotage section.
SD	*Sicherheitsdienst*, secret service branch of the SS.
SHAPE	Supreme Headquarters Allied Powers, Europe.
SIPO	*Sicherheitspolizei*, security police of the Gestapo and SD.
SIS	Secret Intelligence Service, British, also known as MI6.
SMERSH	'Death to Spies', counter-intelligence service of the Red Army.
SOE	Special Operations Executive, British originally Section D of SIS.
SS	*Schutzstaffel*, or protection squad. The original title for Hitler's bodyguard.
SO2	Sabotage Section SOE (Naval).
Station X	GC & CS, Bletchley Park.
Ultra	Ultra decoded encrypted Axis radio communications classified 'Ultra Secret.'
W/T	Wireless Telegraph.
WTA	War Trade Agreement.

Prologue

In February 1939 Rear Admiral John Godfrey was appointed Director of Naval Intelligence (DNI). His appointment was to prove an excellent choice. He was a man of a similar type to Sinclair, who had been DNI between 1919 and 1921, replacing Admiral Sir Hugh Sinclair 'Blinker' Hall. Hall (nicknamed after his incessant blinking),[1] had held the post for most of the World War I and was described as 'a genius in his own sphere and brilliantly successful.'[2]

Godfrey was fortunate to have Hall's support and wrote:

> To no one am I more indebted than Reggie Hall. He came to see me on 27 March 1939 and thereafter very unobtrusively offered me access to his great store of knowledge and judgement on the strange commodity, intelligence about which I then knew hardly anything. He realised that I needed contacts and these he provided in large quantities.[3]

In the early months of World War II, British Intelligence was largely in disarray. Sir Hugh Sinclair, who had been the director of SIS (MI6) since 1923, was in 1939 suffering from cancer of the spleen and died on 4 November. The day before, still working from his sick bed, he had recommended in a letter to Sir Alexander Cadogan, Permanent Under-Secretary at the Foreign Office, that Stewart Menzies should succeed him.[4] Menzies was not seen by others as the obvious choice. No wonder Keith Jeffery in his history of MI6 should title his first chapter on World War II 'Keeping Afloat.'[5] At the time SOE had not even been thought of, and so much of the burden of intelligence gathering and control would fall on Naval Intelligence.

In Spain, Naval Intelligence was fortunate to have inherited the excellent network created by Blinker Hall's inspired appointment, Lieutenant Colonel Charles Julian Thoroton RM, known as 'Charles the Bold', who organised and ran British Naval Intelligence in the western Mediterranean during World War I. One of his most impressive recruits to the Allied cause was the Spanish businessman Juan March. March remained loyal to Britain through two world wars, although he supported the Nationalist cause in the Spanish Civil War. His maritime empire supplied thousands of agents to the network.[6] Admiral Godfrey, Winston Churchill, Captain Alan Hillgarth, the British naval attaché at the British Embassy in Madrid, and Ian Fleming were all beneficiaries of Thoroton's recruitment of March. In 1934, March had alerted Thoroton, who was still living and working in Spain that Wilhelm Canaris, later head of the Abwehr (German Military Secret Service), was 'our best ally in Europe at that moment.'[7]

Francisco Franco, military dictator of Spain in 1939, came from a naval family and had a great admiration and fear of the Royal Navy. With the start of World War II coming only months after the Civil War, Franco saw that Spain was in a dire position. It was unable to feed itself and overseas trade and possessions were at the mercy of the British blockade and fleet. These factors would be part of the reason that Franco, although ardently pro-Axis in the end, would maintain Spain's neutral position throughout the war. Franco would rule his country for thirty-nine years, dying in a hospital bed on Thursday 20 November 1975 at the age of eighty-two. Half a million Spaniards trooped past his open coffin to pay their respects as he lay in state. He was buried in a mausoleum at the Valley of the Fallen, an hour's drive north of Madrid. This is marked by a vast granite cross 150 metres high, the largest ever erected on earth, which stands on top of the Risco de la Nava, an imposing hill of brown rocks. Into the hill was tunnelled a huge crypt, longer than the nave of St. Peter's in Rome, its interior richly decorated with statuary, tapestries, and bronze.[8] By 1975 it was said to be a shrine to all those who had died in the Civil War, rather than what it is, a huge piece of Fascist religious architecture, the last to be erected in Europe.[9]

Due to luck, and Franco's ability to bend with the changing winds of fortune, he and his regime survived, in stark contrast to his two, more powerful potential allies. Adolf Hitler died by his own hand on the afternoon of Monday 30 April 1945 in the Fuhrer Bunker, Berlin, his thousand-year Reich in ruins. Two days earlier, Benito Mussolini, the *Duce,* had met his end on the shore of Lake Como. Trying to reach Switzerland, he and his mistress Clara Petacci had been captured by partisans and shot. Their bodies were taken to Milan and hung on display in the Piazzale Loreto. Of course it was not just a matter of luck, other factors were crucial. The anti-Nazi influence of Admiral Canaris on Franco. The dedication and daring of Allied diplomats and intelligence agents working to secure Spain's neutrality while preparing in case Spain joined the Axis or was invaded by the Nazis. This is their story.

CHAPTER I

The Ideas Man

On 13 June 1940 Commander Ian Fleming of the Royal Navy Volunteer Reserve was flown to Le Bourget airfield, near Paris in France. It was not the first time he had gone there in recent weeks. France was lurching toward defeat and Paris was expected to fall soon. The Admiralty in London and Winston Churchill were desperate to know what would happen to the powerful French fleet. Contact had been lost with its commander Admiral Francois Darlan who Churchill described at the time as becoming '… very important. My contacts with him had become few and formal.'[1]

Admiral John. H. Godfrey, Director of Naval Intelligence, wanted to re-establish contact in order to give the First Sea Lord and the PM the best advice. He wanted to go himself but that was impossible. So he sent his personal assistant Ian Fleming.[2]

Fleming wrote later that it was his suggestion that he, with a wireless operator, should go to France to find Darlan and stay with him: 'I cannot imagine what made me suggest this, except perhaps my usual desire to escape from Room 39 and get some fresh air.'[3] Indeed Godfrey was to write about Fleming: 'He had plenty of ideas and was anxious to carry them out but was not interested in and would prefer to ignore, the extent of the logistics background inseparable to all projects.'[4]

In June 1940 Ian Fleming had been in Naval Intelligence less than a year. He was thirty-two and a colleague at NI described him as '… tall and dark, elegant in his uniform and elastic-sided sea boots, with the worried down-the-nose look, and the heavy loping gait.'[5]

Ian Lancaster Fleming was born on 28 May 1908 at 27 Green Street in Mayfair, weighing in at near nine pounds, the son of Valentine and Evelyn Fleming. His father Valentine was the son of the wealthy Scottish banker Robert Fleming. In 1910 he was elected Tory MP for South Oxfordshire, and in 1914 he rode off to war with the Oxford Yeomanry and was soon promoted to Major. On 20 May 1917 Valentine Fleming was killed in action at Gillemont Farm. His last message to HQ was: 'My squadron holds its locality.' He was awarded a posthumous DSO. Winston Churchill wrote an appreciation in *The Times* praising his devotion to duty, observing that: 'As a young yeomanry officer he always took the greatest pains to fit himself for military duties ...' and '... there were few more competent civilian soldiers of his rank.'[6] Evelyn St Croix Rose, Ian's mother, came from Irish, Scots and Huguenot descent. She was beautiful, headstrong and a law unto herself. Robert Harling, a long-time friend of Ian's, called her a 'snob' while Noel Coward thought she was cold.[7] Ian had an elder brother Peter, and two younger brothers named Richard and Michael. He also had a half sister Amaryllis, born in 1925, and fathered by the artist Augustus John.[8] During the Great War and after the death of her husband Valentine, Evelyn was left to bring up her sons. Ian proved the most difficult. He hated the things the rest loved, like horses and dogs. He loathed family gatherings and holidays in Scotland. In 1915 Ian and Peter were sent to boarding school. In general, Ian disliked the experience but found escape in reading, devouring the likes of Sax Rohmer and his Fu-Manchu books, along with Buchan, Poe and R. L. Stevenson.[9]

Like his creation James Bond, Ian Fleming went to Eton, but retained few fond memories of the school. He was overshadowed by his elder brother. Peter was a success in most things and in 1926 went off to Christ Church Oxford with a string of honours. Though Ian underperformed academically, he did excel at athletics and was a good football player. He broke his nose in one match and had to have a small plate inserted, which his mother felt gave him the air of 'battered nobility.'[10] He even managed to run a car, an old Standard Tourer, garaged nearby in term-time against school rules, in which he ran illicit trips to London. There was also trouble with girls, again out-of-bounds in term time.[11] He avoided being expelled unlike his fictional hero James Bond, whose '... aunt was requested to remove him'[12] according to *The Times* obituary in *You Only Live Twice*. Fleming instead, with his mother's agreement, left a term early to start cramming for the Royal Military College Sandhurst entry examination, where he passed sixth in the country. Evelyn and Ian held high hopes for his future career in the Army, yet given the strict discipline at the military college and his track record at schools he was almost bound to fail and in May 1927 he duly resigned after a string of troubles. For his mother, the disgrace was acute. However she did not wash her hands of him, and instead sent him to the Villa Tennerhof in Kitzbühel Austria for further education.

Kitzbühel is a small medieval town in the Tyrol named after the river and surrounded by the Eastern Alps. Ernan Forbes Dennis, a former British diplomat and spy, had rented the Villa Tennerhof and made it into a school for those wanting to learn German. Peter Fleming had spent the summer of 1927 there to improve his German. It was then that Ernan learnt of the troubles Ian had suffered and offered to help. Ernan later recalled of Fleming's arrival: '… all he could do successfully was to make a nuisance of himself. For he was a rebel, like most second sons.'[13]

It was Ernan and his wife, the writer Phyllis Bottome, who got Ian to buckle down and work. Phyllis in particular encouraged him to write some short stories. For his education, they set the main goal as the Foreign Office examination for which competition was fierce, with most places being taken by Oxford and Cambridge students. The course he undertook with Ernan was much wider than any he could have acquired at a university. They instilled a love of books in him, and not just for reading but as an object in their own right, for he would become a keen collector. All these influences would lead him to make a living with his pen. He also found the freedom at Kitzbühel to explore the company of young women without his family breathing down his neck. One of his fellow pupils admired the effect he had on the female sex calling him 'irresistible to women.'[14]

His car had made it to Austria but was soon wrecked in a collision with a train at a level crossing. Fleming had been returning from Munich one dusk and a field of tall corn had obscured the railway track. Neither train driver nor Ian saw each other until it was too late. The train sliced off the front of the Standard, engine and all, depositing it fifty yards down the track. Ian was unhurt but was badly shaken. In another adventure he courted death by skiing in a known avalanche zone. He was buried to his shoulders but escaped with only minor injuries. This may well have been the source for the avalanche scene in *On Her Majesty's Secret Service* in which the avalanche misses Bond by feet: 'The ground shook wildly and a deep crashing roar filled his ears. And then it had passed him and given way to a slow, heavy rumble.'[15] This gave Ian credence among his fellow students and with the local girls.

After a year Ernan sent Fleming to Munich to stay with a German family and become a day student at the university. At this time, Hitler and the Nazis held some of their biggest rallies in the city and the country but they made little impression on Fleming.

In July 1929 he was back in Kitzbühel. Ernan felt he was nearly ready to sit the Foreign Office exam, but first sent him to Geneva to improve his French. In the Swiss city, Fleming acquired a black Buick two-seater sports car and a fiancée – Monique Panchaud de Bottones, a slim, dark-haired beauty who lived near Lake Geneva. Her father was a respected local landowner and his chateau produced good wine. Fleming now began to take the prospects of the Foreign Office more seriously now that he was thinking of marriage. He took a short-term post with the League of Nations to give him some insight into international affairs. Back in London for Christmas he found his mother hopeful he would become a diplomat, even agreeing to meet his Swiss girlfriend.

Sixty-two applicants sat the Foreign Office exam over ten days in September 1931. There were only three places available and an agonising four-week wait for the results. Fleming came twenty-fifth, and got the lowest marks for his English essay – 20 out of 100.[16]

It was another bitter pill to swallow, and a bigger blow to his ego than Eton or Sandhurst had been. His mother scuppered his romance, stating they were far too young and she was a distraction for his career prospects. Monique was sent packing back to Geneva in tears. Fleming later told Ralph Arnold, a fellow student at the Villa Tennerhof, 'I'm going to be quite bloody-minded about women from now on. I'm just going to take what I want without any scruples at all.'[17]

It was through Evelyn that he obtained a trial post at Reuters, the news agency, for six months. He had no journalistic experience but it was a job that suited him. He first worked in the news room but got out to cover motor racing events at Brooklands. Then in 1933 he was sent to cover the trial of six British engineers in Moscow who were accused of espionage and sabotage. They worked for the Vickers Electrical Company installing and supplying heavy electrical machinery. Vickers was one of the few favoured foreign firms working in the Soviet Union. Through the seven days of the trial Ian gained much firsthand experience of this communist state at work, which would fuel his later fiction. At Reuters he became a good reporter and it was there that he 'learned to write fast and above all, to be accurate.'[18] On 23 April he left Russia and on his return to London he was asked to appear at the Foreign Office to report his views on Russia to some mysterious unnamed officials. It was likely his first contact with the Secret Intelligence Service. First though, he had to deal with a huge tapeworm he had picked up in Moscow which left him unable to work for three days. He nicknamed the tapeworm his 'Loch Ness Monster.'[19]

Reuters were pleased with his work and offered him the plum job of 'Far-Eastern Correspondent' working out of Shanghai. He was excited to go even though the salary at £800 a year was not good given his lifestyle. Sir Roderick Jones of Reuters wanted him to go to Berlin first to see how a foreign office was run and put his good German to use. He might even be able to obtain an interview with Hitler. However, Fleming turned the package down, as he had been offered a job in a merchant bank. His ageing grandfather Robert Fleming was behind it, and he made plain that no special provision was to be made for Ian or his brothers in his will. He regretted his move into banking and later called it a: 'beastly idea giving up all the fun of life for money', but that he had been 'pretty well pushed into it from all sides.'[20]

Thus began his six years as a merchant banker and then a stockbroker. However, unlike journalism, he had no real natural aptitude in the financial world, but still made a great deal of money from it. He spent it as fast as he could make it, on golf, gambling, and women. He became known as a 'Glamour Boy' in the party sect.[21] As one fellow stockbroker said of his efforts in that field: 'As a stockbroker, old Ian really must have been among the world's worst.'[22]

In 1939 he returned to Moscow, this time to cover a trade mission for *The Times* and took leave from his stockbroking firm. He found the Russian capital a depressing city. Sefton Delmer, covering the same event for another paper, thought Fleming was there not only for a newspaper but the government too, given Ian's thinly veiled comments about secret agents. On the train journey home, Soviet customs at the border went through Ian's luggage with a fine-tooth comb. They took particular interest in some Russian contraceptives Ian had.[23]

Back in London on 24 May, four months before Britain went to war, Fleming received an invitation to lunch at the Charlton Grill with Rear Admiral John Godfrey, the new Director of Naval Intelligence, who had been in the job for just three months. The admiral was on the lookout for an assistant. Godfrey was fifty-one in 1939, and tall with a ruddy complexion. Fleming was introduced to his host by a man he knew well, Admiral Aubrey Hugh-Smith, who was the brother of Lance Hugh-Smith, the senior partner in the firm of Stockbrokers he worked for. Fleming had little idea why he was there and the two admirals did not explain much to him.

While captain of the battle-cruiser *Repulse*, Godfrey was notified in August 1938 that it was intended he should relieve Vice Admiral J. A. G. Troup as Director of Naval Intelligence early in the new year. He was concerned as the post usually led to retirement so he asked the advice of Admiral Sir Dudley Pound who reassured him: 'I think your prospective appointment as DNI is an excellent one and when I go to the Admiralty I will make certain that it is their intention to send you to sea afterwards.'[24]

On his appointment he sought out people with intelligence experience for advice on his new role as DNI. He saw Admiral Hugh Sinclair, Director of SIS known as 'C' and his deputy, soon to succeed him, Colonel Stewart Menzies. Among others, Admiral 'Blinker' Hall came to see him, who at the time was nearly sixty-nine and one of the most renowned figures in the intelligence world. Godfrey wrote of that visit: 'From then onwards we met frequently.'[25] He went further: 'To no one am I more indebted than Reggie Hall, the DNI during the Kaiser's war. He came to see me on 27 March 1939 and thereafter very unobtrusively offered me full access to his great store of knowledge and judgement on this strange commodity, intelligence, about which I then knew hardly anything.'[26]

Hall also suggested he should get a good personal assistant. During World War I he had obtained the services of the stockbroker Claud Serocold who had a quick mind and was not hamstrung by naval tradition. David Kynaston wrote of him that he '… concentrated more on the fun aspects of life being considered something of a playboy.'[27] Thus Godfrey sought out someone of a similar ilk.

At their lunch date, Godfrey told Fleming that he might like to be ready for a special post if it came to war. Ian was keen to help in any way he could. A few days later he received a letter from the Secretary of the Admiralty Norman Macleod, who thanked him for the 'offer of your services' and that the Admiralty 'would probably desire to avail themselves of your offer should hostilities break out.' The letter assured him that he would be 'earmarked for service under the Admiralty in the event of emergency.'[28] A short time after the letter reached Fleming, Godfrey telephoned to arrange a meeting at his offices. He wanted him to start work on a part-time basis. This suited Fleming well enough and he spent most weekday afternoons in July visiting the Admiralty after lunch. It was situated along the Mall close to Captain Cook's statue. To enter, he would have to show his pass to the retired sergeant of the Royal Marines who manned a small desk at the Quadrangle leading off to the bowels of the building. He would follow the corridor on the left which brought him to a black door with the number 39 on it in white numerals.

Entering Room 39 the tall windows opposite faced west onto the 'garden of No 10 Downing Street straight opposite, the Foreign Office St James Park Lake-Guards War Memorial composition to the right of it, and to the left the elegance of Horse Guards the Treasury and old Admiralty …'[29]

There could be up to fifteen people working in the large office at desks jammed among metal filing cabinets. The government issue furniture made life uncomfortable and the cream painted walls made it feel like the newsroom of a daily paper. Room 38 was next door – the domain of the DNI.

No one dominated the group. The room had no leader, and the Royal Navy officers in the section had all given up trying to impose any kind of routine or discipline in what was known among the 'Secret Ladies' and typists as 'the zoo.'[30]

Yet they all knew their jobs and the work got done. Each desk dealt with a different aspect of intelligence and was given a code number. The department was designated the Naval Intelligence Division 17. Fleming's desk was 17 F and he dealt with other intelligence and security organisations. His desk overlooked Horse Guards Parade and was six feet from the door of Room 38. As Godfrey's personal assistant people had to get by him to see the DNI.

At a party held by Shane and Ann O'Neill in September, Fleming arrived in his new lieutenant's naval uniform with the two wavy gold rings of the RNVR on his sleeves. One of the women called him a 'chocolate sailor' referring to the man on the Black Magic advertisements. To Fleming's chagrin, the name stuck.[31]

However within the confines of Room 39 Ian Fleming was anything but a 'chocolate sailor.' There he became a '… skilled fixer and a vigorous showman', and he seemed to transmit the energy and wide-ranging curiosity of his first chief. Never, as a colleague put it, did Fleming 'sleep with a problem.'[32]

In the early months of the war the NID became the mainstay of British Intelligence. SIS was in turmoil after the death of its chief Admiral Hugh Sinclair in November 1939, followed closely in the same month by the Venlo Incident when two agents were enticed across the Dutch border and captured in Germany. Special Operations Executive was not formed until June 1940 with Churchill's instruction the next month to 'set Europe ablaze.' Thus NID had to shoulder the burden with all sorts of people beating a path towards its doors, and way beyond its principle role of collecting intelligence about the war at sea.

On 8 September Fleming was promoted to commander, with three wavy rings on his uniform. The higher rank gave him more confidence to confront seniors at the Admiralty and within the other services. He would even do so with cabinet ministers he came across in the course of his duties, which was the purpose of the promotion.

As Donald McLachlan put it: 'Fleming suffered not at all from very senior officer veneration. He was ready – indeed, more ready than Godfrey himself – to stand up for a case against a sceptical Vice-Chief of Naval Staff or Director of plans. This easy confidence made him very effective in defence of the DNI's sideshows …'[33]

During the Phoney War, Fleming dreamed up various schemes, like his project to watch U-boat movements from the remote Baltic German Frisian islands inspired by Erskine Childers *The Riddle of the Sands,* as he recalled in 1960:

The last time I had paid serious attention to these island names – Wangerooge, Spiekeroog, Norderney, Borkum – was when, as a young Lieutenant R. N. V. R., I had studied them endlessly on Admiralty charts and put up a succession of plans whereby I and an equally intrepid wireless operator should be transported to the group by submarine and there dig ourselves in, to report the sailings of U-boats and the movements of the German fleet.[34]

The idea formed the basis for the plot in his short story *From a View to a Kill* where a group of Soviet Military Intelligence agents bury themselves in an elaborate hideout in the woods near the NATO SHAPE (Supreme Headquarters for Allied Powers in Europe) HQ, which was established in April 1951 at Rocquencourt near St Germain on the western suburbs of Paris. From there they ambush NATO motorcycle dispatch riders before Bond locates the hideout:

It was like the opening of a hinged Easter egg. In a moment the two segments stood apart and the two halves of the rose bush, still alive with bees, were splayed widely open. Now the inside of the metal caisson that supported the earth and the roots of the bush were naked to the sun. There was a glint of a pale electric light from the dark aperture between the curved doors. The whine of the motor had stopped. A head and shoulders appeared, and then the rest of the man. He climbed softly out and crouched, looking sharply round the glade. There was a gun – a Luger – in his hand.[35]

Vice Admiral Norman Denning, who worked with Fleming at the time, felt a lot of his ideas 'were just plain crazy' yet '… a lot of his far-fetched ideas had just the glimmer of possibility in them that made you think twice before you threw them in the wastepaper basket.'[36]

All the while Ian had been itching for some sort of adventure, and a proper role in the war. He got his chance at last when the Germans attacked the Low Countries and broke through the Ardennes Forest into France in the spring and early summer of 1940.

CHAPTER 2

France 1940

Geoffrey Cox, foreign correspondent of the Daily Express, found Paris in the spring of 1940: 'So beautiful in those last days of May and early June. Dawn came clear, tinted, gentle behind Notre Dame, midday was a blaze of sunshine on the chestnuts along the Champs Elysees, on the red umbrellas on the cafe terraces, in the evening the sun went down behind the Arc de Triomphe and the soft spring night came slowly over the boulevards.'[1] Yet at that time, 150 miles to the north, long lines of men were waiting on the beaches of Dunkirk to be rescued as they were bombed and strafed by the Luftwaffe.

Sometime earlier Patrick Whinney, a former naval officer, became an 'Admiralty Messenger', whilst coveting a permanent appointment. It was in this role that he was sent to Paris, Toulon, and Marseilles where he found that: 'The changeover from peace to war footing meant that each post, each ship, needed new confidential and secret books ...' A heavy workload for the Messengers, with so many bags in fact that Whinney observed at times '... there was scarcely room for me in the railway compartment or the cabin on board ship.'[2]

Returning from a big delivery to Paris he was ordered to report to NID, where he was interviewed by Commander (Kipper) Bradford. He found a charming man who chain-smoked using a long cigarette holder. His first question to Whinney was: 'Do you speak French?' In fact he had little better than schoolboy French, but claimed to be fluent calling it the 'mildest exaggeration'. So he was sent to Paris as assistant to the naval attaché. Whinney had joined the Royal Navy in 1925 and served for seven years, reaching the rank of sub-lieutenant, before being released on medical grounds with an eye condition. With his new appointment he was given the astonishing choice to return to his old rank in the regular navy, or as a full lieutenant with a second ring in RNVR. Two rings would mean extra pay which clinched the matter.[3]

On his arrival in Paris he soon met the naval attaché, the charismatic Captain Cedric Holland, who had the nickname of 'Hooky' due to his long nose. Whinney met Ian Fleming in Paris and London on many occasions, and he became their main contact with NID. He found the Director's personal assistant had 'extraordinary versatility' and: 'There was nothing that I ever discovered which he could not do better than most other people.'

Although at times he could be extremely rude, especially to senior officers, Whinney found him to be 'polite' and 'considerate, perhaps because, although not technically junior to him, we had far less important appointments.'[4]

Ian's main role in the early days of spring in France was to aid the new naval attaché in Paris, Captain the Hon Edward Pleydell-Bouverie, who had taken over from Hooky Holland in April. The latter had been appointed to command the new aircraft-carrier *Ark Royal*. Patrick Whinney thought it the oddest time for Pleydell-Bouverie, known as 'Ned', to take over for 'He took over a success story which was beginning to gallop to total disintegration.'[5]

Pleydell-Bouverie spent as much time as he could close to the commander of the French Navy Admiral Francois Darlan. The French commander was stocky with a ruddy complexion, a vain man who always wore his hat to cover his bald head. Whinney thought of him as a man without friends but he took the trouble to know about everyone on his staff: 'He was highly intelligent with the Achilles heel of vanity. He made sure that no decision of what he thought to be of importance was taken by anyone but himself – a factor which caused many delays. It was something that took us a long time to grasp.'[6]

In September 1939 Darlan had moved his operational headquarters from Paris to the village of Maintenon 50 miles west of Paris, which had excellent communications and an airfield nearby. A complex of hutted offices was built in the grounds of the Chateau de Maintenon for his 400 staff. Away from the political turmoil of the capital, Darlan was able to run his headquarters more like a ship. Personnel were forbidden to have their families in the village, and everyone had to obtain special permission before 'going ashore'.[7]

Lieutenant S. M. Mackenzie arrived at Maintenon in November. At the time Hooky Holland spent half his time in Paris and half at Maintenon. The French Ministry of the Navy had remained at Rue Royale in Paris. The liaison team at Maintenon consisted of Whinney, Mackenzie, who had replaced Charles Morgan, and two retired Royal Marine colour sergeants. They all lived at the Villa des Cigoynes on the outskirts of the village, which had cobbled streets, several small shops and a fine village square. Nearby was the Chateau which was once the home of Louis XIV's mistress, before belonging to the Duc de Noailles. Mackenzie says the villa was 'within walking distance of the offices' and they had a staff of four French sailors, 'but due to the sensible French system of conscription our Maitre d'hotel, Germain, was in fact the "patron" of the local Maintenon pub, and the cook, Maurice, in peacetime ran a restaurant in Paris.'[8]

Life for Whinney and Mackenzie consisted of deciphering endless messages from the Admiralty by teleprinter which were then passed on to the French. They had a constant stream of visitors, including Admiral Pound, and even the Duke of Windsor. Mackenzie was on leave when the Germans invaded Holland and Belgium but returned on 16 May. He found the naval attaché's office in the Embassy was in a 'major flap' about the possible need for evacuation. Later, after calm was restored, he was sent back to Maintenon.[9]

Arriving in Paris on 10 June only days before the Germans marched in, Ian helped organise moving the different British intelligence operations while the country was falling apart under the German onslaught. He managed to obtain a large amount of funds from the Rolls Royce office in the city which was a front for SIS. His main contact with the SIS in France was with Peter Smithers, one of his recruits to NID. Smithers had been laid up in Hasler Naval Hospital Portsmouth suffering from measles when Ian contacted him and arranged an interview. His interview with Ian was hasty. He was hurried over to Broadway, the SIS headquarters near St James's Park, where his handler Jimmy Blyth sent him to Paris to report to Commander Wilfred 'Biffy' Dunderdale. He was the exuberant Odessa-born station chief, a Sidney Riley type of character, who wore hand-made suits and gold cufflinks and was chauffeured around Paris in a Rolls Royce. The car was driven by Gresev, a Russian émigré who fought for the Whites in the Russian Civil War and was a former captain in the Imperial Guard. Biffy and Gresev had been school friends before the revolution in Russia. Another member of his motley crew was 'Uncle Tom', Biffy's right-hand man Tom Greene. Patrick Whinney thought they were an odd pair: 'The Irishman, six foot four or five, and weighing not less than about sixteen stone, with a cavernous mouth, and huge hands, made Biffy look even more like a music-hall dandy. But it was Biffy who commanded.'[10] He got his sobriquet Biffy from his prowess as a boxer in the navy during World War I. He was another friend of Ian Fleming, and later claimed some of his own stories found their way into the Bond novels.[11]

Smithers was posted to the SIS Office in the rue Charles Floquet near the Eiffel Tower, where he debriefed Dutch tugboat captains. At one point he lived in the Hotel Vouillement, and recalled air raids on the city and taking shelter in the basement. With the Germans closing in Smithers moved to the Chateau le Chene, an SIS safe house at Sologne, in the Loire Valley.[12]

Ian then went with Pleydell-Bouverie hoping to meet Darlan and his staff at Maintenon. Darlan was spending a lot of time in Paris for crisis meetings. Patrick Whinney takes up the story: 'When Ian arrived in Paris he was met by Ned [Pleydell-Bouverie] who brought him straight down to Marceau [Maintenon] where the two of them made a vigorous approach to the French top brass to discover what if any were their future plans.'[13] They got to see Darlan briefly who passed them onto his staff and learned from them that if the Germans reached Paris the French Naval HQ would move to Tours. Ian immediately drafted a report on the meeting for the Admiralty which Whinney sent, before Ian made his way back to London.

Back in London Ian outlined the difficulties Captain Edward Pleydell-Bouverie was operating under. He was still trying to bring about a close relationship with Darlan and his staff. He had only been in the job for two months and had already managed to rub the French up the wrong way by questioning their will to continue the fight. On catching up with Darlan it became obvious to Ian how serious the rift had become. He then suggested to Godfrey that he should return to France and become the link with Darlan and his staff.

At 3am on 13 June, Pleydell-Bouverie, Mackenzie and the two Marine colour-sergeants clambered into a Citroën with a French driver and set out for the new headquarters at Tours. Patrick Whinney stayed at Maintenon the next morning to send the last messages to London, as files were being burnt out in the grounds and trucks moved off with cabinets and personal belongings, heading south for the Loire Valley alongside thousands of refugees. He left early the following morning via back roads to avoid the mass of people leaving Paris for the south.[14]

Miss R. Andrew, an English nurse working at the American Hospital in Paris, set off with five colleagues in a Buick for Chateauroux on Monday 10 June, to set up an office there. She remembered: 'Millions of Paris inhabitants all had the same idea as us about leaving Paris and the roads were jammed with cars even before we reached the Porte d'Orleans. It was a very hot day and soon everyone's engines began to boil as we edged along in low gear.'[15]

Patrick Whinney's journey was seventy miles shorter than Nurse Andrews but by then the situation was even worse. He set off in 'glorious' weather and tried to stick to the B roads as he had been advised. He found them 'completely deserted' so much so it was hard to believe 'people were killing each other only a few miles further north.'

Eventually he had no alternative but to join the main route, which he found jammed with all sorts of vehicles, including handcarts, and people on foot. Every vehicle seemed overloaded with people and possessions. He found evidence of German aircraft having strafed the road as there were a few dead bodies on the brown grass verges, which most people were careful to avoid. His ten hours on the roads left him exhausted and when he reached Tours all he wanted to do was sleep. He felt desperately sorry for the people on the roads some of whom had been travelling for days. He found the plight of the children the worst: '... most of them showed no emotion beyond a dull wide-eyed stare' yet 'not many of them cried. Perhaps they were past it.'[16] Geoffrey Cox, the *Express* newspaperman, felt the same about the children. The journey to Tours 'was marked for me by dark-eyed tired children, staring from the interior of darkened lorries and of crowded cars as the line of traffic moved a few paces, and then jerked to yet another stop.'[17]

On 14 June Paris fell. The French Admiralty had set off for Tours the day before followed by Fleming. The next day Ian relayed a message from London to Darlan urging him to bring his fleet to Britain. Ian had his reply transmitted back to Godfrey. Like a lot of the French High Command, Darlan had lost touch with the reality of the highly fluid battle. In the reply there were phrases such as '... if anything really grave occurs' and 'For the moment the war at sea will go on as before.'[18] It is often indicated that Ian Fleming only saw action once while on board the destroyer HMS *Fernie* during the Dieppe raid of 1942. He was by then no longer a 'chocolate sailor' stuck behind an admiralty desk. However this rather ignores France 1940, when Maintenon, Tours and Bordeaux were all bombed during the time Fleming was there. He may also have been caught in the strafing of the refugee columns on the roads he will have travelled.

On 16 June the government led by Paul Reynaud capitulated to be replaced by the Vichy government under Marshal Petain. Godfrey now had the luxury of direct contact with Fleming in Tours and was much better informed on the state of French morale. However, he was now far from confident the French Fleet would sail for British ports. He was able to inform the First Sea Lord Albert Victor Alexander and Admiral Pound, who were about to fly to France to try and stiffen French resolve. He had also been advised by Lord Tyrrell, former ambassador to France, that in his opinion 'Darlan was a twister' and not to be trusted.[19]

In Tours, Patrick Whinney noticed that demoralisation had set in among the French officers: 'Before that things had happened too quickly to allow time for much thought. Most had hoped for a miracle to save Paris, some had believed that it would not, could not fall.' They hoped for another miracle like the battle of the Marne in 1914. Whinney recalled: 'Only a few faced the truth. And that is not being cynical or unkind. I think we would have thought much the same about an attack on London.'[20]

It was the last Fleming saw of Darlan and his staff who having come under air attack at Tours set off for Bordeaux. Bundling his wireless operator into a car, Ian set off in pursuit along the roads of south west France choked with refugees and military units.

However he was soon told to forget about Darlan and help with the British evacuation from Bordeaux and its estuary of the Girande leading to the sea. The town was packed with those desperate to get away. The French and British General Staffs were there. The British ambassador with a large party, officials of all kinds, dislodged servicemen, refugees and wealthy British nationals. Smithers was there with his SIS people, their wives and mistresses.

Mackenzie and Pleydell-Bouverie only spent a night at Tours before moving straight onto Bordeaux, in a French Admiralty Citroen. They spent a night at the roadside before reaching the southern city on 16 June. There they started to organise the evacuation of British passport holders to Britain, of which there were hundreds besieging the consulate. Mackenzie says Ian Fleming arrived the following day, while on the 18th, the destroyer HMS *Berkeley* docked. On board was the First Lord of the Admiralty Alexander and Admiral of the Fleet Pound, their mission a last-ditch attempt to persuade Darlan to bring the French fleet to Britain, or at least take it beyond the reach of the Germans.[21]

Patrick Whinney's journey to Bordeaux, was 'more difficult' than the one to Tours. He had been dreaming about an omelette for a long time on the road. When he arrived in the city people were having dinner. He found Fleming and Mackenzie at a restaurant near the consulate and their empty plates showed they had already eaten. Asked if he had eaten he confided to them of his desire for an omelette, to which Ian burst into laughter confessing he had 'just eaten the last omelette in the entire square.' Patrick found out Ian was not joking which did not improve his mood. However he was able to tell them Darlan was staying in the naval barracks on the outskirts of the city. Ian told him not to lose touch with the French admiral.[22]

One task Ian was given was to make sure a large quantity of aircraft engines and spares found a place on the evacuation ships, and did not fall into enemy hands. This tall well spoken RNVR officer exuded a confident air amidst the dockside chaos. He duly found space in a ship to supervise the loading and the engines made it safely back to England.

The SIS staff was taken aboard the cruiser HMS *Arethusa* in the Girande estuary. However Smithers was ordered off and told to report back to Bordeaux where Commander Fleming would give him further orders. He found Ian burning papers at the British Consulate and told him he was to act as flag lieutenant for the First Sea Lord Alexander, who was meeting Admiral Darlan for dinner that night.

In the meantime Fleming and Smithers drove out along the estuary to the anchorage at Le Verdon, past abandoned cars – many Rolls Royce and Bentleys – crammed with luggage. At the quayside there were hundreds of people milling about trying to get a ship back to England. Ian aided by Smithers swiftly took charge, persuading, cajoling or just plain bullying the captains to let these people board. He told one skipper: 'If you don't take these people on board and transport them to England, I can promise you that if the Germans don't sink you, the Royal Air Force will.'[23] He paid a local ferryman to take people out to the larger ships with rolls of francs he had taken from the SIS safe in Paris. Ian and Smithers stationed themselves on the quayside insisting that only two cases per person could be taken on board and checking passports, interrupted from time-to-time by German aircraft. They worked through the summer afternoon and into the evening until everybody had been taken off.

Nurse Andrew and her colleagues who were left at Chateauroux were soon told to go to Bordeaux and return to England or risk internment. There they met an 'adorable young man in Naval Uniform' organising the evacuation. She hoped he got a medal for his efforts. Later in a *Sunday Times* article she identified him as Ian Fleming. She missed at least two ships there, due to sight-seeing trips, but would later return to England from St. Jean-de-Luz.[24]

That evening the French and British General Staffs dined at the Chapon Fin Restaurant in Bordeaux. Alexander's attempt to convince Darlan to throw in his lot with Britain or sail his ships to neutral ports failed. It was a sombre affair. Few could engage in the occasion, lost in their own concerns. Fleming and Smithers in particular were exhausted after the day's efforts.

Patrick Whinney was probably the last British officer to see Admiral Darlan at Bordeaux when he delivered a proposal from Admiral Pound to send every French ship he could to the West Indies. He found Darlan at the barracks walking across the parade ground. Darlan did not return Whinney's salute or acknowledge his 'good morning' as normal: 'Instead he looked me up and down as if he had never seen me before, and then grabbed the envelope from my hand. His only acknowledgement was a snapped out "Bien", before he turned on his heel and walked away.' The next day Whinney and Mackenzie were ordered to leave Bordeaux for Bayonne where a substantial number of British refugees had gathered.[25]

Alexander and Smithers returned to England in a Sunderland flying boat and Ian would go to Portugal. Godfrey needed him to see Alan Hillgarth, the naval attaché in Madrid, and assess the effect the German victory might have in Spain.

Quite how Ian got there is unclear. To have gone overland would have been extremely unlikely, and as his objective was to get to Madrid if going overland, why go to Portugal? He possibly travelled by sea. The Portuguese Consul in Bordeaux, Aristides de Sousa Mendes, worked tirelessly issuing visas. The demand was so great that he ignored his government's policy that was aimed at trying to keep Jews out of Portugal. Instead he issued visas to all regardless of nationality, race or religion. Many of these refugees went by sea.

Sousa Mendes paid for this humanitarian act with his career and the ruin of his family by a furious Dr Antonio De Oliveira Salazar, dictator of Portugal.[26] The report of the PVDE, the Portuguese Secret Police who controlled Portugal's borders, put entrances of refugees by land at 30,854, by sea 6,843, and by air 5,843 in 1940. The influx was so great that it led to the Spanish closing the border with France, and an increase in tension between Lisbon and Madrid.[27]

Ian could have perhaps taken a flight from Bordeaux. Two weeks before Sir Samuel Hoare's flight south to take up his post as ambassador in Madrid, he had refuelled at Bordeaux where he found the 'aerodrome was nominally still in use.' His flight was going via Lisbon and would be the last British civilian flight to land at Bordeaux. He recalled: 'Our arrival created little interest amongst the handful of employees who were still on the aerodrome and it was with a feeling of foreboding that having lunched, we quitted France ...'[28]

John Pearson in his book *The Life of Ian Fleming* claims that Fleming returned to England: 'HMS *Arethusa* was waiting off Arcachon to take away the British ambassador and when she sailed Lieutenant (Commander) Fleming would sail in her.'[29]

This is maybe more likely as he could then have got a flight to Lisbon. BOAC started operating a flight from Heston aerodrome, west of London, to Lisbon on 4 June. In September 1938 it was to Heston that British Prime Minister Neville Chamberlain returned from Munich displaying the paper signed by him and Adolf Hitler promising 'peace for our time'.

What makes this more likely is that Mackenzie and Whinney say they saw Ian Fleming at the DNI office in London after they had arrived on 26 June. Whinney recalls that Fleming greeted them after they had briefly seen Admiral Godfrey with: 'Hello, you monkeys, where have you been? And what have you been up to?' After reporting on their adventures they were sent on leave.

They had left Bordeaux on 20 June for Bayonne where they were to help in the continued evacuation of British Nationals. At Bordeaux there had been quays where the ships could come in, but at St. Jean-de-Luz they had to be ferried out to the larger ships in small boats. There they worked for days getting people away, including King Zog of Albania along with his family and his treasury. Nurse Andrew finally got away on the SS *Emrick*, which was the same one the king had boarded.

On 25 June, Mackenzie and Whinney were taken off by the Canadian destroyer *Fraser*. They were among the last British officers to leave France, who had surrendered the week before. Unfortunately their adventures did not end there. On the return voyage, in poor visibility and rough seas, the *Fraser* was cut in two by the cruiser *Calcutta* which hit the destroyer just forward of the bridge. The *Restigouche*, another Canadian ship, rescued most of the passengers. Whinney recalls leaping across from one destroyer to the other: '… it seemed a longish drop, and then capable hands steadied me on deck.' The *Fraser* lost forty-five people in the collision and *Calcutta* lost nineteen.[30]

In Lisbon the only flight Ian could get to Madrid was with Lufthansa, who at first refused him as an enemy alien. Never noted for taking no as an answer Ian persisted, pointing out that flying from a foreign country, as a commercial airline, they were duty-bound to take him. Thus, late in June, he arrived in Madrid for his vital assignment with Hillgarth. Here in the Spanish capital, events for Britain had become even worse. The Franco regime had changed the war status of Spain from 'neutrality' to an undefined 'non-belligerence' which showed a clear sympathy for the Axis. On 10 June Mussolini's Italy had entered the war. Many expected Spain to follow suit.

A year before, when Admiral Godfrey had taken up the reins of NID, he was wise enough, no doubt with advice from Blinker Hall, to have Commander Alan Hillgarth appointed assistant to the naval attaché in Paris which at that time took responsibility for Spain. During this time, Hillgarth would reside in Madrid. Soon after, the Paris office was moved to Lisbon. Then Hillgarth was promoted to naval attaché for Madrid. Godfrey had met Hillgarth when he was consul at Palma during the Spanish Civil War, when the *Repulse* was sent to Majorca to take off British subjects caught up in the fighting. Alan had lived in Spain for years, understood the Spanish, and had many good contacts within the military and navy and with the Franco regime. Godfrey might well call him a 'super-Attaché'.[31]

In the Compiegne Forest north of Paris on 22 June 1940, the Nazis stage-managed the surrender terms which France had to accept. They heaped humiliation on the defeated by using the same railway carriage that had been used for the armistice in 1918. Hitler even sat in the same seat Marshal Foch had used in the old wooden carriage. A week later Adolf Hitler paid a brief visit to Paris to see the Eiffel Tower, the Arc de Triomphe, the Paris Opera

House and, most important to him, Napoleon's Tomb. He now probably considered himself a military genius like Napoleon. As he was leaving the tomb he is reported to have murmured: 'That was the greatest and finest moment of my life.'[32]

Article 8 of the 1940 armistice between Germany and France stated that all French Navy ships were to be: 'demobilised and disarmed under German and Italian control' and all Atlantic bases in the occupied zone were now at the disposal of Germany.[33]

Darlan had assured Churchill '… that whatever happened the French Fleet should never fall into German hands.'[34] However, Churchill and the war cabinet felt unable to accept the risk. Thus Operations *Grasp* and *Catapult* were put into effect to seize or destroy the French ships. On 3 July the Royal Navy overcame French ships and submarines in the harbours of Portsmouth, Plymouth, and Alexandria in Egypt. The only casualties were when two British officers, one seaman and a French warrant officer were killed in a fight on the submarine *Surcouf* in Plymouth.

However there was a large fleet in the Algerian ports of Mers-el-Kebir and Oran. Force H at Gibraltar, under Vice Admiral James Somerville, was given the task of dealing with this force. The British had managed to steal the code and cipher books from the French submarine *Narvel* in Malta. These were sent by flying boat to NID and Bletchley Park, thus giving Somerville the advantage of reading the dispatches of the French Fleet.[35]

Force H had been formed partly to compensate for the loss of the French Mediterranean Fleet. It was able to lend support to the Atlantic or the western Mediterranean as required. At this point Somerville had under his command the battlecruiser *Hood* and the battleships *Resolution* and *Valiant,* the carrier *Ark Royal,* two cruisers and eleven destroyers.

Early on the morning of 3 July, Somerville's fleet arrived off the Algerian coast ready to put Operation *Catapult* into action. The former Paris Naval Attaché now commanding *Ark Royal,* Captain Cedric 'Hooky' Holland, was sent ashore to give the French commander Admiral Marcel-Bruno Gensoul a six-hour ultimatum: to join the British, go into internment, sail to the French West Indies and disarm, scuttle their ships or be destroyed. Gensoul thought the British were bluffing and played for time so that his ships could raise steam.

Force H opened fire at 17:30. The battlecruiser *Strasbourg,* although sustaining some damage, and five destroyers, broke out and managed to reach Toulon. All other ships in the two ports were sunk or crippled within minutes. The battleship *Bretagne* exploded and sank, with 37 officers and 940 ratings killed. The French lost 1,297 men.[36]

The ruthless British action against the French Fleet at Mers-el-Kebir boldly underlined Churchill's rhetoric that Britain and her Empire would fight on. Meanwhile Hitler's speech to the Reichstag on 19 July 1940, claimed that he was the victor and that he could '... see no reason why this war must go on.' In Britain, this was treated with contempt.[37]

Count Galeazzo Ciano was impressed by the British action and resolve, as were many around the world, and he wrote on 4 July: 'For the moment it proves that the fighting spirit of His Majesty's fleet is quite alive, and still has the aggressive ruthlessness of the captains and pirates of the seventeenth century .... British morale is very high and that they have no doubts about victory, even though it may come only after a long time.'[38]

CHAPTER 3

Naval Attaché

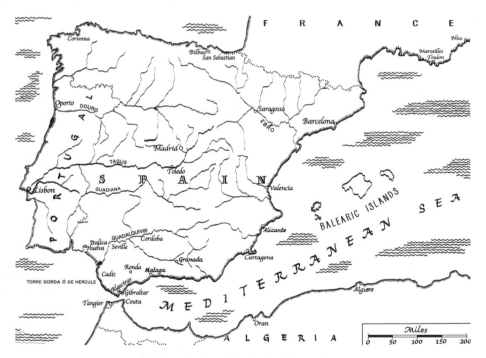

General map of the Iberian Peninsula.

Sir Samuel Hoare arrived in Lisbon on 30 May 1940 with his wife Lady Maud. He was sixty, balding and with a stooped bearing. He had a nervous disposition, though his smile was bright and infectious and he had a gregarious nature. He found the Portuguese capital bright with: 'vivid colours of the jacarandas and the many exotic trees and shrubs, the radiant facades of the baroque churches and palaces, the silver setting of one of the worlds noblest rivers combined to make a superb prospect of external beauty.'[1] Yet he was still depressed by the war news.

They stayed two nights at the embassy as guests of Sir Walford Selby, the ambassador for Portugal, who was an old-fashioned gentleman nearing retirement. David Eccles, a Scot, had managed the Central Mining and Investment Company before the war, specialising in Spanish railways. With the coming of hostilities he joined the Ministry of Economic Warfare, and was posted to Spain and Portugal to conduct economic warfare against the Axis. He arrived in Lisbon in April to take over the commercial side of Embassy business. He found Selby had 'many delightful qualities' but lacked the 'stamina to be head of the mission' during time of war. He did not have the confidence to deal with Salazar, the dictator of Portugal, so once Eccles was settled in he took over all dealings with him.[2]

Eccles was amazed at Hoare's self-confidence and ignorance when he met him with Selby. Hoare, the new ambassador to Spain, told them he had only agreed to the appointment after pressure from Churchill and the King. He was confident he would soon have Franco eating out of his hand and he would quickly obtain a guarantee that Spain would remain neutral for the duration of the war. Then he expected to be moved on to be Viceroy of India. He estimated it would take no more than a few weeks, two months at the most, in Spain.

Selby, Eccles says, was 'struck dumb' by Hoare's confident stance and it was left up to him to describe what he was likely to find in Spain. He told him that the people in the cities were starving, the secret police were ruthless, and they had heard from reliable sources that Franco was close to joining the war beside Hitler. On learning this, Hoare turned 'pale' and said he had been deceived and that his mission was hopeless and would therefore return to London. Eccles said that at the time 'Selby and I rallied him as best we could ...'[3]

The next day a telegram from London did not improve Hoare's mood when it told him to: 'Await further instructions before proceeding to Madrid ...' A day was spent waiting in Lisbon, whilst glued to the radio which was full of bad news.[4]

Eventually, they received the order to move on, and on 1 June they in Madrid. Flying over Portugal and Spain Hoare found Portugal 'verdant and varied' with an impressive 'smiling landscape' but the Spain of Estremadura and Castile was a country like many deserts he had flown over.[5]

Hoare remained fearful, and tried to hold the British Airways plane at Barajas airfield in case they had to leave in a hurry. He had even taken the precaution of carrying an automatic pistol and kept it with him night and day. Before leaving he had learnt how to use it in London. A bodyguard, who was a detective from Scotland Yard, also accompanied them. Arthur

Yencken from the Embassy was there at Barajas to meet them. Sir Samuel knew him fairly well having played tennis with him before. He told Hoare that there had been orchestrated demonstrations at the Embassy to welcome him, and they were chanting 'Gibraltar Esponal'.[6] However by the time they had arrived into the city they had dispersed for siesta. The Embassy needed repairs, so for the first few weeks they stayed at the Ritz Hotel. It had been a hospital during the Spanish Civil War but had been newly restored to a high standard. For Hoare however it proved far from ideal as it was full of Abwehr (German Military Secret Service) agents. They watched him round the clock and his telephone was tapped. It was not the haven of rest that he had enjoyed in Lisbon. In the surrounding area, people were often beaten up by Falange thugs and the wife of a German diplomat jumped from the top floor of the hotel upon learning that her husband had been recalled to Germany. It was so intolerable that they started looking for a house.[7]

Sir Samuel was soon firing a barrage of letters back to Britain announcing his displeasure. He addressed one to Lord Beaverbrook on 6 June 1940: 'If I had known the difficulties of this place. I never should have come here.' To Neville Chamberlain on the same day: 'Living in Madrid is like living in a besieged city.' To Lord Halifax who had asked him to take the post he wrote three days later: 'It seems futile to talk about all these things while the battle is going on.' And on 11 June: 'You cannot imagine how isolated I feel here.' He also addressed a letter to Winston Churchill on 12 June: 'At present I am not at all sure whether I shall be able to do any permanent good.'[8]

Immediate help was at hand to help him steer through the chaos. He had the excellent council of Military Attaché Brigadier Bill Tor and Naval Attaché Alan Hillgarth. Bill Tor helped him find a suitable house with his good knowledge of Madrid. The house was in the Castellana area within a brisk walk of the Embassy. The only disadvantage was that his next-door neighbour was the German Ambassador Baron von Stohrer.

Hillgarth was swift to advise Hoare, in writing, of his view of the state of the Embassy and its staff. He said they were a 'defeatist' bunch and needed 'a drastic reorganisation' and that the 'Special Branch here is not allowed to be efficient.'[9] After ten days in Madrid, Hoare wrote to Churchill to say that he had an '… excellent Naval Attaché in your friend Hillgarth'. He described him as a great 'prop'.[10] Hillgarth reported to DNI on security at the embassy where he found the staff lacking in the basics of security and likely too 'careless or deliberate [with their] disclosure of information by members of staff, of whom there were at one time over 400 in the Embassy alone.' He felt the need for a 'full time security officer, but he must be at least First Secretary's rank and should not be a career diplomat.' Who he found was often 'the most careless of all'.[11]

George Hugh Jocelyn Evans was born on 7 June 1899 at 121 Harley Street, the second son of the Surgeon Willmott Evans. He would, in 1926, change his name to Alan Hillgarth having first used the name as a nom de plume in his writing career. He was descended from Evan Evans, who was a Second Surgeon's mate in the Royal Navy of the 18th century. A further seven generations of the Evans family became naval surgeons. Hugh, aged 12, was sent to Osborne College on the Isle of Wight, which was the preparatory school for the Royal Navy, and with his olive complexion and dark hair, he was dubbed 'the little dago'.[12]

On the whole, he enjoyed life at Osborne. In the summer of 1913 the cadets took part in the Spithead Review aboard the battleship *Bulwark* which he found 'absolutely topping'.[13] In May 1914 he moved on to Britannia Royal Naval College at Dartmouth, to start the two-year course to make him a naval officer. However the outbreak of war changed that as all cadets were sent off to join fighting ships for the war effort. He joined the crew on the Cressy-Class armoured cruiser *Bacchante* which had been laid down in 1899 and would soon become obsolete. On the day war was declared, Cruiser Force C, of which *Bacchante* was a part, was on patrol in the North Sea. Afterwards, back in Deal, they learned they had sailed through a minefield where another cruiser had blown up and sank with the loss of 150 men.

Weeks later, Cruiser Force C provided a screen to intercept the movements of German ships during the battle of Heligoland Bight but was not directly engaged. *Bacchante* took on casualties and Hugh worked in the sick bay witnessing harrowing scenes. He told his mother that they brought the wounded and dead back to Chatham.[14]

By the end of 1914 *Bacchante* was in the Mediterranean. On 17 December Hugh sent home a photograph of himself from Gibraltar. In January, the ship was back in home waters whilst briefly docked at Devonport before heading back to the Mediterranean on convoy duties. Soon after, she joined the fleet in Egypt and arrived at Port Said in February 1915.[15] After serving mainly in the Canal Zone, the *Bacchante* joined the Gallipoli campaign and arrived at the Allies, main naval base in Moudros on 12 April. The ship supported the landings at Gaba Tepe, a headland north of Cape Helles at the tip of the Gallipoli Peninsula. Her midshipmen, including Hugh, were in charge of the ship's launches which were used to tow barges full of Anzac troops ashore.

Bacchante had a lucky escape. She had been on bombardment duties around Suvla Bay when she was relieved by *HMS Triumph* on 24 May. They had been warned that German U-boats were in the area. *U-21* had left Wilhelmshaven on 25 April for the eastern Mediterranean and it reached Gallipoli on 25 May. At first the anti-submarine patrols, spotting her periscope, forced her away. A torpedo was fired at *Vengeance* but was spotted and avoiding action was taken. However, Commander Otto Hersing skilfully stalked the *Triumph* off Anzac Cove and at 12:25 U21 struck. Hersing fired torpedoes and one hit home. The destroyer *Chelmer* saved most of the crew on *Triumph* by putting her bows close into the stern of the sinking ship and a lot of men were able to escape, without getting wet, onto the *Chelmer* decks. However, seventy-five men were lost with *Triumph*.[16] Hugh wrote to his mother on 31 May about the sinking of *Triumph*. He was not even sixteen at the time.

During the time the vessel was sinking and the boats were picking up survivors, the Turks and Germans were firing at them. 'Shrapnel burst over us, and I should say that a fair percentage of the people who were killed were hit by shrapnel bullets while in the water. It was ghastly.'[17]

Much of the time with the *Bacchante* at Gallipoli, Hugh spent with the picket boats on various duties assisting the troops. He often visited the trenches, writing to his father in July that he was only fifteen yards from the Turkish lines in no-man's-land. He said that dead bloated bodies gave off a sickening stench.[18] The horrors of Gallipoli would haunt him for the rest of his life.

On 4 November he was transferred to the Beagle-Class torpedo-boat destroyer *Wolverine*, a much smaller vessel with a crew of 96 compared to the 750 on *Bacchante*. *Wolverine* also took him away from the carnage of Gallipoli and Captain Algy Boyle of the *Bacchante* who he felt 'had a down' on him.[19] He joined his new ship in Malta where she was refitting and to his delight he found his new skipper was a 'treasure'.[20]

In April 1916 *Wolverine* was bombarding Turkish coastal defences when it came under small arms fire and midshipman Evans was wounded. He was transferred to a hospital ship and, via Malta, sent home to England to recover.

Fit again he served on the battlecruiser *Princess Royal*, which was not a happy time as he was court marshalled for being asleep on duty but later acquitted.[21] He was soon back in the Mediterranean on the sloop *Lily*. He started writing short stories about Gallipoli to pass the time. The first to be published appeared in *Sketch* magazine in July 1918. He stayed in the navy when the war ended, witnessing some of the events of the Russian Revolution and Civil War while serving in the cruiser *Ceres* in the Black Sea.[22] These events were inspired his first novel *The Princess and the Perjurer* which was published by Chapman & Dodd in 1924.

The novel featured a scene where a ship arrives at Constantinople packed with White Russian refugees. There were soldiers, Cossacks, civilians, women and many children. There were wounded too, and those stricken with disease. There were even dead bodies of those who had perished with exhaustion. Others, unprotected from the rain and from the cold, without sanitary arrangements of any sort, some of them nearly naked, were unable to move: 'Those who looked at me had in their eyes a dull, glazed stare, devoid of any emotion ... They were of every class, I knew. Refugees from the Crimea might be princes or peasants. You could seldom tell by looking at them, so begrimed were they by filth, so far sunk in despair.'[23]

At the registrar's office in Gibraltar, on 18 October 1921, Hugh married a nurse named Violet Mary Tapper. She was 27 and he was 22. The marriage only lasted a few weeks during which time they stayed at the Hotel Reina Cristina in Algeciras before she disappeared. She would go on to do this to other partners. Finally, in 1924, she divorced Hugh for adultery.[24]

In September 1922, after eight years of service, Hugh was placed on the retired list at his own request.[25] However it is likely, like thousands of the others, he may have been a victim of the 'Geddes Axe' when in 1922–23 defence spending was slashed from £190 million to about £110 million. These economies were named after the chairman of the National Expenditure Committee Sir Eric Geddes. Thousands of servicemen were released prematurely while ex-servicemen suffered pension cuts.

Hugh did not have the burning ambition to stay in the navy. In 1923 he commuted his annual pension of £97 for a one-off lump sum of £1,370.[26] He then took up his pen to become a writer and in the following years wrote and travelled a lot. In 1924 he obtained a master's certificate from the Board of Trade which qualified him to command private vessels, but he had to get it replaced a year later after the motor yacht *Constance* caught fire and exploded in the Spanish port of Almeria, which was owned by Sir Cecil Harcourt Smith. Hugh had taken her from Monte Carlo bound for Gibraltar. There was talk of gun-running to Morocco.

Two years after leaving the navy he was calling himself Alan Hillgarth. His second novel *The Passionate Trail* was published in 1925 by Hutchinson. It was set in Egypt, and the hero Harry Chester foils a plot against British rule in Africa hatched by a Mad Mardi type of figure. He also falls in love with plenty of 'exotic' women. It seems as if he was clearly influenced by the likes of John Buchan and Rider Haggard.

On 3 September 1926 it was announced in *The Times* that he had changed his name to 'Alan Hugh Hillgarth Evans'. In 1928, by deed poll, he dropped the Evans to become Alan Hugh Hillgarth.[27]

In 1923 he was in Ireland and he produced a 1,000-word report entitled 'Bolshevism in Southern Ireland'. Who this was for remains unclear.[28] He completed the novel *The War Maker* in 1925 published by Thomas Nelson & Sons. This was his third different publisher so clearly his 'pot boilers' were not a great success. This time, the hero Shaun McCarthy is offered five thousand pounds to run guns to Rif tribesmen in Morocco. This was probably influenced by his time in Ireland. Soon after, he went to Morocco.

After Morocco, Alan set off for the Americas sailing around South America in an ocean-going yacht. There are hints that he worked for the government as a King's Messenger to deliver confidential documents to British Embassies and Consulates around the world.[29] The cruise ended after several months at Palm Beach Florida where he stayed at the Yacht Club. Here he contributed several articles to sailing journals, including one to *The Rudder* on the Duke of York's Trophy international race. *What Price Paradise*, his next book, published by Houghton Mifflin in 1929 was based on his time at Palm Beach and was the story of the rampant commercialism he found there. He also sold articles to the *Daily Telegraph* on smuggling alcohol during the Prohibition.

He returned to England in 1926 for a few days and worked on the London Underground during the General Strike. He was promoted to lieutenant commander in the Navy in 1927, which was unusual as he was still on the retired list. Could this possibly have been his reward for the work he had done for the Admiralty?

In 1928 Alan set off on a treasure hunt for lost gold to Sacambaya in the Bolivian Andes. It had been long rumoured that there was a colossal hoard of gold that had been hidden by Jesuit priests at or near the monastery of Plazuela in the high Andes. King Charles V of Spain had banned these priests from the New World for meddling in politics. Their wealth was based on the exploitation of gold mines in the area. Other earlier expeditions had found nothing. The 1928 undertaking was led by Dr Edgar Sanders, a Swiss national, who had led two previous reconnaissance trips to the area in 1925 and 1926. A company was set up for the far bigger 1928 trip, where members were expected to invest and take part. It is not known how much Alan invested.

They took masses of equipment with them which on the final leg up to Sacambaya had to be transported by mules. Alan was not impressed by the valley which he called: 'a poisonous place – a dark, dirty valley shut in by hills.' This valley was infested with biting insects and snakes, and it was boiling hot during the daytime and freezing at night.[30] Having arrived in March it was a fiasco by November and after months of hard work they had found nothing. The enterprise was abandoned for the year. Alan never returned. In 1930 the company was wound up. Somehow Alan became the record keeper, keeping boxes of documents and a silver crucifix which had supposedly been found on one of the earlier trips. He kept in touch with Sanders. In later years stories abounded about other expeditions but they never found anything. One local guide, asked why no gold had been found replied: 'It's a gringo treasure.'[31]

During the Sacambaya fiasco, Alan was distracted by his scandalous love affair with Mary Hope-Morley, a dark-haired beauty, a married woman of thirty-two, and estranged from her husband the Hon Geoffrey Hope-Morley. Mary's mother Winifred was the daughter of the 4th Earl of Carnarvon, a noted statesman, while her brother, the 5th Earl of Carnarvon, was the Egyptologist who discovered Tutankhamun's tomb in the Valley of the Kings. Mary's marriage to Geoffrey was dissolved on 3 December 1928 on the grounds of Mary's adultery with Alan, and was cited as taking place at the Savoy Hotel. In January 1930 Alan and Mary were married and their son Jocelyn was born in September. The marriage freed Alan from financial worries as Mary, once Geoffrey had been granted his 'decree nisi', had settled to give her a generous allowance of £4000 a year. Soon after, *What Price Paradise* came out in America but sales were again poor.

The 150-foot twin-masted Dutch built schooner *Blue Water* was bought by Alan in 1929. He set off, complete with a crew and cook, for the Mediterranean, stopping at Majorca that summer as news broke of the Wall Street Crash.

In 1930 Alan and Mary purchased an old finca called 'Son Torrella' which was twelve miles inland from Palma. They were both enchanted by the old farm house and the island, and it was far cheaper in the circumstances to live in Spain. Over two years they restored the house, adding running water, bathrooms and electricity, whilst furniture was obtained locally along with a few pieces sourced from England. A large painting of Mary's great-great-grandmother was delivered by the battlecruiser HMS *Hood,* by a group of petty officers who delivered it to Son Torrella.

Alan's next novel, *The Black Mountain*, was based on his adventures to try to find gold at Sacambaya, and it was published in 1933 by Ivor Nicholson & Watson, his fifth publisher. The reviews were favourable and the film rights were sold in America for $5000 although the movie was never made. The book, like the others, did not sell well.

In December 1932 Alan was appointed the acting 'Vice Consul' in Palma by the British government. Though it was an unpaid post, he could at least be reimbursed for expenses.

Winston Churchill and his wife Clemmie visited Majorca in 1935 and stayed at Pollensa. Winston had come to the island to paint. They were invited to Son Torrella for lunch, which was an oasis of tranquillity. Sharing many common interests, including books and writing, Alan and Winston became friends, and it proved to be an enduring friendship.

Mary and Alan at this time enjoyed a golden period in their lives, yet around them Spain was in political turmoil. The country had fragmented and there were numerous political parties and labour unions which held seats in parliament. Governments formed and fell and soon it spiralled toward civil war. As Hugh Thomas puts it: 'So now there was to spread over Spain a cloud of violence, in which the quarrels of several generations would find outlet. With communications difficult or non-existent, each town would find itself on its own, acting out its own drama, apparently in a vacuum. There were soon not two Spain's, but two thousand.'[32]

That cloud of violence would soon find its way to Majorca. Alan, as the official British representative on the island, would find his diplomatic skills strained. In a dispatch to the Foreign Office, he observed that the average Spaniard on the whole loathed all foreigners '… and is so extremely individual that he loathes most of his fellow countrymen as well.'[33]

War broke out in July 1936 between the left-wing Republican government and the Nationalist Forces led by General Francisco Franco. Hillgarth had known Franco from the time the general had been in command of the Balearic Islands defences.

MI6 was involved in flying Franco to Spain. Major Hugh Pollard, sporting editor of the magazine *Country Life,* was an ardent Catholic Fascist sympathiser, and had been a police advisor during the Anglo-Irish war of 1919–1921. He arranged a chartered flight from Croydon Airport, using a de Havilland Dragon Rapide (G. ACYR), which flew the Spanish general from the Canary Islands to Morocco, which allowed Franco, '… to kick-start the armed challenge to the Republic.'[34]

The expatriate community may have thought briefly they were safe on Majorca since there had been no fighting on the island since the 15th century. However, Ibiza, fifty miles to the south, was invaded in early August. The Republicans quickly took that island and brutally stamped their authority there by attacking the church where twenty-one priests were killed and many churches torched.

The battlecruiser *Repulse* had already evacuated some 400 foreign nationals from Majorca. Most were British but there were also Germans, French and Americans. Alan had been on holiday with his family in England when hostilities broke out. He left Mary and Jocelyn behind and returned to Palma on the destroyer HMS *Gipsy*. On arriving, his main preoccupation was to deal with the expatriates who had refused to leave and he reported to the Foreign Office that there were 'eighty-eight' who refused.[35]

On 16 August a force of 2,500 men landed on Majorca from Republican warships. Four days later, Alan reported their attack had failed and that revenge was now being taken: '… Communists have been shot every night, but this cannot last long as there are not many left to shoot.'[36]

The British and French policy of non-intervention in Spain left Alan in an awkward position in the largely conservative Majorca. He had no time for the Communists and although he inclined toward the Nationalists he detested Fascism. During this time, Majorca was being built up as an Axis base with many German soldiers and Italian airmen arriving. The Axis bombers were within easy range of Valencia, Cartagena, and Barcelona, and there were bombing missions flying off every day soon after. Alan reported this to the FO. He observed that if the Republican cause were to succeed on the mainland, Majorca was likely to: 'turn to some power for protection and in the present conditions that power would certainly be Italy.'[37]

Mussolini's Italy supplied far more support to the Nationalists in Spain than Germany did. There were about 75,000 Italian military personnel serving in the country, and 4,300 would die compared to about 300 Germans killed, and 200 Soviets fighting on the Republican side.[38]

After a few months Mary returned to the island arriving on a British destroyer and they lived in a rented house in Palma. Once the threat of invasion had receded, and the Spanish Army had installed a telephone at Son Torrella, they returned to their farm. Alan was free to move about the island to check on the remaining expatriates. He became skilled at treading the thin line between the two sides, managing on one occasion to get the former Republican mayor of Palma, and his wife, off the island by smuggling them onto a British destroyer. Yet at the same time he developed a close working relationship with Vice Admiral Francisco Moreno Fernandez who commanded the Nationalist forces on the Balearic Islands. But as the war dragged on and became more savage, Alan wrote of the vice admiral that: '… it became increasingly difficult to get him to see reason.'[39]

The British government recognised the good work he had done and in April 1937 he was awarded an OBE. Robert Graves who had lived on Majorca but left before the war wrote to congratulate him, observing that he must 'be getting tired of it by now'. Admiral Somerville, on the other hand, felt he should have received the CMG (Companion of the Order of St Michael and St George) for the 'exacting work' he had done.[40] By the end of 1937 the number of British subjects on the island had risen to 137 as several returned to their homes despite the fact that Italian propaganda, Alan wrote, had made the British and Britain: 'more unpopular here than she has ever been since we were last at war with Spain.'[41]

Alan worked tirelessly to save Spanish lives on both sides. He rescued Fernando Morenes y Curvajal, el Conde del Asalto, who had been captured and held by the Republicans and was awaiting execution on a prison ship in Barcelona harbour. Learning he would soon be shot, Alan bluffed his way into see him and smuggled him out dressed as a Royal Navy officer, going as far as to shave off his moustache.[42] The two families became firm friends after that. Alan was instrumental in obtaining the surrender of Minorca to the Nationalists in 1939. HMS *Devonshire* took the delegation from Majorca to Port Mahon, and then the ship was used as a neutral meeting venue for the two sides. In spite of the Italians bombing the island while this was going on, much to the anger of the cruiser's captain G. C. Muirhead-Gould, the surrender was concluded. The *Devonshire* then took 450 Republicans to Marseilles.

Duff Hart-Davis wrote of this:

> As usual, Alan played down his own role in the proceedings, but his intervention was his single most important act during the whole war, and must have saved more lives than all the rest put together. It was his friendship with (Conde de) San Luis, his total command of Spanish, his steady nerve, his ability to commandeer a British warship, and his reputation as a diplomat with Spain's best interests at heart, that made Minorca's peaceful transfer of loyalty possible: by averting the threat of a Nationalist invasion, he prevented hundreds of deaths and wholesale destruction of property. For this he was remembered on the island with intense gratitude for the rest of his life, and for more than twenty years after his death.[43]

At the end of the war, Alan sent a memorandum to the FO that the Spanish were now concerned that a European War: 'would force them into active participation on the side of the Axis, a thing they do not want ...' But would find difficult to avoid believing Germany 'is invincible'.[44]

The Spanish Civil War had cost Alan not only financially but in time away from his writing and his family. Admiral Sir Dudley Pound Commander-in-Chief of the Mediterranean during most of the civil war recommended that Alan should be promoted to Commander on the retired list as recognition for his efforts over the three years. The Admiralty turned it down as he had not completed enough service on the active list.

When Admiral Godfrey became DNI, he addressed the glaring omission of there being no resident naval attaché in Madrid. The Paris naval attaché was meant to cover Spain, which was a wholly inadequate arrangement. By June 1939 he had convinced the Treasury and Foreign Office to appoint an assistant to the NA in Paris to reside in Madrid. This was just the first step. The next step was to transfer the post to Lisbon, before finally upgrading to the naval attaché in Madrid.[45] Godfrey and Alan met in 1938 when the *Repulse* came to Majorca. They found they had much in common having both served during the Gallipoli Campaign as junior officers. Alan proved a great help. He had a mission to visit the British Legation at Caldetas near Barcelona, and was worried his ship might get caught up in Italian air raids. However Alan, through his contacts within the Spanish Command and Italian Air Force, obtained the undertaking promise that no raids would be conducted in the area during the *Repulse* visit. Godfrey called it an outstanding feat 'in practical diplomacy'.[46] In August 1939 Alan took up the post of NA in Madrid and was recalled to the navy's active list.

David Eccles arrived in the Spanish capital in November and found there was 'a great deal of damage' from the civil war. He was soon at work and wrote to his wife Sybil:

> We had our first meeting today. It is curious how difficult it is to realise that England is at war and that we must bend our efforts to winning as soon as possible. If we were not at war we could certainly give some very welcome and very valuable assistance to the reconstruction of this country. As it is it will be more difficult, but we shall manage something.[47]

The task facing the new naval attaché to Madrid was daunting. The British Ambassador, Sir Maurice Peterson, had treated his role casually and chose to reside in Paris. There had been no NA in Madrid for sixteen years. His predecessors had done little in the country and, as Alan wrote: '[had] no knowledge of the place or people and no influence whatever.'[48]

CHAPTER 4

The Network

When Tom Burns crossed the border from France into Spain, in February 1940, he had been working for the Ministry of Information for just four months. Before that he had been a Catholic publisher. He was thirty-four, handsome, debonair and with Latin looks. He was Chilean born, and his father David Burns was a Scottish banker. His mother Clara was also Chilean born from British stock. He might have been flustered as his companion Denis Cowan, who had recruited him into MoI, had been recalled to London. At Hendaye in south west France they had checked with the British consulate before crossing the border. There an official letter was waiting for Cowan marked 'urgent'. It instructed Cowan to return to London and for Burns to continue onto Madrid alone.[1]

Cowan had served as a neutral observer during the civil war implementing the non-intervention policy and was therefore not trusted by the Nationalists, who believed the observers had favoured the Republic. Cowan's and Burn's mission to Spain was a reconnaissance trip to set up a propaganda department at the British Embassy in Madrid. The Spanish Ambassador to London, the Duke of Alba, had got wind of the mission and had complained to the Foreign Office about Cowan's 'pro-Republican sympathies'.[2]

So Tom took the grey Humber in which the two men had 'bowled along' the roads of France and alone headed south skirting the Pyrenees. The high peaks still had snow on them but he found the valleys were alive with the green shoots of spring. He missed Cowan. They had got on well during the journey. They shared the sense of adventure that the open road instilled and, like the weather, their mood had improved as they moved further south.[3]

It was a landscape Tom was familiar with. He had walked the Pyrenees as a schoolboy, following in the writer Hilaire Belloc's footsteps. He had even approached him for advice on crossing the mountains. Shortly after his journey began, he had become lost, but he soon found his way again aided by a priest and some friendly villagers. Motoring south toward Burgos he recalled his time there in 1937, driving an ambulance donated by English Catholics to the Nationalist headquarters during his summer holidays. His companion travellers on that occasion had been Gabriel Herbert, a volunteer nurse, and a mysterious former soldier, whom he thought might be a spy.

Burgos had been the old capital of Castile: '… a grave reserved, conservative city, the rising triumphed without difficulty and with scarcely a shot fired.' The Condesa de Vallellano said, 'The very stones are Nationalist here.'[4]

It became Franco's headquarters, well chosen as it was the birthplace of Rodrigo Diaz de Vivar, El Cid Campeador, the legendary 11th century knight and mercenary. The Cid's remains, and that of his wife Jimena, are in the 11th century cathedral. The diminutive Generalissimo wanted to be Spain's new El Cid at the head of a holy crusade to liberate Spain from communists, freemasons, and foreigners.

In 1939 Burns found Burgos had lost the 'sense of urgency' it had during the civil war and was instead like 'a woman with nothing to do but confront the chores and tedium of solitary life.'[5] Beyond Burgos lay the great plains of Castile which were new to Tom then. It was harvest time when the now famous writer Laurie Lee had walked across this sea of waving, ripening crops before the Civil War broke out:

> Green oaks like rocks lay scattered among the cornfields, with peasant's chest-deep in the wheat. It was the peak of harvest, and figures of extraordinary brilliance were spread across the fields like butterflies, working alone or in clusters, and dressed to the pitch of the light-blue shirts and trousers, and with broad gold hats tied with green and scarlet cloths. Submerged in the wheat, sickles flickered like fish, with rhythmic flashes of blue and silver, and as I passed men straightened and shielded their eyes, silently watching me go, or a hand was raised in salute, showing among its sun-black fingers the glittering sickle like a curved sixth nail.[6]

The landscape Tom drove across was markedly different to what Laurie Lee had witnessed, and far from that which Don Quixote and Rocinante had plodded through. It was instead a 'limitless table land' of brown naked soil destroyed by war and interspersed with trenches and barbed wire and burned out villages. He was grateful to finally see the clear outline of Madrid before him.[7] The Spanish capital also showed the gaping wounds of war having been in the front line for three years. Reporting to the Embassy, Tom was told to come back on Monday. But a room was booked for him at the Palace Hotel, which was built in 1912 on the Plaza de las Cortes. It had been one of the largest hospitals during the civil war, and one of the first buildings to be restored.

Tom was tired out by the time he reached the Palace after he had driven for about 300 miles across some of the most war-torn roads in Europe. When he arrived at the hotel: 'A group of journalists were predictably to be found at the bar but I had no inclination to mix with them …' All he wanted was his bed.[8]

On Monday 19 February Tom reported to the Embassy. He soon realised it was understaffed and chaotic. Yet the Assistant Press Attaché Bernard Malley, a former teacher at El Escorial and fellow Catholic, would prove to be a fountain of excellent advice. Known at the Embassy as *Don Bernardo* Tom soon found that, 'he gleaned information and exercised influence in areas seldom reached by the career diplomats.'[9] He had built up contacts in Spain over many years.

From the start, Alan Hillgarth and Tom got on well together, with the former proving a good guide to the Madrid nightlife. Alan was accomplished at mapping out the numerous espionage groups in the city with all their pitfalls. He was then engaged on building up the British Intelligence gathering network across the Iberian Peninsula. He had already built a good rapport with the Nationalist Naval officers from his days in Majorca, as acknowledged by an NID report to the other British intelligence services that he was: '… already on excellent terms with the Spanish naval authorities who both like and trust him.'[10] Yet Hillgarth was lucky to have inherited a legacy stretching back to World War I. It was a legacy that helped him with one of the most important contacts he could have, that of Juan March, referred to as 'The Pirate'.

By the time that World War II had started, Juan March was one of the wealthiest men in Spain. He had started smuggling tobacco, and anything else that might make a profit, from North Africa to Spain. In the first war he had brokered arms deals to both sides. He had been instrumental in transferring the £2,000 needed for the hire of the Dragon Rapide DH 89, which was used to fly Franco from the Canary Islands to Spanish Morocco. The money was paid into the account of Kleinwort Benson & Sons, a London merchant bank. He also financed the transfer of Franco's African Army to Spain by air.

He was born in Santa Margarita, Majorca, in 1880 and was the son of a farmer. March had come to know Hillgarth on Majorca probably before the civil war. One story has him interned by the Republicans before the civil war, but Philip Vickers wrote: '… he escaped by bribing all his jailers and taking them with him to Paris at his own expense.'[11]

It is inconceivable that at some point Alan did not hear about, or even meet, Charles Julian Thoroton, former Colonel of the Royal Marines, who had run British Naval Intelligence in Spain during World War I. It was Thoroton who affectionately called March 'my pirate' and he secured his services for the

Allies with his: 'smuggling, commercial and maritime empire provided some 40,000 agents to the network.'[12]

Major Thoroton arrived in Gibraltar in 1913 and was appointed senior naval intelligence officer for the colony on 12 September. The author Alfred Edward Woodley Mason was head of operations in Spain, best remembered for his 1902 novel *The Four Feathers*. However, Mason was more often inclined to act as a field agent, leaving Thoroton as the director. Late in 1916 Mason sailed around Spain in a steam yacht supplied by Blinker Hall: 'with a large, mixed house party' whose 'careless sightseeing formed an excellent cover under which he made a careful search for German submarine bases.'[13]

The 'cover' cannot have been that good because he was recalled by Hall having become too well known. He was replaced by the then Colonel Charles Thoroton known as 'Charles the Bold' by those within NI.[14] It was Thoroton who, in May 1915, during a meeting with March, had convinced the wily businessman to support the Allies. He became Thoroton's most important source. Sir Basil Thomson, assistant commissioner of the Metropolitan Police and head of the CID at Scotland Yard, had responsibility for catching spies. When the war broke out, his services were secured for the Admiralty and War Office. He wrote in his diary about the German attempts to turn March over to their side:

> He keeps the government quiet by bribing officials and occasionally permitting captures of cargo, but he turned over the services of his staff to watch the coast for German submarines. The Germans offered him money, and he replied they might as well offer him an elephant, and then they tried a decoration, and he said he could buy things to hang on his coat whenever he wanted them. Then they tried a lady from Hamburg, who first would and then would not, though he offered her 30,000 pesetas. This infuriated him. Thoroton had told him she was a spy. He said he did not care what she was. He meant to have her. Thoroton became nervous, but early this month he [March] returned triumphant from Madrid with a scratch across his nose inflicted by the lady, who resented having received only 1,000 pesetas. Now the smuggler [March] is in harness again.[15]

Thomson thought the 'lady from Hamburg' might have been the actress Beatrice von Brunner, whom he had arrested in 1915. It seemed that she had been turned by NI and sent to Gibraltar to infiltrate German spy rings, but they rumbled her and tried to poison her.[16]

In 1919 Thoroton retired from the Royal Marines after twenty-six years of service. The Spanish government had even sought his retention as he knew more about Spain and had better contacts than their own Secret Service.

Thus he served as a Commissioner to the Federation of British Industry in Madrid for five years. It was a continuation of his wartime work but for commercial and financial purposes, and so was in effect industrial intelligence.

In 1923 he retired to his villa Stella Maris, Pedregalejo, Malaga, although he had use of a property in Madrid courtesy of the government. He lived in Spain until the start of the civil war and retained his links with March. He also had a house in England, The Grove at Canford Cliffs, Bournemouth, which remained in his family after his death, before it was later demolished. We know he visited his old friend Marshal Louis Lyautey in Morocco in 1933 who called Thoroton a personal friend and a 'friend of France'.[17] Thoroton probably left Spain for the last time just before or just after the outbreak of the civil war and died in Britain on 17 January 1939. He remains a shadowy figure especially because he destroyed most of his own papers. It was Alan's work with March which built up his network in his early months as naval attaché in Madrid: '... in this Hillgarth was Thoroton's beneficiary.'[18]

The enemy Alan Hillgarth faced in Spain in the early months of the war was powerful and well established. Admiral Canaris had in February 1937 started the Abwehr stations in the Iberian Peninsula. He built up a large number of agents and contacts with an intricate communications web. He also created 'several dummy firms-including Rowak Hisna, Carlos Hinderer & Co and Transmare to serve as blinds to handle financial transactions ...' Transmare was the biggest, with interests in Spanish Morocco and South America. Ladislas Farago wrote: 'It was managed by Canaris's sole truly intimate friend in the world, an obscure Russian exile known as Baron Ino, whose real name was Baron Roland Kaulbars.'[19]

Well in advance of World War II, Canaris had built up the elaborate Kriegs-organisation (War Organisation) or KO Stations. In the end there would be six major KOs abroad in Spain, Portugal, Switzerland, Sweden, Turkey, and China. The first to be operational was in Madrid housed with the embassy, and in adjacent buildings there were about eighty Abwehr staff, plus OKW Oberkommando der Wehrmacht (German Armed Forces High Command) radio intercept teams and a branch of the RSHA, the supreme state security department set up in 1939 to supervise the other security organisations. About half the embassy staff in 1939 was working in intelligence, and towards the end of the war that ratio would increase. They were dependent on good relations with the host country because the KO personnel were 'built in' with the diplomatic service. This would later cause great problems but in the early years of the war, the Spanish authorities turned a blind eye to this abuse of the diplomatic code.

There were other smaller KOs in the country in San Sebastian, Barcelona, Seville, and in Spanish Morocco. These worked from the German consulates present in the region. In addition there were Abwehr agents in all the Spanish ports.[20] Walter Schellenberg on a mission for the RSHA passed through Madrid in 1940 and visited the Embassy.

Madrid was one of the most strongly developed centres of the German Secret Service. Apart from active espionage and counter-espionage, its military sector included between seventy and a hundred employees who lived and worked in one of the extra-territorial buildings of the German Embassy. There, we had one of our most important short-wave listening posts and decoding stations. There was also a meteorological station with sub-stations in Portugal the Canary Islands, and North and South Africa. This station was of decisive importance to our Luftwaffe and U-boat operations off the Bay of Biscay and in the western Mediterranean area, while the centre at Madrid also supervised the surveillance of the Straits of Gibraltar.[21]

The Abwehr enjoyed another advantage of being able to work closely with the Spanish Secret Service, the 'Sirene' run by General Martinez Campos, an old friend of Canaris.

To make matters worse for Hillgarth he soon found out that SIS were weak in Spain and, against his better judgement, found he had to shoulder this responsibility as well. He believed that the naval attaché should not have: 'knowledge of the organisation or the sources of SIS or expect to see reports.'[22]

After his appointment in Madrid he began to recruit agents for this task. He had the help of his skilled assistant Lieutenant-Commander Salvador Augustus Gomez-Beare, known as the 'Don'. He was born in Gibraltar of Anglo-Spanish parents and could easily pass for Spanish being fluent in the language. He had served in all three branches of the British Armed forces and had suffered injury in the Royal Flying Corps, whilst during the Civil War he had seen action with the Nationalist Army in military intelligence. In 1939 his offer of service to Britain was accepted and he was commissioned into the RNVR. He set to work quickly travelling hundreds of miles across the country on errands. He was at home with all levels of Spanish society from dock workers to the aristocracy. Alan called him 'invaluable'.[23]

With financial backing from SIS approved by Sir Stewart Menzies, Alan was able to bribe an officer in the Spanish Secret Service to obtain a list of the key Abwehr agents. Meanwhile, according to Keith Jeffery, he had set up 'his own counter-intelligence system, code-named "Secolo" targeting German attempts to sabotage British ships in Spanish ports. Some positive work was at last being done.'[24]

However, as with Thoroton, Hillgarth's most effective ally would be Juan March. He was fifty-nine when the war broke out. He was now bald, wore thick spectacles, looked frail and walked with a stoop, but he still had a keen mind. Many thought him nothing short of a criminal. Alan wrote that he was: 'the most unscrupulous and the richest man in Spain besides one of the cleverest.'[25]

Some accounts cite that Alan was first introduced to March in September 1939 by Sir Maurice Peterson, but this is unlikely to have been his first meeting.

He already knew him from Majorca, when Alan had been vice-consul in Palma during the civil war. Their respective homes had only been a few miles apart.[26]

In their first Madrid meeting March broached the subject to him of buying all the German ships which were interned and laid up in Spanish ports, totalling fifty-nine. He intended to pay the Germans for the ships in pesetas paid into Spanish banks which could not be drawn on until the end of the war. Once he had control of these ships, Britain could use them and Spain could have the money. Alan was taken with the idea, and he sent March off to London under the cover of a business trip to see Godfrey, but with a warning for the admiral not 'to trust him an inch'.[27] Godfrey was impressed by March even though they had to use an interpreter, and wrote in his diary of their meeting on 23 September:

> He explained that he 'had control' of all Spanish ports except on the north and north west coasts (meaning I suppose from Vigo to San Sebastian) and, believing the future of Spain was bound up with that of Great Britain, he would do all in his power to help us. If we received reports of U-boats taking fuel from a Spanish oiler or in a Spanish port, he asked us not to sabotage the ship or create fires and explosions in the port as we used to do in World War I. Instead would we let him know and he would see that it did not happen again. The same applied to 'incidents' in Spanish ports which should be minimised rather than exaggerated. He explained that the port authorities were under his control. He said that Franco would never let the German Army into Spain. He wanted the relations of Spain and England to be friendly and tranquil and would do all he could to achieve this end. We kept in touch and he passed me valuable information which was never incorrect.[28]

Churchill had wanted to see 'Senor Marche' but the meeting did not take place. However he wrote to Godfrey that he felt March: 'may be able to render the greatest service in bringing about friendly relations with Spain' and they should not be put off because: 'he made money by devious means in no way affects his value to us at this present time or his reputation as a Spanish patriot.'[29] Of course Churchill was well aware of the service March had already provided for Britain in World War I through his own correspondence with Thoroton who had stayed in touch with him up until his death. Thoroton wrote a three-page letter to Churchill from the Villa Stella Maris in May 1936 about his concerns for Gibraltar. The letter ends with the hope he has, 'written enough to rouse your interest but not so much as to bore you.'[30]

From the start of the war, the Germans had planned to resupply U-boats off Cadiz, Vigo, and Las Palmas de Gran Canaria, and Franco had indicated a willingness to help. In August 1939 they started to put the plan into operation only for Franco to cancel the arrangements by letter on 4 September.[31] But only four days later, he changed his mind and allowed it to move ahead. An interned German tanker was to be used in the operation, and supplies were to be provided by Spain, beginning on a dark winter's night off Cadiz in January

1940. However, no doubt through March's network, British intelligence was alerted and, in the face of stiff British and French protests, Franco cancelled further activity. Alan reported to Godfrey in February that they had bribed customs officials at Vigo and other ports in order to make it impossible for German submarines to call there. However the fall of France would change that.[32]

Rather like Thoroton before him, Hillgarth came to trust March and later wrote that he was: 'a very clever man but a scrupulously honourable one. He always carried out his undertakings and always stood by those who trusted him.'[33]

While Burns was in Madrid, he helped Hillgarth lobby London for more funds and personnel to extend the propaganda and intelligence operations spreading out from Madrid across the entire Iberian Peninsula. He was back in London in April pressing MoI and the Foreign Office for a larger network of press and information offices across Spain to be directed by the Madrid Embassy.

His experienced friend and colleague Paul Dorchy was sent to Barcelona to open an office. Supplying him with adequate resources proved more difficult, so he encouraged Dorchy to write to MoI. 'There is an enormous amount to do and people are eager for British propaganda but my hands are tied until someone comes out from Madrid with some sort of credentials …'[34] It was not until the MoI and Foreign Office stopped arguing about who was responsible for him that he obtained the funds and staff required.

In March Alan was promoted to acting-captain. He was now working under the code-name 'Armada' and never revealed any sign of his involvement with intelligence, through his use of third-party agents. Through the 'Don', Gomez-Beare, they had built up a large network of help from dockworkers, customs officials, bar-owners, taxi drivers and shop owners, who would act as their eyes and ears.

On 10 May, hours after the German Blitzkrieg struck the Low Countries and France, Churchill was chosen to replace Chamberlain as prime minister. Three days later he asked the House of Commons for a vote of confidence in the new administration: 'After reporting the progress which had been made in filling the various offices, I said: "I have nothing to offer but blood, toil, tears, and sweat." In all our long history no prime minister had ever been able to present to Parliament and the nation a programme at once so short and popular.'[35]

A month later Alan flew to London with another ambitious plan to offer Churchill which March and himself had cooked up. It was to gain favour with anti-German forces in Spain by bribing high-ranking Spanish officers to pressure Franco in to staying out of the war. Churchill gave his enthusiastic support. Alan had the rare privilege of direct access to the prime minister who trusted his judgement about Spain. He was also glad to have him in Madrid to keep an eye on Hoare, the new ambassador, who he was not entirely comfortable with.

Once again it was March who set up the operation in Spain to make it appear wholly Spanish. It was referred to as the 'Chivalry of St George' from England's patron saint slaying the dragon upon gold guineas that had been used by England to subsidise military allies. March laundered the money through Spanish banks and businesses. A group of Spanish general officers were brought into the fold and they received large payments for promising to discourage Spain's entry into the war.

The money was drawn secretly from an account with the Swiss Bank Corporation in New York. During the course of the war $13 million in bribes were paid out.[36] In 1940 alone, $10 million would be paid out, the same amount as Spain's exports to Britain that year. At an exchange rate of four dollars to the pound, it was a large amount by the standards of the time.[37]

However all did not start smoothly as the Foreign Office and Treasury were against the idea fearing the real source was bound to leak out. This delayed the payments for months and undermined the scheme.

On his return to Madrid, Alan faced further crisis with the war situation going from bad to worse. Operation *Dynamo* had evacuated the BEF from France on 3 June but Britain could now face invasion. At the same time he had to deal with his highly nervous new ambassador Sir Samuel Hoare, who had been a senior Conservative politician and close to Chamberlain. He had served in World War I as an infantry officer on the Western Front and later with intelligence in Italy and Russia and was a diplomat of great experience. Hoare gave Churchill his assessment of Spain's position on 10 June after Italy entered the war: When I arrived on 1 June I found the whole of Madrid in a state of nervous excitement. It was evident that the Italians and Germans were making a frantic effort to push Spain into the war simultaneously with Italy.[38] Two days later, Franco changed the stance of Spain from neutrality to non-belligerency. Hoare quizzed him over this change of status, later recalling: 'His answer was that, as the war had now come into the Mediterranean, it was necessary for Spain to show its direct interest in what had happened and to be prepared for all emergencies.' However he added that this did not mean the 'Spanish Government had departed from their general policy of abstention from the war.'[39]

The head of the Foreign Office, Alexander Cadogan, was among many who were glad to see the back of Hoare. He told a colleague that there were 'lots of Germans and Italians in Madrid, and therefore a good chance of S. H. being murdered.'[40]

Hoare did not waste time in his new post. He requested £500,000 to specifically bribe Foreign Minister Juan Beigbeder, and others. On 27 June he wrote to Churchill about the 'state of nerves in which Spain and Madrid find themselves after the Germans arrived on the Pyrenees' but that he was trying his best to appear 'calm' in the sea of troubles.[41]

Alan never took to the opinionated Hoare but was impressed with the way he knuckled down to work. He was also more upbeat about the situation writing to Churchill that 'Things are going quite well' and that, 'Sir Samuel Hoare is doing better than any diplomat I know could do.'[42]

Ian Fleming, after leaving Bordeaux and making his way via Lisbon to Madrid, was there to assess the situation on the ground in Spain and to report back to Godfrey. He also needed to lay the foundations of a stay-behind sabotage and intelligence gathering operation within the Iberian Peninsula, in case the Germans invaded. He arrived in late June and stayed with the Hillgarths in Madrid. They then went by road to Gibraltar taking Mary along with them to give the outing the cover of a sightseeing trip. Mary was not impressed with Ian as a NI officer, especially when he forgot his wallet at a restaurant.[43]

Their main aim from the trip was to establish an office in Gibraltar. On the way they met Colonel William Donovan, the United States intelligence chief, who was on a fact-finding visit to Europe. They briefed him on the vital efforts being made to keep Spain neutral. From Gibraltar, Ian went onto Tangier to create a haven there in case the Rock should fall.[44]

CHAPTER 5

The Wayward Royals

Another headache for the staff at the British Embassy in Madrid was that they had to deal with the Duke and Duchess of Windsor, who both proved to be peevish, arrogant characters. They had been staying at a rented villa at Cap d'Antibes on the French frontier with Italy along with a small staff. For a while the Duke, as a major-general, had been attached to the British Military mission at the French general headquarters. On 28 May 1940, at his own request, he was transferred to the Italian frontier. He was still there when Italy declared war in the second week of June. The local British consul Major Hugh Dodds urged him to leave without delay.[1] Yet he dithered for thirty-six hours hoping for instructions from London. On the morning of 17 June he telephoned Major-General Edward Spears and asked him to arrange a Royal Navy warship to pick him up from Nice. Spears was, at the time, the liaison for Churchill with the French government and told the Duke in no uncertain terms that no ships were available and that he should make his way by car to Lisbon as the roads were open.[2]

Two days later the Duke and Duchess and their entourage, in a convoy of three cars and a hired van containing their luggage, set off for Barcelona. Dobbs, who had been ordered to leave, led the way in a Bentley with diplomatic number plates. Spears's advice that the roads were open was not all that accurate as they were choked with refugees and soldiers. However they encountered little trouble reaching Aries by nightfall on the first day. The next day, when they reached the Spanish border, the border officials denied them entry as they had no visas and they could not issue any. Telegrams to various officials and Hoare in Madrid managed to procure the orders for transit papers. They crossed the border into Spain at six that evening and reached their hotel in Barcelona by midnight.[3]

The next day the Duke and Duchess travelled through to Madrid having first sent a telegram to the Foreign Office and one to Hoare that they were proceeding onto the Spanish capital. Bad weather en route forced them to spend the night at Zaragoza.[4]

Sir Samuel Hoare had only been in Madrid three weeks before the Duke arrived, and he had only met Franco once. He wrote to Churchill before the Duke arrived to say that rumours were rife in the Spanish press about his arrival and that Churchill 'had ordered his arrest once he set foot in England' and that he had come to Spain 'to make a separate peace'.[5] He asked the Foreign Office if he would be acting correctly by entertaining the Windsors and, also, to say that he wanted them out of Spain as soon as possible.

On 22 June he received instructions to pass them onto Lisbon where a Flying Boat would be leaving on 24 June for England. However that was quickly changed. The Duke's younger brother, the Duke of Kent, was due to arrive in Lisbon on that day for an official visit. Dr Antonio De Oliveira Salazar, the dictator of Portugal, was well aware of the abdication crisis and the feud within the house of Windsor. He did not want them in the city at the same time and the two Dukes had made it clear that they had no wish to meet. Hoare was told to keep the Duke of Windsor in Madrid until his brother left Lisbon on 2 July.[6]

The German Ambassador in Madrid, Dr von Stohrer, contacted the German Foreign Minister Joachim von Ribbentrop about the imminent arrival of the Duke of Windsor's party. As far as he knew they were en route to Lisbon to return to England. The Spanish Foreign Minister, Juan Beigbeder, wanted to know if the Germans would be interested in their delaying the Duke so that they could contact him.[7]

The next day Ribbentrop replied to Stohrer advising him, if possible, to detain the Windsors in Madrid for a couple of weeks, but in no way should this appear to be a German directive. He also felt it was better to deal with Ramón Serrano Suñer, the Interior Minister, rather than Beigbeder. After Stohrer consulted with Franco and Suñer they agreed to delay the Duke who they hoped might act as a peacemaker. The Spanish appointed the diplomat Javier Bermejillo to accompany the Duke and report back on his views.

On the evening of Sunday 23 June the Windsors arrived in Madrid. The city came as a shock even though they had travelled across the war-ravaged country – the city's wounds were still stark. However they were booked into the Ritz which had everything the Duke and Duchess could need. Hoare was a friend of the Windsors going back many years and he met them soon after their arrival. They were glad to get news they could trust about the war even though most of it was bad. As the Duke and Duchess settled down in Madrid waiting for his brother to leave Lisbon, Hoare worried about the German propaganda that the Duke had quarrelled with the British government over the war. He was also concerned the Duke would refuse to return to England unless he was given reassurances about his future. However he was pleased with the attitude the Duke and Duchess displayed: 'Far from making any defeatist remarks they went out of their way to show their belief in our final victory.'[8] However, that was their public persona. Hoare might have seen the Duke's stay in Madrid with a different light had he known of the contact established with Beigbeder within two days of his arrival. He had invited the Windsors to stay in Spain as a guest of the Spanish government.

Put at the Duke's disposal would be the Palace of the Moorish Kings in the remote mountain town of Ronda in Andalusia. The offer tempted him, especially if Spain remained neutral. As he had not been offered a British position, he felt that Spanish retirement was appealing. On 26 June he sent a telegram to Churchill asking if there was any hurry for him to return home.[9] Arranged by Bermejillo, the Duke and Duchess went on sightseeing trips to Toledo, the Escorial and some of the civil war battlefields.

On 28 June Hoare gave a large cocktail party in honour of his royal visitors which drew over five hundred guests to the Embassy. Many of them were friends of the Duke and Duchess and the majority of the Spaniards were those with Nationalist leanings. Hoare was dismayed at the growing rift between Churchill and the Duke. The Duke wanted to know what job he would be given before he came home, but Churchill, under pressure from the Royal Court, could only say it would be better for them to come home first 'where everything can be considered.'[10]

The Duke had also contacted the Axis powers through Bermejillo asking if they would agree to protect the Windsors' two houses in France, which proved to be an ill-judged act. Ribbentrop replied to Stohrer that he should let the Duke know confidentially through the Spanish that they were looking after the properties, but that nothing should be passed to him in writing. This was to keep the British government in the dark.[11]

On 1 July Hoare informed the Foreign Office that the Duke and Duchess would be moving onto Lisbon the next day. However, he warned that this did not mean they would move on to England until the Duke was happy about his reception.[12] The Duke had a habit of telling people what they wanted to hear. The Italian Count Vittorio Zoppi commented that the Duke was 'hedging his bets, adopting a policy of wait-and-see.'[13] The Duke made one condition plain at this time for their return to England and that was that the Duchess was to be received by the King and Queen for fifteen minutes. Failing this he was willing to serve anywhere else in the Empire.

Hoare was glad to see the back of the Windsors and wrote to Churchill to say that he had done 'his best' while they had stayed in Madrid. Hoare went on to say: 'He was certain that this is the moment to end the trouble and if it is not ended now, the rift between them and the rest of the Family will become deeper and possibly more dangerous.'[14]

Around midnight on 2 July Berlin received the report that the Duke had left Madrid for Lisbon. Stohrer reported that he had understoood the Duke would return to Spain if his wife was not recognised by the royal family. He was also thought to be against Churchill and the war. Apparently Ribbentrop was furious when the report reached him, raging against the Madrid Embassy and the Spanish as a whole.[15]

The Windsors crossed the border into Portugal on the morning of 3 July in blazing weather. The British Ambassador in Lisbon, Walford Selby, was an old friend of the Duke, and he had only expected the royal party to stay for two nights. Two Sunderland flying boats were ready and waiting to take them all home. He had been instructed that they were not to stay at the Embassy so they were booked into the Hotel Palacio in Estoril. It was the finest hotel on the Lisbon coast. At the time it was full of foreign visitors: Americans, British, and French. It was close to the Estoril Casino, the largest in Portugal, and the haunt of rich aristocrats, as well as spies, smugglers and diamond traders.[16] Hours before the Duke and Duchess were due to arrive, the manager telephoned the British Embassy to explain that he could not accommodate the royal party due to lack of space and security concerns. However he offered an alternative in the villa of Ricardo Espirito Santo in Cascais on the same stretch of coast as the Palacio. The suggestion, though, had really come from Dr Salazar. David Eccles had met Salazar for the first time on 9 May and was 'immensely impressed' and thought he possessed 'good sense and charm' and that he was 'the best-looking dictator in Europe'.[17]

His choice to accommodate the Windsors at the estate of Espirito Santo, Boca do Inferno, was astute. There the Duke would be easier to guard away from the mass of guests at the Palacio and he would get detailed reports about his movements and who he saw. British officials soon began to raise concerns over the suitability of Espirito Santo to host the royal party. He was called the 'Holy Ghost' by the British as he seemed to be everywhere, and was known to be a close friend of the German Ambassador Baron von Hoyningen-Huene. The Baron ran a bank called Banco Espirito Santo, which was a large private bank that traded heavily with the Germans. Selby came in for some criticism for allowing it to happen, although it was the Air Attaché Wing Commander P. R. T. Chamberlayne who booked the accommodation. In Selby's defence, despite being out-foxed by Salazar, there was little room in the city that was not already crammed with refugees and he was assured Ricardo Espirito Santo would not be staying in the villa at the same time.

Portugal was vastly different to Spain in 1940 and must have come as a breath of fresh air to the Windsors after the war-ravaged and starving country they had come from. Lisbon by contrast was a colourful city, with flowers growing everywhere. The city was vibrant with noise from the trolley-trams rattling along their rails and bells ringing. While the lights had gone out in the rest of Europe, Lisbon came alive in the darkness with neon advertising signs and white street lamps. 'Lisbon at first sight – the streets-and wall-gardens – seems more like Italy – Naples or Sicily – than anything I've seen in Spain' observed David Eccles in May 1940.[18]

Although there was some sympathy for the Axis powers within the government, Portugal favoured Britain as they were their 'oldest ally', especially as they had fought together during World War I.[19] Salazar wanted to stay neutral, but privately like the majority of Portuguese, wanted Great Britain to win. The capital was overcrowded with the influx of refugees and had become a hive for spies and international espionage, while the Portuguese Secret Police, the PVDE, were everywhere and renowned for their brutality. The Windsors crossed the Tagus Estuary by ferry to Lisbon on the evening of 3 July. The villa was at Cascais, a small fishing town seventeen miles west of Lisbon.

Selby was at the villa to meet them and was alarmed to find Espirito Santo and his wife there to greet them. The ambassador handed the Duke a telegram dated 1 July from Churchill ordering him, as he was still a serving officer, to return to England immediately.[20]

The Duke then agreed to return to England without delay or conditions. However overnight circumstances changed again. At the Embassy the next day, he saw David Eccles who gave him the latest telegram from the Foreign Office. The telegram read that Churchill had offered the Duke the governorship of the Bahamas, and it was hoped he would be able to travel direct from Lisbon to Bermuda. The Prime Minister argued that this was the best answer to 'the grievous situation in which we all stand. At any rate I have done my best.'[21]

The Duke was stunned at first. He felt the post was a minor one and beneath him. He asked Eccles for his opinion. Eccles said he would 'take it'.[22] After all, he would be safe there and he would be serving the country. The Duke thought about it over lunch before replying to Churchill to accept the appointment. Selby was glad to hear it was settled when Eccles told him. Eccles, on the other hand, somehow doubted it would 'be an end of it'.[23] He wrote to his wife Sybil on 4 July that he thought the Bahamas job was a 'cunning solution'. Eccles did not like the Windsors, and thought the Duchess was a 'poor creature' and that the Duke was 'pretty fifth column, but that's for you only.'[24]

During the Windsors' stay at Cascais, the Duke passed the time playing golf at the Estoril Club and visiting the British Embassy. He played several rounds with Espirito Santo who was the main sponsor of the club. The Duchess liked playing bridge. On other occasions, there were outings to the Casino, the British Hospital in Lisbon, and even to a Portuguese bullfight. All the time they were shadowed by the PVDE, Portuguese Secret Police, and SIS. The PVDE supplied Salazar with detailed daily reports.

David Eccles was at the villa at Cascais twice a week and he found himself being seduced by the Windsors' charm which he found 'hard to resist'. Yet he still called them 'the arch-beachcombers of the world' and he said that he found Wallis 'vulgar'.[25]

On 8 July the Spanish diplomat Bermejillo who had been with the Windsors in Madrid arrived in Lisbon and was met at the airport by the Duke's chauffeur, as reported by the PVDE. He had come to report on the Windsors' houses in France and their missing luggage. He met the Duke several times over the next few days and was often seen carrying document files. On 13 July he returned to Madrid, reporting the Duke's views on the war and his concern over his properties and lost luggage. The Germans and Spanish decided to delay the return of the luggage and the maid who had been sent to collect it, in the belief that they would not leave without it. The Duke tried to telephone Bermejillo on 28 July but he did not answer.

It was not until 24 July that Walter Schellenberg of the SD was ordered to report to Ribbentrop. He was told to go to Portugal and convince the Duke not to return to England but to stay in a neutral country, and that they were willing to offer him 'fifty million Swiss francs if he were ready to make some official gesture dissociating himself from the manoeuvres of the British Royal Family.'[26]

Schellenberg was born in Saarbrucken in 1910. He attended university at Marburg and Bonn, studying medicine, but later switched to law. After graduating, he joined the SS in May 1933, before later joining the SD. The SD was founded in 1931 and led by the former naval officer Reinhard Heydrich a prodigy of Admiral Canaris. He built it up into a powerful surveillance and information gathering agency. Schellenberg proved to be one of its most effective agents. He was used on foreign assignments, and achieved spectacular success with the abduction of two British Secret Service agents from the Dutch border town of Venlo in November 1939.

Ribbentrop went on to explain to Schellenberg that the Fuhrer wanted the Duke to live in Switzerland. If the SIS tried to force the Duke into some move against his wishes, Schellenberg was to 'circumvent the British plans, even at the risk of your own life, and, if need be by the use of force.' Schellenberg says he was 'stunned' by the proposition and voiced his concerns. But Ribbentrop brushed them aside insisting everything was already in place. He then telephoned Hitler who was in favour of the operation code-named *Willi*. The Fuhrer spoke to Schellenberg to tell him he was 'relying on him'.[27] Ribbentrop went on to say that 'in the near future the Duke expects to have an invitation to hunt with some Spanish friends.'

During this hunt Schellenberg would have an ideal opportunity to speak with the Duke. From there he could be 'brought into another country'.[28]

Having grave reservations about the mission he met with Heydrich before he left who voiced his concern that Schellenberg was 'much too valuable to me to waste on this affair.' He did not like the plan and advised him to take two good men with him who could speak the language. With them he would have some protection. Heydrich said of Schellenberg: 'Certainly if I were head of the British Secret Service I would settle your hash for you'.[29]

Schellenberg flew from Berlin to Madrid on 25 July arriving at six that evening. The next day he flew onto Lisbon taking off at four in the afternoon and landing at seven that evening.[30] Before leaving Madrid he had seen Stohrer at the Embassy who had no news for him about where and when the hunt would take place. They had a long conversation in which the Ambassador warned him about the undue optimism about Spain entering the war. He said this with the hope that he would convey this view to Berlin.

In Portugal he quickly grasped the layout of the house where the Windsors were staying, and became familiar with the servants and the police of the PVDE in their pay. He saw the Ambassador Baron von Hoyningen-Huene who 'welcomed me cordially'. Schellenberg told him about his mission and his view that it could not be done. Von Huene had heard the Duke was far from happy but, in his opinion, it had all been exaggerated. He thought that there was a real danger of straining relations between Portugal and Germany over this.[31]

After six days, Schellenberg wrote that he had a clear picture of the Duke and that he had no intention 'whatever of going to live either in a neutral or enemy country.'[32] There were crude attempts to intimidate the Duke with activities such as having people throw stones at the windows of the villa which the PVDE tried to blame on the SIS. A bouquet of flowers arrived with a note warning them about the SIS intending to move them on by force, and that a Portuguese friend had their interests at heart. David Eccles was not impressed with SIS at the time saying: 'we could have done without the Secret Service in Portugal. They were always getting it wrong, and they were always getting into trouble.'[33]

During this time the head of the PVDE Captain Agostinho Lourenco had for ten years been running the security police and ruthlessly rooting out opposition to the New State. He showed the same determination when dealing with refugees and foreign agents. However he tried not to offend either side. His master Salazar had quiet control, with many of the agents supposedly working for the Germans or the British first and foremost working for Lourenco.

Another development that would clearly scupper the plan Schellenberg had been given was when the Windsors announced a move to the Hotel Aviz in Lisbon. They felt they had overstayed their welcome and were abusing the hospitality of Espirito Santos. This would stymie Schellenberg, as he would have no influence at the Aviz which was looked on as a British hotel used widely by the SIS. Meanwhile a friend of the Duke, the Spaniard Miguel Primo de Rivera, in league with Serrano Suñer, sent the Duke a letter which was delivered by the Abwehr agent Angel Alcazar de Velasco who was a Spanish journalist who had interviewed the Duke in Madrid. It made the Duke aware of a plan to bring the Windsors to Spain if he so desired. All that was required to implement the plan was twenty-four hours notice. They would go to the hilltop town of Guarda under the cover of a hunting trip. The town was two hundred miles north-east of Estoril and thirty miles from the border. There would be no trouble with the border guards. Once across the border they would be guests of the Spanish government and free to do as they wished.[34] On 30 July Stohrer reported to Berlin the Duke's reaction to the letter – he said he would think the matter over and give his answer in forty-eight hours.

Two days before Stohrer reported to Berlin, Sir Walter Monckton, who worked for the Ministry of Information, arrived by Flying Boat. Churchill asked him to go to Portugal, knowing he was a friend of the Duke. Churchill wanted him to make sure the Duke was aware of the peril he was in and that he should sail for Bermuda on 1 August. The Foreign Office had received a telegram from the Duke asking for a week's delay. There is little doubt that Churchill had got a whiff of what was going on. Monckton came straight to the point by making the Windsors aware of a suspected German plot to kidnap them. It came as a shock to the Duchess, but was the Duke naive enough to believe he was only talking to the Spanish government through the Primo de Rivera letter? This is the letter that suggested they could live in Spain. The Duke soon changed his mind about delaying their sailing. Monckton stayed with them at Cascais and he arranged for a detective to accompany the Windsors to Bermuda.[35]

On 29 July Schellenberg wrote that the 'Spanish plan collapsed completely' and in his log '*Willi will nicht*' which translates as 'Willi says no'.[36] The report he sent to Berlin drew cold replies. He soon received a telegram from Ribbentrop that: 'The Fuhrer orders that an abduction is organised at once.'[37]

On the evening of 1 August Schellenberg watched the American ship *Excalibur* sail from the tower room of the German Embassy through binoculars. He, like everyone else involved on both sides, was glad to see the back of the 'Wayward Royals'. However he was worried about the reception he might face in Berlin. Luckily for him, the interview with Ribbentrop went better than he had expected. He was told the Fuhrer, although disappointed, agreed 'with your decisions and expresses his approval of the manner in which you proceeded.'[38]

That August Admiral Canaris, after his visit to Spain, returned to Germany via Portugal where he 'found little evidence of British activity.'[39] However he was well aware of Operation *Willi*, and he would have seen many of its documents. It is likely he would have looked on the whole affair as a joke given his keen sense of humour.[40]

CHAPTER 6

Felix and Sealion

Ian Fleming flew back from Tangier, having done as much as he could, via Lisbon to London. He wrote to Hillgarth thanking him and Mary for their hospitality and kindness to him and praising Alan's excellent work as naval attaché in Madrid. NI was fortunate to have such a strong team 'in our last European strong hold' resulting in the 'great contribution you are all making to winning the war.' Later in the same letter he turned to *Golden Eye*:

> 4/ You will by now have a signal about receiving Golden Eye messages. Mason Macfarlane has no objection, and C. N. S. (Commander Naval Station) is about to give his decision, which I have no doubt will be favourable.

He finished with Portugal:

> 7/ I discussed the inclusion of Portugal in Golden Eye on my way through Lisbon, and got the Naval Attaché's reaction on a very general plane. This has been put up to the Planners, and I have no doubt that the answer will be "Yes," and that Owen will be instructed to go down to Gibraltar to report to the delegation.[1]

Back in England he may not have felt as optimistic for by that time the Battle of Britain was raging and the preparations to defeat the threatened invasion seemed insufficient. On 12 August the Luftwaffe struck its first hard blows at the RAF airfields and radar stations in southern England. For a week they launched heavy raids, on 15 August flying 1,786 sorties before cloudy weather intervened.[2]

A month earlier Adolf Hitler had issued his directive No 16: 'As England in spite of the hopelessness of her military position, has so far shown herself unwilling to come to any compromise, I have decided to begin to prepare for, and if necessary to carry out, an invasion of England.'[3] In the weeks prior to issuing this order Hitler faced several dilemmas. The first and most pressing was Britain's refusal to make peace. For weeks he had savoured the glory of victory and soaked up the acclaim of his generals that he was a military genius. However the British attack on the French Fleet at Mers-el-Kebir on 3 July had shaken him from his dream of a short war. It was clear that Britain intended to fight on.

He faced five options, none of which were very attractive. The first was Operation *Sealion*, which was a planned cross-channel invasion of England that would be a risky undertaking. Hitler was not averse to gambling but he feared such operations. Perhaps subconsciously a seaborne invasion worried him because he could not swim and often said: 'On land I am a hero, on the water I am a coward.'[4]

The second option was an air assault. However the Luftwaffe was not designed to be an independent strategic air force and had no four-engine heavy bombers and those it did have carried too light a bomb load and were lightly armed. The third was a siege of the British Isles but the German navy had too few submarines. The fourth was a Mediterranean strategy but that might not work, as it was unlikely to be decisive alone. The fifth, a grand strategic alliance against the British Empire but the prospective allies to achieve this were seen as unreliable, especially Soviet Russia who he saw as an enemy.[5]

For most of July he continued to be frustrated and lacked drive. However preparations for the cross-channel invasion got under way. In his mind he likely saw it as another gamble but was it a risk he was willing to take, or was it just a bluff? During this time there was no sign of any interest in Spain.

It was General Alfred Jodl, Chief of the operations Staff, 'a major figure among the small coterie of soldiers and politicians surrounding Hitler'[6] who focussed the Fuhrer's mind on Spain. On 30 June he presented a six page survey on the direction of the war. He was not in favour of a cross-channel invasion in 1940 preferring a siege to bring Britain to its knees. After that he briefly mentioned the 'indirect approach' through attacks on the British Empire, requiring the support of other nations which included Spain. With their good links with the Franco government, operations against Gibraltar and through Spanish Morocco to the Suez Canal could be considered.[7]

On the following day Hitler met Dino Alfieri the Italian Ambassador to Germany for a 'brief chat'.[8] Three days later Alfieri reported on the meeting to Count Galeazzo Ciano, Mussolini's son-in-law and Foreign Minister, who wrote in his diary:

> Alfieri has reported on the conference with Hitler. I am convinced that there is something brewing in that fellow's mind, and that certainly no new decision has been taken. There is no longer that impressive tone of assurance that surfaced when Hitler spoke of breaking through the Maginot Line. Now he is considering many alternatives, and is raising doubts which account for his restlessness. Meanwhile, he doesn't answer Mussolini's offer to send

men and planes to participate in an attack on England. On the other hand, he offers us air force assistance to bomb the Suez Canal. Obviously he does not trust us that much.[9]

On 7 July Hitler was in Berlin for the French victory celebration. Count Ciano was there for the same reason and spoke with him and received a 'warm reception' from the Fuhrer. As to the invasion of England he was told that 'the final decision has not been reached' but that he appeared 'calm and reserved'.[10] Ciano later spoke with Field Marshal Keitel at some length. He felt that a strike at Gibraltar was the best way of subduing Britain, whereas the cross-channel attack had too many uncertainties.[11]

Unable to make his mind up, Hitler went to his mountain retreat the *Berghof*. On 21 July he met with Admiral Erich Raeder to review the alternatives again. He reiterated his dislike of *Sealion* with Britain's control of the sea.

On 10 July Field Marshal Wilhelm Keitel asked Admiral Wilhelm Canaris to lead a team to Spain to assess the feasibility of taking Gibraltar as Canaris was considered the German 'expert' on the country. Within ten days, Canaris had set off for Spain.[12] The team consisted of Colonel Hans Piekenbrock, a competent professional soldier and head of Section 1 of the Abwehr, Secret Intelligence abroad. He was much taller than Canaris, his chief, who only stood at about five feet four inches. Piekenbrock had a good sense of humour and the two men often travelled together. Colonel Hans Mikosch, another member of the team, was an engineer and Major Wolfgang Largkau represented the artillery. Captain Rudolf Witzig was an assault engineer who had taken part in the capture of the Belgian forts at Eben Emael, and the last member was a captain from a parachute regiment.[13] On 22 July they all travelled through Spain by different routes with false passports and in civilian clothing.

As soon as Canaris was in Spain he felt the country lift his spirit with its 'constant exhilaration'. Fluent in Spanish and, in the right dialects, he could easily pass for a local 'whose home these worn Sierras, windowless churches and mud-built villages were.'[14] He enjoyed the food and wine at small wayside inns, and liked driving the dusty hard roads in powerful cars – such as the American Buicks or Packards. He had first visited the country during World War I.

Wilhelm Franz Canaris was 53 in 1940. He was born in the small mining town of Aplerbeck near Dortmund Westphalia, and was the son of the wealthy industrialist Carl Canaris. He joined the Imperial Navy Academy at Kiel on 1 April 1905, where a military infantry course was followed by nine months of naval training. A fellow cadet found him 'slow to speak but quick to listen'.[15]

By the time World War I started, Canaris was serving in the South Atlantic on the light cruiser SMS *Dresden* as an intelligence officer. He soon gained a reputation for being reliable and competent. The *Dresden* had been part of Admiral Maximilian Graf von Spee's squadron that had sunk the British Pacific Fleet at Coronel, with the loss of two armoured cruisers and nearly 1,600 men. For three months the Germans had been masters of the South Pacific before the powerful British ships closed in and they decided to flee via the south Atlantic. The British Fleet caught up with Spee's ships off the Falkland Islands and, on 8 December 1914, the battle cruisers *Inflexible* and *Invincible* sent them to the bottom of the Atlantic. Only *Dresden* escaped due to its superior speed.

For several months *Dresden* played a game of hide-and-seek with the British, much to the chagrin of the Admiralty in London. Canaris played a major role in arranging clandestine meetings with supply ships. However, the *Dresden* was finally cornered near Chile by HMS *Glasgow* which opened fire despite both ships being in neutral waters.

In Chile the crew of the *Dresden* faced internment for the rest of the war. However many of the crew managed to escape, the first of which was Canaris, who could speak Chilean Spanish with no foreign accent. Olga Krouse entertained several of the *Dresden's* officers at her parent's villa and remembered Canaris: 'He had dark hair and skin and was well educated in manner. He did not look German. Neither was he good-looking, but he had an attractive personality.'[16] She witnessed the first part of his escape after her brother-in-law supplied him with money and a forged passport. Watching from a window, she saw Canaris leave 'dressed as a peddler wearing clothes and a cap which seemed to cover his face almost entirely. He had exchanged his heavy German suitcase for a canvas bag.'[17]

Canaris got to the capital Santiago and obtained a Chilean passport from the German Embassy in the name of Reed Rosas. By Christmas he had crossed the Andes by donkey and on foot but contracted malaria. In Buenos Aires he took time to recover and was helped by the local German community. Fit again, he took the Dutch steamer *Frisa* back to Europe.

Canaris got on well with the English passengers on board the Frisa, becoming a popular player at the bridge tables. The ship's first port of call was Plymouth, but no suspicion had been cast on Senor Rosas. Canaris disembarked at Rotterdam and from there, still using his Chilean passport, crossed the border into Germany.

These exploits cemented Canaris's name within the German Navy. His name would also have come across the desk of Commander Mansfield Cumming 'C' of the SIS, and maybe even brought to the attention of Winston Churchill at the Admiralty for the first time.

Back in Berlin he was awarded the Knight's Cross in September 1915, and shortly after joined the ND (Geheime Nachrichtendienst) the security intelligence service. Early the next year he was sent to Madrid, an ideal appointment with his perfect Spanish, to provide accurate intelligence on Allied shipping movements. Again he used his pseudonym of the Chilean Senor Reed Rosas. He took a flat not far from the German Embassy, a place he never visited as it was under constant observation by Allied agents. However in his flat he met with Hans von Krohn the naval intelligence officer from the embassy and Eberhard von Stohrer, a first secretary, to discuss the Allied ship movements. At the time, few knew Canaris other than by his code-name 'Kika' meaning 'peeper'.[18]

'Kika' soon built up a network of agents and informants across all the main Spanish ports to gather information on Allied shipping. He obtained the services of several Spaniards who were day workers in the British colony of Gibraltar. Intelligence from these sources was given to Krohn who then signalled the Austrian naval base at Cattoro where it was passed to the U-boats. The submarines at the time could not be re-supplied beyond their Adriatic bases which restricted their operational range, a shortcoming Canaris set about changing.

He cultivated relationships with several wealthy Spanish businessmen and financiers like the man he knew as 'Ullmann' who came from a German Jewish family who had migrated to Spain, and came to play an important part in Canaris's life. The Spanish industrialist Horacio Echevarrieta was another, one of the richest men in Spain, with interests in banks, newspapers, and shipping. Both these men were more interested in making money rather than supporting Germany.

With a large budget Canaris was able to buy the services of Spanish ships to resupply U-boats at sea. The ships were commissioned by Reed Rosas for use in South America, but trials took them to the bay of Cadiz where at night they rendezvoused with submarines to supply fuel and provisions.

Cummings, the head of the SIS, realised the importance of monitoring U-boat movements around Spain, and agreed early in the war to leave control of the service on the Iberian Peninsula to the head of the Naval Intelligence Division Captain William Reginald Hall, known as 'Blinker', from his constant blinking. Hall sent his personal assistant Dick Herschell to Spain to set up a permanent operation there. Lord Herschell was a German linguist who had been working in Room 40, the cryptanalysis section at the Admiralty, working from the Ripley building at Whitehall. Herschell had good connections in the country being a personal friend of King Alfonso XIII and his wife Queen Victoria Eugenie. These contacts proved invaluable, far outstripping those of the German Ambassador Prince Ratibor.[19]

To control the operation in Spain, Hall appointed A. E. W. Mason, an author who had once been a Liberal MP. He was a keen mountaineer and yachtsman and, although 49, he had managed to enlist in the Manchester Regiment by the ruse of reducing his age by twelve years. Hall had Mason transfer to the Royal Marines. Around this time Reed Rosas had come to the attention of the British who sent the Captain Stewart Menzies to 'Kill or Capture' Canaris. However Canaris got 'wind of' the British interest in him and he promptly disappeared.[20] Canaris left Spain in February 1917. It was during this first period in the country that he met the young Spanish Army Officer, Francisco Franco, who was as enigmatic as Canaris himself.

Suffering from recurring malaria, and still using his Chilean passport, Canaris headed for Germany by train. However he was arrested by Italian police at Genoa, who had been tipped off by French Intelligence that Reed Rosas was a German spy. This information was gained from a source within the German Embassy in Madrid that had heard the name there.

Clearly ill and claiming he was en route to a Swiss clinic, Canaris talked himself out of a Genoan jail. But the border guards at Domodossola were not fooled and removed him from the train on which he had been a passenger and locked him up. He was arrested with a priest and his subsequent release may have been due to Vatican pressure.[21]

He was put onto a ship bound for Marseille, where the Italians hoped the French authorities would deal with the Chilean-German, whoever he was. But Canaris's luck held. The ship's captain was Spanish and he bribed him not to dock at Marseille, or any other French port. Instead he was put ashore in Cartagena, still feverish with malaria. By March he was back in Madrid, where he applied for active service. Hans von Krohn told him he would have to remain in Spain for the time being. He spent another six months building up more contacts. However neither he nor Krohn knew his spy rings had already been compromised by Room 40 breaking the German ciphers.

Blinker Hall had taken over control of some aspects of Room 40's work and put his energy behind not merely collecting naval intelligence but also into systematic diplomatic code breaking. The key to this was the amount of wireless traffic between Berlin and Madrid.[22] When examined, it was found a high proportion were messages from and to military and naval attachés. Also some of these messages were still being coded in the Verkehrsbuch (VB) codebook which had been obtained in 1914.

Madrid was of great importance to Germany as its centre of trade and communications with the rest of the world, and controlled the biggest espionage network outside of Germany. This was a great coup for Hall and his team which led to a prolific source of intelligence.[23]

These intercepts were very detailed and revealed German espionage activities in Spain down to individual agents and spies. For example in June 1916, Berlin informed the Madrid Embassy that agent 'Arnold' was on his way to help organise the destruction of ships transporting iron ore from Spain to Britain. An embassy official questioned this as ore was always transported by Spanish ships, and did this mean the ban on attacking neutral ships had been lifted?[24]

Canaris finally left Spain in October 1917 and was picked up by *U-35*. The businessman Juan March had learnt of the operation through his huge network of workers and agents. His ships were known to supply U-boats with fuel and supplies. Once the operation had been completed however they promptly supplied the British with the locations and routes the submarines were using in the Mediterranean, often ending with the destruction of the U-boat supplied. He was more than happy to be paid by both sides but soon became aware that the Allies were the better bet. With information from March, two French Submarines, the *Topaze* and *Opale*, were supposed to ambush *U-35* but they bungled the mission and Canaris managed to reach the U-boat in a fishing smack and had to scramble onto the casing as the submarine prepared to dive, and fled for the Adriatic.[25]

Back in Germany Canaris joined the Submarine service in Kiel. It was there he met Erika Waag, the woman he would marry after the war. After completing training he was posted to Pola and joined *U-34* as second in command. The submarine took a heavy toll on British merchantmen in the Mediterranean.

The entry of the United States into the war tipped the strategic balance decisively against Germany. In October 1918 all U-boats in the Mediterranean were ordered home. By that time Canaris had risen to command his own submarine, *U-128*. He reached Kiel on 8 November to find the ships of the High Seas Fleet gripped by revolution and mutiny and flying red flags. Three days later the war ended, as did the world Canaris had been brought up in. The navy he loved suffered a complete breakdown in discipline. Yet the officer corps soon rallied to undermine communist attempts to control the navy. Canaris, although no longer a field agent, was quick to act during the communist attempt to take over Germany during 1918–21, aiding the assassins of the communist leaders Rosa Luxemburg and Karl Liebknecht. The German communist threat ended after the failure of the uprising in 1923.

In the 1920s Canaris's linguistic skills were well used on trips to Japan, Spain and Sweden, where weapons and ships were secretly purchased for the German Navy, largely ignoring the terms of the Treaty of Versailles. In Spain he was able to reactivate links with the Spanish Navy and within two days of his arrival in Madrid in June 1925 he had re-established contact with many of his old agents in most of the important ports. He had been instrumental in starting a secret U-boat construction programme with Japan in 1924 before it was discovered by the British and the programme was switched to Spain.[26] With the help of his old friends Ullmann and Echevarrieta, he was able to set the financial wheels in motion. Both men were now able to realise their long-held dream of setting up a Spanish arms industry and helping Germany with her illegal submarine programme was a small price to pay.

Younger officers within the Spanish Navy were also keen to help. The U-boats of World War I had gained a legendary reputation and they were eager to obtain craft for their own navy. It soon became apparent that the only man they could do business with in Germany was Canaris, who understood the 'Spanish Mind.' In a few short months, Canaris had '… placed himself at the centre of the interlocking circles of German and Spanish naval rearmament. From now on nothing concerning relations with the Spanish Navy in Berlin took place without Canaris's approval.'[27]

In January 1921 the German military intelligence service was reborn as the Abwehr, but at this time it was a tiny organisation with only a handful of officers and some clerical staff at HQ. By 1933 its chief was a naval officer, Captain Conrad Patzig, who had reluctantly taken the appointment which army officers looked down on as a dead-end job.[28] As Patzig was in the navy, the Abwehr came under their remit, which was to prove good for both services.

It was Grand Admiral Erich Raeder, head of the Kriegsmarine, who wanted to keep the Abwehr in the navy's control. He knew Patzig did not have the heart for the job, and so appointed the then Captain Wilhelm Franz Canaris to the post. Although Raeder was not overly fond of Canaris, he knew of his reputation and skill with intelligence work. Canaris accepted with enthusiasm, as at the time he was languishing in command of the coastal defences at Swinemunde. He sped across the country to Berlin to take up his new appointment on 1 January 1935. Patzig had hated the job, and whilst showing Canaris around the five-storey HQ of the Tirpitzufer, he asked him if he knew what he was getting into, especially with the Nazis. Canaris replied: 'I'm an incurable optimist. And as far as those fellows are concerned I think I know how to get along with them.'[29]

OKW had taken the initiative over Spain and Gibraltar by sending Admiral Canaris on his fact-finding mission. On 23 July 1940 the group reached Madrid. There Canaris met with his Abwehr chief in Spain, Commander Wilhelm Leissner, code-named Gustav Lenz. Leissner had spent many years in South America at various jobs when he joined the Abwehr in 1937. Canaris immediately assigned him to Spain where he stayed until 1945.[30]

Leissner and the team visited the Spanish Minister for War, General Juan Vigon, and two of his staff, Colonels Martinez Campos and Don Ramón Pardo. They outlined their mission to plan a possible assault on Gibraltar with Spanish help. Vigon's response was not encouraging, and to their surprise he revealed there was no Spanish plan to capture the Rock, and that there would be great problems in such an operation. Surprise would be almost impossible to achieve and difficulties with railways and roads would hinder the movement of large artillery pieces.[31]

Later Vigon took Canaris, Piekenbrock and Leissner to meet Franco. The *Caudillo* seemed more optimistic than his war minister. He thought the operation was possible, but was concerned over the fate of the Canary Islands if such action was taken, not to mention the economic issues of such a plan.[32]

The next day, Canaris and his team journeyed onto Algeciras with Colonel Pardo assigned to go with them. They used three houses in the town: Villa Leon, San Luis and Villa Isabel. The first of these had a view of Gibraltar Bay. These houses became popular and Ladislas Farago thought the number of visitors to Algeciras from the secret services had reached comical levels comparing them to: '… a veritable avalanche of reconnaissance ventures until Spain became the popular tourist attraction of the Abwehr.' These missions overlapped one another, and reduced their assignments to '… a brief period of mainly hilarity in the Abwehr which was not otherwise noted for its sense of humour.'[33]

For two days they observed Gibraltar from various vantage points. Colonel Mikosch, in the disguise of a Spanish official, inspected the neutral zone and took a Spanish flight around the area. The formidable obstacles to an attack were noted as well as the irregular wind currents which ruled out the use of glider or parachute troops. On 27 July they discussed their findings and reached the conclusion that the Spanish would have to provide more information and better maps.

Most felt Vigon was right that surprise was not possible and transport through Spain would be difficult. Shortly after this they returned to Berlin, where Canaris, Piekenbrock and Mikosch prepared a plan of attack.

The assault force would need to be made up of two infantry regiments including mountain troops, two combat engineer battalions, an engineer construction battalion, and a company of mine experts. Up to twelve artillery regiments with heavy guns of 21cm (8 inch) and 88mm anti-aircraft guns were required, so 160 guns in all to give them a three to one advantage over the defenders. After a heavy bombardment by artillery and dive bombers, the infantry would go forward behind a drumfire laid by the artillery. They expected three days of heavy fighting to take the town and the Rock.[34]

As the proposals for this formal assault were filed, a different approach was considered. In late July another mission went to Algeciras led by Captain Hans-Jochen Rudloff who had been the leader of the Abwehr Company during the French campaign. His orders from Canaris were to explore the possibility of sending troops through Spain, without being detected, travelling in civilian clothes in closed trucks and making sure to avoid towns and cities. It was estimated that it would take three days to reach southern Spain, during which time other troops would move by sea and artillery would be dispatched to the port of Ceuta. But it soon began to unravel. Moving large bodies of troops through Spain without dectection was thought to be impossible. Anoter difficulty was that the cranes at Ceuta were not big enough to unload the heavy guns required. This plan was promptly shelved and Canaris did not present it as an option to his superiors. Neither operation had yet been assigned a code name.[35]

Hitler was not idle while these outings were gathering at Algeciras. Three days after seeing Raeder he told General Wolfram Freiherr von Richthofen, commander of the VIII Air Corps and distant relative of the World War I flying ace, to meet him in Berlin. There he told Richthofen the struggle against Britain was to be intensified and one option was to attack Gibraltar. The Spanish were likely to demand to participate. If the British counter-attacked on the Iberian Peninsula Germany would move in. He asked him to go to Spain and see General Vigon whom he knew to be a good friend of Richthofen and, via that officer, send a message to Franco.

Richthofen met Vigon at Biarritz on 28 July to tell him about the Fuhrer's idea. Vigon informed him of the *Caudillo*'s interest in the plan which others had voiced, but that he was uneasy about entering the war at this stage.

By now *Sealion* was coming under closer examination and disagreements between the army and navy had increased. On 31 July Hitler met with his advisors for a major study of the operation. It was agreed 15 September was the first possible assault date. If the arial attack were to lead to air superiority the landings would take place. If not they would be postponed until May 1941.[36] Indeed the naval staff favoured an invasion the next spring. They argued that the navy was far too weak, not to mention that the weather in the channel was unpredictable and presented great hazards for the invasion fleets, none of which were purpose-built for the task.[37]

With the Army wanting to land at dawn, the periods of 20–26 August and 19–26 September would be suitable due to the favourable tides. The navy could not be ready by August and September was nearing the bad weather season. Even in the best of conditions the motley invasion fleet, made up of Rhine barges and Steamers, would cross the channel slower than Caesar's legions 2,000 years before. They expected to lose 10% of their lift capacity due to accidents and breakdowns before the Royal Navy and RAF put in an appearance. Raeder used these arguments to insist on a narrow front invasion from Dover to Eastbourne, adding the Luftwaffe would be unable to protect the long front favoured by the Army from Dover to Portland. General Franz Halder, Chief of Army General Staff wrote in his diary that the army rejected the navy's plea for a short front which revealed 'irreconcilable differences' between the two services and would be tantamount to putting the 'troops through a sausage machine'. However Hitler would decide in favour of the Navy.[38] Hitler's proviso that failure to gain control of the air 'under the circumstances was tantamount to postponement.'[39]

An odd omission by many at OKW was to question the lack of intelligence they had on Britain and the British. Keitel complained to Ciano about this in July: 'The intelligence available on the military preparedness on the island and on the coastal defences is meagre and not very reliable.'[40] The information coming from the Abwehr was erratic and they constantly over-estimated British strength citing the defending army between 23 August–17 September at about 35 divisions which was six divisions more than they actually had.[41] In September the Abwehr tried to address these shortcomings by sending a large group of spies to the UK, but they were poorly trained and were captured quickly.

The one serious leak at the time which affected the British was through another channel, a cipher-clerk working at the United States Embassy in London, Tyler Kent. He got involved with Anna Wolkoff, the daughter of a White Russian Admiral, who held extreme anti-Semitic and pro-German views. She was a member of the 'Right Club' which was a right-wing fascist group.

Kent kept copies of the messages he had seen, and began showing them to members of the group, including highly secret correspondence between Churchill and Roosevelt. In one instance, a message referred to fifty old US destroyers which were given to Britain in exchange for the use of Caribbean bases. This would 'have strengthened the hand of American isolationists whose influence Churchill was struggling to diminish.'[42]

The leaders of the 'Right Club' had a contact with the military attaché of the Italian Embassy. On 23 May details of the old destroyers' arrangements were transmitted by the German Embassy in Rome to Berlin. However the club was under surveillance by MI5 and the Italian diplomatic telegrams decrypted by British codebreakers revealed almost all the US Embassy despatches to President Roosevelt were being passed to Rome. The US Embassy was alerted and all of the group's members were arrested on 18 May. The group was led by Archibald Ramsay, a maverick Tory MP, and a former army officer in World War I with a good record. Kent was sentenced to seven years, Wolkoff to ten and Ramsay was interned until the end of the war.

It appears as if Canaris, although heavily engaged with Spain and able to visit Turkey at the time, paid little attention to *Sealion*, which was the bigger and more active operation. This is odd given the energetic part he played in Germany's war effort between September 1939 and November 1940. Colonel Oscar Reile of the Abwehr was to become one of the services's early historians and wrote of the hard-working Canaris of that time: 'His membership in the resistance movement was one thing but premeditated treason was another. The fight against Hitler on the home front had nothing to do with the struggle against enemy secret services.'[43] Canaris was trying to be all things to all men.

Canaris rendered excellent service during the Norway victory and as a result was promoted to the rank of full Admiral. Yet what he had seen in Poland had sickened him. When Hitler had first come to power Canaris had admired him saying 'You can talk to the man' and that he could be 'reasonable'.[44] However when the SS was formed in 1938 and the General Staff lost much of its power, which passed to the new High Command under Hitler, Canaris began to see the writing on the wall, and began to turn against him. The invasion of Poland confirmed his worst fears. He witnessed the horror of the SS burning the synagogue in Bedzin with 200 Jews inside.

He complained to Keitel about 'extensive shootings' and that the Polish 'nobility and clergy were to be exterminated.' Keitel replied to say that it was Hitler's decision and warned him to go no further with his protests if he wanted to survive.[45] There had been murmurings in the German General Staff about deposing Hitler, but their lack of action had led Canaris to despair of the generals and to accuse them of moral 'cowardice'.[46]

From 1938 Canaris, a Catholic all his life, had established a close personal link to the Vatican. He had known Pius XII from his days as Nuncio Head of the Catholic diplomatic mission in Berlin, the equivalent of an embassy. His offices were used as a secret mediation, and as a link via the British Minister at the Holy See, Sir Francis d'Arcy Osborne. There was a risk in this to the Vatican and Catholics in Germany and Austria, should use of this avenue find its way to the Nazis. Dr Josef Muller was the main messenger Canaris used with the Vatican through the Pope's German adviser Cardinal Ludwig

Kaas, who was a Catholic priest as well as a professional politician.[47] Various details were leaked through the Vatican to Britain about possible plots against Hitler and the Nazis, but they were not taken seriously.[48] Muller was sent to Rome to warn the Allies about the attack in the west scheduled for 10 May 1940. Muller was almost rumbled on this occasion by the SD, but due to his quick thinking he deflected suspicion away from himself by having the date 1 May and point of entry Venice stamped in his passport after his mission by a friendly border guard, as the information about the leak reached Hitler on 1 May. The SD continued to eye the Vatican with suspicion but was no match for the Machiavellian labyrinth of that organisation.

When Churchill became prime minister, the British government began to take this strange link more seriously. Churchill would later write: 'Our excellent intelligence confirmed that Operation *Sealion* had been definitely ordered by Hitler.' He already had some idea of German Naval plans too.[49] None of this information could have come to him via any ground reconnaissance, or through Ultra decrypts. Ultra was the signals intelligence obtained by breaking high level encrypted enemy radio traffic. It was not until May that Ultra began breaking significant codes, initially for the Luftwaffe. This 'information' must have come from a source within the German High Command. Only a few senior officers would be privy to such details, one of whom was Canaris. Historian Ian Colvin wrote: 'The hand of Mr Churchill seems to have been guided at this time by somebody to whom the innermost counsels of Hitler were revealed.'[50]

One of Ian Fleming's roles in the early months of the war was to act as liaison between the various intelligence organisations: SOE, MI6 and MI5, who poured oil on troubled waters whilst trying to avoid upsetting anyone.[51]

On 19 July SOE had come into being with Churchill's directive to 'set Europe ablaze'. Admiral Godfrey had set up NID 17 early in 1940 'to coordinate intelligence' between NID and the others. SOE had been spawned by SIS and had a troubled relationship with its parent. This was not helped by the two directors who could not stand each other. Colonel Stewart Menzies 'C' hated the highland warrior Brigadier Colin Gubbins who was the head of SOE. It did not help either that the two organisations had conflicting remits. SIS largely dealt in covert operations whereas SOE were saboteurs out to make trouble. In such an environment, Fleming proved to be ideal at smoothing over hostility between the factions which would be particularly useful in Spain.[52]

Fleming made regular visits to Bletchley Park. They were having difficulty breaking the German Naval Enigma at Hut 8. Ian was sent by Godfrey to talk to Dillwyn Knox. 'Dilly', as he was known, was a brilliant classical scholar, papyrologist and cryptographer who in 1917 succeeded in breaking much of the German naval codes. It is unlikely Fleming was ever privy to the Ultra sources, but would have known about the code-breaking going on there. It was not until December 1941 that Dilly broke the Abwehr's Enigma Key, before he died of stomach cancer in 1943. [53]

However the British had a stroke of luck when Arthur Owens was recruited by the Abwehr agent Nikolaus Ritter in 1938. Owens often passed himself off as a fanatical Welsh Nationalist. He had already briefly worked for SIS in 1936 when selling batteries for ships in Germany, by relating what he had seen in the shipyards of the Kriegsmarine in Kiel. In 1939 he was supplied with a miniature German wireless set he picked up at Victoria Station. He reported this to his handler Inspector Gagen of the special branch and the radio was examined by MI5. He was interred, rather to his surprise, in Wandsworth Prison under the Defence Regulation 18B but MI5 decided they could use him as a double agent and gave him the code name SNOW.[54] Before his release they began transmitting with the radio from the prison, but John Burton, a prison warder and former Royal Signals soldier, took over his role with the radio. After his release, Owens travelled to Antwerp for the first of several meetings with the Abwehr. He returned from these meetings with codes and

Operation *Felix* plan 1940–41.

instructions which led to the breaking of the Abwehr's hand ciphers. This in turn helped Bletchley reconstruct some of the Abwehr's Enigma keys.[55] The deception of the Abwehr, which began from a Wandsworth prison cell, would lead to the Double-Cross System which was to play a vital part in Operation *Neptune*, the D-Day landings in Normandy in 1944.[56]

What the British did not know at this time was how far the Germans had gone in planning their attack against Gibraltar. It would not be until 9 November 1940 that it was assigned the code-name *Felix* by OKW.[57]

Two weeks later, Hitler signed the order for the invasion of Britain at the beginning of August 1940. General Jodl visited the OKW's planning section, the National Defence Branch KTB at Bad Reichenhall, in the Bavarian Alps. He told its head, General Walter Warlimont, Hitler had made up his mind to invade Russia and thus Operation *Barbarossa* was born.

Barely a week before, thanks to the Fuhrer dithering so much, Warlimont and his staff were ordered to produce two further studies on Africa and Gibraltar. The planners had been unable to resolve the problems with *Sealion*. Now they were told to cancel their plans as the cross-channel assault on Britain had, at the very least, been postponed. What soon became apparent from the two projects of Egypt and Gibraltar was that the two forces could cooperate in attacking the British in the Mediterranean. However it was equally apparent the big stumbling block was Franco and whether Spain would agree to the move against Gibraltar. It would be a German operation, yet they could be seen to give the Spanish 'control for propaganda purposes'.[58]

On 9 September von Richthofen was sent to San Sebastian, Franco's summer headquarters, to try and find out when Spain would join the war. However the *Caudillo* was concerned about participating in a long war. He decided to send his brother-in-law Ramón Serrano Suñer, the Interior Minister, with a large entourage to Berlin on 16 September to see Hitler. Beigbeder, the Spanish Foreign Minister, did not go as he was seen as being too close to Sir Samuel Hoare and the British.

On the day they arrived, Serrano Suñer spoke with Joachim von Ribbentrop the German Foreign Minister, and the two men hedged around the main issue of Spain's entry into the war. Suñer was shocked by Germany's wish to have a Canary Island ceded to them as this had not been mentioned before. The next day he met Hitler for an hour and informed him that Spain would declare war once material difficulties had been resolved. Spain feared the Royal Navy, if they were to declare war, in regard to their Atlantic islands. Hitler closed the conversation with the view that he and Franco should meet, and this was a proposal which Serrano Suñer agreed with. Hitler followed this up with a letter to Franco.[59]

Franco's reply to Hitler's letter is dated 22 September. He thanked the Fuhrer for the 'cordial reception' of his minister. He noted the German wish to use Spanish bases, and said Germany would, as an ally, be free to use them as long as they would remain under Spanish control. He also rejected any German enclaves in Spanish Morocco for the same reason.

He feared a move against the Spanish Atlantic Islands by the British should Gibraltar be attacked. Spain was strengthening the defences there and they would welcome German aircraft in this respect. He finished with his most 'sincere feelings of friendship and I greet you'.[60]

Serrano Suñer had a second meeting with Ribbentrop on 17 September which did not go well. Ribbentrop restated that Germany required one of the Canary Islands. Suñer would not hear of Spain ceding any territory. He suggested, instead, that maybe they should take one of the Maderia Islands from Portugal, a British ally.[61] The only real agreement reached by Serrano Suñer's mission to Berlin was that Hitler and Franco would meet and settle matters. Franco had suggested this should take place at the Spanish border.

A week later Hitler and Ribbentrop spoke with Count Ciano. They complained about Spanish demands for aid without any contribution to the German war effort. Ciano wrote in his diary that Hitler did not 'speak about the current situation.' Instead, he concentrated on the Spanish 'intervention' which he felt 'would cost more than it was worth. He proposed a meeting with the Duce at the Brenner Pass and I immediately accepted.' Ciano noted that there was no more talk of an invasion of England, and that the Fuhrer seemed worried at the prospect of a 'long war.' He also thought that Ribbentrop was 'nervous' and also noted that the Germans were 'impeccably courteous toward us Italians' while it was starkly apparent the Spanish mission 'was not successful'.[62]

Serrano Suñer had gone onto Rome from Berlin where he complained bitterly to the Duce about German demands. Mussolini showed 'little enthusiasm for Spain's early entrance into the war.' Their intervention could affect Italy's role and prospects.[63]

Meanwhile the British, knowing full well that Spain was likely in the near future to join the Axis, were failing to make much headway in preparation for a potential invasion of Gibraltar other than through the efforts of NI. The SIS found Sir Samuel Hoare a 'difficult colleague'.[64] When, in September 1940, three men passing as Belgians were arrested on the border with France as British agents by the Spanish Security Police, they then confessed to working for the SIS. Hoare promptly ordered the passport control officer, who was the SIS representative, to go home. He also wanted the new SIS head of station,

Leonard Hamilton Stokes, to go as well. It was clear that Hoare was in a funk as he often was when he saw 'agent provocateurs' everywhere 'exciting anti-British demonstrations and harassing the lives of British subjects.'

David Eccles was in Madrid during August 1940 and he found the city to be 'hot and tension is running high'. He put it down to: 'the Germans have been stung to fury by their failure to get Spain into the war.'[65]

Leonard Hamilton Stokes had been setting up an early warning network against a possible German invasion in the border area with France. Much of this was now lost he complained to 'C' Menzies about 'YP' (code for Hoare) as becoming 'extremely difficult' and the 'SIS had suffered' as a result. Menzies understood that the Germans were trying to shut the SIS in Spain down and '"YP" had fallen for it'. In the end the passport control officer was sent home while Hamilton Stokes stayed despite being far from happy with having to work with Hillgarth who seemed to be able to manipulate Hoare.[66]

During August in London, Ian Fleming began work on the stay-behind operation for Spain and Gibraltar should the Germans move in. Where did the name *Golden Eye* come from? Ian would later name his Jamaican home *Goldeneye* after all. It seems likely that he was reading the Carson McCuller's novel *Reflections in a Golden Eye*. Maybe the name, in some way, reminded him of Spain. The novel was not published until 1941 by Houghton & Mifflin, but was serialised in the October–November 1940 issue in the *Harper's Bazaar* magazine.[67]

CHAPTER 7

Meeting at Hendaye

By the time Hitler met Benito Mussolini, the Duce, at the Brenner Pass on Friday 4 October, he had dismissed the visit of Serrano Suñer to Berlin as futile. He was now caught in a morass of inactivity. What was clear was that negotiations with Spain had ground to a halt. Much of the bewilderment of the meetings with the Spanish minister could be laid at the door of Ribbentrop. Most people who had to deal with the German foreign minister took an almost instant dislike 'to his preposterous vanity and to his overbearing methods in trying to get his own way.'[1]

Ciano wrote in his diary about the meeting at the Austrian-Italian border: 'Rarely have I seen the Duce in such a good mood and in good shape as at the Brenner Pass today. The meeting was cordial and the conversations were certainly the most interesting that have taken place so far. Hitler put at least some of his cards on the table, and told us about his future plans.'[2]

Ciano put these broad plans in order: First, *Sealion* was over. Second, Hitler hoped to bring Vichy-France into the anti-British coalition. Third, greater importance was to be given to the Mediterranean. Key to this was to bring Spain into the war and to take Gibraltar and improve the German position in Morocco and the Canaries, thereby facilitating the control of Portugal through Spain. He observed that Hitler 'was energetic and again extremely anti-Bolshevik' and he recorded him saying: 'Bolshevism is the doctrine of people who are lowest on the scale of civilization.'[3]

The meeting at the Brenner Pass might have pleased the Duce but it still left Hitler groping for a course of action. He needed Franco to come into the fold and stop his prevarication. Then he could group the continental powers against the sea power of Britain, which was a policy that Napoleon had failed with. Still unsure, he retreated to the *Berghof*. Four days later he was back in Berlin and met with Raeder, Keitel, and Jodl. Raeder did most of the talking. The Fuhrer seemed preoccupied. He asked just one question about the feasibility of sending troops to the Canary, Azores, or Cape Verde Islands. He asked Raeder and the Navy to study the problem. After this he flew back to his mountain retreat.

In Spain, Britain, through the efforts of Sir Samuel Hoare, had managed to gain the confidence of Colonel Beigbeder, the Spanish Foreign Minister, who felt Britain was far from beaten. The two men became friends. Yet Hoare felt that his friend had become over confident when he, the British ambassador, was being closely watched by the Germans. Beigbeder went out of his way to demonstrate his friendship with 'Don Samuel' which Hoare had warned him about, saying: 'But no words of caution would deter him from showing to the world his contempt for all Germans and Germanophiles.'[4]

Yet, in the Civil War, Juan Beigbeder had helped Franco with vital Nazi contacts at the start. He was one of the main proponents of expanding Spain's dominion in Morocco and north-west Africa, which was a policy close to Franco's heart. It was also Spain's main colonial experience at that time. It reflected the close association Spain had with the Muslim world through centuries of history. Beigbeder told Hoare 'we Spaniards are all Moors'. Hoare thought that his 'dark, thin Quixotic figure was more in keeping with the Riff and the desert', rather than a room at the Ministry of Foreign Affairs.[5]

In June, with France tottering towards defeat, Beigbeder had encouraged Franco to act in Tangier. Spain had sent troops into the Tangier neutral zone on 14 June and had 26,000 troops in Spanish North Africa which had annoyed Hitler. However, Vichy France retained control of its protectorate while Germany became the arbiter of the situation. It was Beigbeder who sent a letter to Hitler and Mussolini outlining Franco's general requirements of entering the war. They would seize Gibraltar, take all of Morocco, parts of Algeria, and extend the territory of the Spanish Sahara. In return, Spain would enter the war on Germany's side provided Germany granted military and economic assistance.[6]

On 18 October, as Hoare had predicted, the friendly Beigbeder was replaced as foreign minister by the pro-German and Falangist Interior-Minister Serrano Suñer, who took on both jobs himself. It had been forced on the Caudillo by Himmler, who felt Beigbeder was too close to Hoare. Franco deeply resented this interference but complied and sacked his friend. He was also becoming infuriated by the activities of the SD in Spain. SD agents had flooded into the country and had set up their own station in the Spanish Post Office to check on the correspondence of the Allied Embassies not using the diplomatic bag, going so far as to frank the stamps with the Swastika. This was pointed out virtually daily by the Allies. There were some heated arguments when Franco learnt that even some of his own letters had been franked by the SD.

After a bungled attempt, by the burgeoning SD, to blow up the plane of the pro-Allied General Jose Enrique Varela by a 'clumsily staged air crash', relations between the Spanish and the SD went from bad to worse.[7]

Schellenberg despaired of the SD in Spain, who seemed to him to be more intent on having a good time with long 'drinking bouts' rather than working. He found out that the owner of a restaurant in Madrid was 'the treasurer of our currency fund.' The local police were paid off and joined in the drinking sessions, while some of the officers were 'counter-agents, who reported everything that happened to other intelligence services.' The code used by their main transmitter had been lost. The whole set up was a shambles and the information they supplied was 'complete nonsense'. However Schellenberg felt that 'It was a frightening thought that information based on such work had actually been passed to the top leaders.'[8]

At last, reluctantly, Hitler came to the conclusion that he would have to meet with Franco to make military progress. On 20 October he set out in his own personal train to meet with Petain, Franco and Mussolini. He met Petain in central France first, and then moved onto Hendaye on the Spanish Border to meet Franco on the 23rd. Hitler brought a large group with him, including Ribbentrop, Keitel, von Brauchitsch and Stohrer who came from Madrid. He had Paul Schmidt who was an excellent interpreter, along with an infantry band which struck up suitable stirring music when the trains arrived.[9] Yet the German Spanish expert was not there. Canaris, who had a close relationship with the Caudillo, and who knew the affairs of the Peninsula so well, was not present. Colonel Erwin von Lahousen of the Abwehr told Ian Colvin that: 'Ribbentrop did not trust his influence and did not want him to be there.'[10]

It likely suited Canaris not to attend for he would then have had to pay lip-service to the Fuhrer's views. He had already advised the Spanish General Martinez Campos, the Spanish Chief of the General Staff, 'that Spain should remain neutral and defend her neutrality.'[11] While in Rome, Serrano Suñer had met with Josef Muller who told him to advise the Caudillo that Spain should avoid war at all costs, on the advice of Canaris, who felt that Germany had 'little hope of winning the war.' He promised that Hitler would not invade Spain. Clearly, Serrano Suñer held a different view, but he would have delivered the message to Franco for it could just as easily have reached Madrid through other avenues. Canaris was careful not to put anything down on paper or in a cipher.[12]

There are conflicting reports about who arrived first at Hendaye. The German diplomat Hans Stille, who was Stohrer's representative, says Franco's train was on time. Hitler was on edge and ready to overwhelm the diminutive Franco like a cat playing with a mouse, ready to intimidate him with his non-stop language as he had done to so many others. However he was to get more than he bargained for with the unflappable, dignified and affable approach of Franco. For the Caudillo was no political fanatic like the Fuhrer or the Duce. His main concern was Spain.

They started by both expressing their delight at the meeting. Franco expressed Spain's thanks for the help Germany had given during the Civil War, and that the two countries were welded together spiritually. He then went on to explain the difficulties that Spain faced which 'were well known to the Fuhrer'. He mentioned his concerns about feeding his people and that Great Britain controlled their essential supplies from the United States and Argentina which would soon be 'intensified by the bad harvests'.[13]

Then Hitler spoke going over what had happened in the war and in particular the hopelessness of the British position. It dragged on for three hours. Paul Schmidt the interpreter described the talks as a 'fiasco'. Even Hitler's trump card of Germany delivering Gibraltar to Spain produced no effect on Franco: 'I really could not tell from his face whether he found the idea a complete surprise or whether he was just considering his reply.'[14]

After lunch in Hitler's restaurant car Franco disappeared for an hour. Hitler was left fuming when Franco explained on his return that he had just had his hour's siesta. The meeting resumed and went on into the evening. Franco talked a lot, explaining the history of Spain in Morocco, about his own personal military experiences, all of which 'bored Hitler to tears'.[15] He would relate this to Mussolini: 'rather than go through that again' he would prefer 'to have three or four teeth taken out'.[16]

Again Franco returned to Spain's needs, but Hitler this time refused to discuss that and dismissed it. The Canary Islands were not mentioned during the meeting. Franco thought afterwards that Britain would fight on even from Canada, and he felt that the seizure of the Suez Canal was vital. However Hitler felt Gibraltar was vastly more significant. Finally the talk ended and they took dinner again in Hitler's restaurant car – soup, fish and fruit salad was on the menu. There was a brief conversation afterwards, and they departed amicably enough but with no real resolution.[17]

The two foreign ministers had met separately and Ribbentrop produced a secret protocol for Serrano Suñer to sign, which pledged for Spain to enter the war, whereas Germany would promise unspecified assistance. Ribbentrop wanted it signed right away but Serrano Suñer insisted he show it to Franco first. The Spanish then produced a supplementary protocol dealing more closely with economic matters and the 'French Zone of Morocco which is later to belong to Spain'.[18] The next morning Serrano showed it to Ribbentrop who was furious. Hitler could not endorse it having already left, Ribbentrop is said to have slammed the door muttering 'Jesuit swine'.[19] It was not until the 4 November that the final draft of the protocol was completed after Italian interests were added. For Germany it was far from ideal and only spoke about Spain entering the war when ready: 'at a time to be set by common agreement of the three powers.'[20]

Hitler had gone to Montoire to see Henri Petain again. The old marshal of France 'was one of the few men who ever impressed Hitler.' Despite this, he told Petain that France was in a difficult position, and once the war was over 'France or England would have to bear the territorial and material cost of the conflict.'[21] However when Petain in principle expressed himself willing to collaborate with the Axis, Hitler softened his approach and agreed that France might recover compensation from Britain. The wily old Marshal, though, was not taken in by Hitler for a moment, later confiding to a friend: 'It will take six months to discuss this programme and another six months to forget it.'[22]

The same day, Ribbentrop telephoned Count Ciano from a small railway station in France. Ciano later wrote:

> He [Ribbentrop] reports on a conference with Franco and Petain and is, on the whole, satisfied with the results achieved. He says the program of collaboration is heading toward concrete results. I do not conceal my doubt and suspicion. Nevertheless, it is essential that the inclusion of France in the Axis shall not be to our detriment. Von Ribbentrop also discusses an impending trip by Hitler to a city in northern Italy, to confer with the Duce.[23]

The meeting with Mussolini took place in Florence on the 28th but it was overshadowed by the Duce's action on the same day. Expressly against Hitler's wishes, the Italians attacked Greece. It was to prove a turning point in the war and would disrupt the Fuhrer's plans for the Mediterranean and Africa. With Mussolini however, he behaved with 'remarkable restraint', and assured him he would give Italy his full support. It would prove to be a costly mistake.[24]

Hitler signed Directive No 18 on 12 November. It allowed for the possibility of France to come into the war on the Axis side. German troops would be committed to Africa to support the Italian offensive against Egypt and Greece. Preparations against Russia would continue. *Sealion* would maintain a state of 'readiness'. However the bulk concerned Spain and Gibraltar. It alluded to the political steps needed for Spain's entry into the war, and the Operation code-named *Felix* would drive the British out of the western Mediterranean through the capture of Gibraltar. The assault on the Rock would fall into four phases: Firstly, reconnaissance of the area for final assault plans where the specialist troops would assemble on the Franco-Spanish border. Secondly, a surprise aerial assault would be launched on the British fleet while German troops crossed the border. Aircraft would fly initially from French bases but would then use Spanish facilities. Then, thirdly, the main assault would follow. Finally, phase four, three divisions would move into Spain to counter any possible British landing. German troops would occupy the Portuguese Cape Verde Islands by air, while small German forces would land in the Canaries to assist the Spanish defence.[25]

The British had little knowledge of the Hendaye meeting although Beigbeder had warned Hoare, a few days before his fall, what was about to take place. After Spain sent troops into the Tangiers International Zone in June, Churchill ordered the Admiralty to prepare for plans to secure the Canary Islands if Spain came into the war. He told Halifax that operations were to be considered against Spain's Atlantic Islands even if the Germans did not move into the Peninsula. The Canaries would be alternative bases to Gibraltar and would also be easier to defend. 'How much do we care whether the peninsula is overrun or not' Churchill said.[26] Halifax and Hoare saw this view as potentially dangerous. Providing Franco or Hitler did not move against Gibraltar it had some merit. Yet there was a good advantage to be had by airing the invasion threats against the Canaries through the Spanish corridors of power.

One appointment by Serrano Suñer was to prove advantageous to Britain. The pragmatic Demetrio Carceller Segura was made Minister of Commerce and Industries and entered the government in September as a Falangist comrade, a member of the Falange, Fascist party of Spain. However he soon 'began to show remarkable independence in his views about Anglo-Spanish trade.' He came from a poor background and by hard work and guile had become one of the richest men in Spain. He was soon reconsidering the economic strength of the British.[27]

Hoare regularly advised London to put their main effort behind the economic weapon. Spain was in a desperate plight and the country had not recovered from the disruption of the civil war. Alan Hillgarth in 1939 had estimated that a quarter of Spaniards faced starvation.[28] The Falange's interference in agriculture had made matters worse, the people hated using the government food stores which were abused by corrupt officials. Britain was fortunate to have such a powerful card that could be used against Franco's regime, but it was a card that had to be played with care. Eccles in Madrid, during the autumn of 1940, warned that 'another bread-less period will see the end of the regime with one sure result, a short period of chaos followed by an Axis occupation.'[29]

Through the naval blockade and the system of 'navigation certificates', Britain in effect controlled a large share of the imports and exports of Spain. Ships were certificated by Britain to pass through the blockade. Hoare was at the centre of the debate. His view was that Britain should increase their economic assistance to Spain whose economy was staggering towards collapse. The critical choice was whether Britain should set conditions or not. Churchill tried to find common ground with the USA. In November Hoare met with Serrano Suñer when he accused the British of 'starving Spain to death'. Hoare found he was making more headway with Carceller Segura, the practical businessman, but even he admitted that if Spain did not receive wheat soon the government might fall. By now Churchill had begun to appreciate how serious this situation was and appealed directly to President Roosevelt in November:

> Our accounts show that the situation in Spain is deteriorating and that the Peninsula is not far from starvation point. An offer by you of food month by month so long as they keep out of the war might be decisive. Small things do not count now, and this is a time for very plain talk to them. The occupation by Germany of both sides of the Straits would be a grievous addition to our naval strain already severe.[30]

However the American administration, backed by public opinion, was against propping up a Fascist Dictator, and had already rejected a direct approach from Spain for a $100 million loan to buy wheat and petrol from the USA. The Canadian government took much the same view. Britain extended the War Trade Agreement in December for an additional £2 million to the original amount granted in March 1940 of £4 million.

This allowed 200,000 tons of wheat from Argentina to be shipped and Britain released 25,000 tons of cereals from its own supplies. The Americans also agreed to a food programme of aid through the Red Cross but refused to match the British loans. So Britain, through food, was keeping Franco in power.[31] Hoare wrote to David Eccles in December to tell him that Carceller Segura was openly saying that he had worked well with him and it was 'the British who helped smooth out the American trouble.'[32] The wrangling over trade would continue and come to include Wolfram (tungsten) of which Spain and Portugal were exporters, but for the moment Britain had gained much ground. Even so, Churchill felt Spain was 'trembling on the brink'.[33]

Carceller had told Hoare, in confidence, that he did not want wheat coming from Germany as he preferred working with the British.[34] Hitler made a grave mistake insisting on conditions before supplying Spain with food. Given all the economic aid Britain had provided it was Hitler, by not ordering his troops into Spain, that proved the decisive factor in Spain's neutrality. Britain and Spain were in no position at the time to resist such a move. Why then did the Fuhrer not grasp the moment?

To expedite Directive No 18 Hitler summoned Ciano and Serrano Suñer to his mountain retreat at Berchtesgaden on 18 November. However in Madrid the Spanish military were losing their enthusiasm about the war. Jose Enrique Varela the minister of the army, a strong, anti-Falangist recommended the trip to Germany should be postponed, but the danger of angering Hitler proved too risky. Ribbentrop met Ciano in Salzburg and told him that Hitler would talk about the Greek Crisis at the meeting.[35]

There, Hitler went into his usual lengthy explanation of the war situation. Turning to Spain he stressed the need for the Spanish to take rapid action. Serrano Suñer replied that, not knowing the agenda beforehand, he could only give a personal opinion.[36] He explained that the Spanish government was deeply involved with the famine issue and they were forced to seek aid from Britain and the USA, while Franco, he knew, felt the Hendaye protocol was too vague in regard to Spain's needs not to mention the concern about Morocco. Hitler responded by saying that once Germany had obtained her objectives, Spain would be satisfied in Morocco. Serrano Suñer did not raise any more questions.

On 20 November General Franz Halder issued orders for *Felix* the assault on Gibraltar. The troops were to be assembled in the Bordeaux-Bayonne-Orthez area. They would pass through Spain on or about 10 January 1941. The axis of advance would be Burgos – Valladolid – Salamanca – Seville to Gibraltar, with two corps of specially selected assault troops to attack the Rock.

The 3rd SS Panzer Division Totenkopf would move to Seville, while 16th Armoured Division and 16th Motorised Infantry Division would move to the Portuguese Frontier. However there was no plan to invade Portugal, and this was just a precaution. 800 aircraft would also be committed to the operation. The plan to invade the Portuguese Atlantic Islands was abandoned.[37] Clearly, the Fuhrer and Ribbentrop felt they had agreement on this.

In Spain the Spanish War Council met in December. The mood at the meeting was gloomy and it was felt that the country was in no state to enter the war.

At the last major *Felix* planning session on 5 December Hitler ordered Admiral Canaris to go to Spain and obtain Franco's final agreement. The Admiral met the Caudillo two days later. The only other person at that meeting was General Vigon. It is unknown what was discussed but clearly Franco would not agree to cooperate with the German plans.[38] Franco did state later that he was worried about British naval strength in regard to the Canaries and the economic state of the country was poor. He gave no alternative timetable to the Germans. When Canaris informed Hitler, he was told to try again. On 10 December he telegraphed Hitler via OKW stating that Franco would not enter the war as long as Britain could inflict great damage on Spain.

With the attack on Russia looming larger, Hitler, exasperated with the Spanish, ordered *Felix* to be postponed.[39] During another meeting on 8–9 January at the Berghof, he stated that he was still attracted by the Gibraltar operation but saw no hope in taking it forward. Spain was too poor, too desolate, and too wide for effective troop movements without the permission of the incumbent regime, Hitler outlined. Having to support the Italians in Greece and Libya meant that there was no question of forcing Spain into the war, although he would still try and persuade Franco.[40]

At his next meeting with Mussolini, Hitler asked the Duce to meet with Franco and try to persuade him to join them. Franco and Mussolini met at Bordighera on the Italian Riviera on 12 February. Franco had refused to fly ever since two of his generals had died in an unexplained plane crash during the Civil War, so he travelled through France by car. Italy was hardly a shining example to Franco of the potential fate of entering the war. The Italian armies were defeated in Greece and Africa, and the Royal Navy had crippled the Italian fleet at Taranto. Yet Mussolini did the best he could to restate the good German position, although he agreed that Franco must decide when Spain would be ready to enter the war. Franco gave Mussolini the same assurances he had given Hitler, including his belief that the Axis would be victorious.

On 22 February Ribbentrop telegraphed Stohrer in Madrid, advising him not to take any further action 'in the question of Spanish entry into the war.'[41]

CHAPTER 8

Operation *Golden Eye*

When Ian Fleming returned to London from Spain and Morocco in August 1940, after a prompt de-brief with Admiral Godfrey, he was given the task of assessing the danger to Gibraltar and drawing up a plan to have in place for stay-behind agents and saboteurs should Spain join the Axis. This was Operation *Golden Eye*.

It came at a time when Fleming had a lot on his plate. The Battle of Britain was reaching its height. The U-boat threat was growing. Ian was fiercely dedicated to his role at NI. He would be at his desk by 6am, and worked late into the night. As a colleague observed, Fleming never slept 'with a problem'.[1] All sorts of ideas flowed from his pen, including scuttling cement barges in the Danube to block the river's traffic, forging Reichsmark's to disrupt the German economy, and luring German agents to Monte Carlo to capture them. One of the more realistic and practical was Operation *Ruthless*, which he hatched in September 1940. The cryptologists at Bletchley Park had already broken the German Army and Abwehr Enigma messages. But the Kriegsmarine three-rotor encoding machine was proving a tougher nut to crack. Admiral Godfrey sent Fleming to see Dilly Knox at Bletchley Park who told him that a German Navy codebook would be of great assistance. So he came up with a plan to capture a German vessel that would be carrying the codebook. He soon identified that the Germans were running an air-rescue boat out of Denmark which would pick up air crews that had ditched in the sea after a raid. If a rescue boat could be lured to pick up a crew of a downed bomber, which would be British in disguise, the crew might be overpowered and the codebook taken. Fleming outlined his idea in a note to Godfrey:

1. Obtain from Air Ministry an air-worthy German Bomber.
2. Pick a tough crew of five, including pilot, W/T operator and word-perfect German speaker, Dress them in German Air Force uniforms; add blood and bandages to suit.

3. Crash plane in the channel after making S. O. S to rescue service in P/L (Plain Language).
4. Once aboard rescue boat, shoot German crew, dump overboard, bring rescue boat back to English port.

In order to increase the chances of obtaining an R or M (a small or larger minesweeper) with its richer booty, the crash might be staged in mid-channel. The Germans would presumably employ one of this type for the longer more hazardous journey.

F. 12.9.40.[2]

A Heinkel III bomber was available. The aircraft had been captured in an airworthy condition from the bomber unit Kampfgeschwader 26. In early February it had made a forced landing near North Berwick after tangling with a Spitfire over the Firth of Forth. It was then assigned to the RAF and flown by the Air Fighting Development Unit, although Group Captain H. J. Wilson pointed out that crashing this type of aircraft in the Channel would result in the collapse of the bombers Perspex nose, and the crew would likely drown before they could get out. However he reluctantly agreed to the operation after the Heinkel's nose was reinforced.

Fleming volunteered to be one of the crew with his excellent German but Admiral Godfrey banned him from taking part, as his possible capture was too great a risk. Rear Admiral Jock Clayton, head of the Operational Intelligence Centre, supported the scheme but wanted to see a more detailed plan. Ian set to work on the details.

The Heinkel Werk Nr 6853 would take off just after dawn following German aircraft returning to base after a raid. When it spotted a German rescue vessel it would cut one engine and produce smoke by injecting oil into the exhaust, send an SOS, and ditch into the sea. The operation was scheduled for the early part of October as German codes were changed at the start of each month. Fleming, with his team, went to Dover to await the next suitable bombing raid, but aerial reconnaissance and wireless monitoring failed to locate any German rescue vessels and they were stood down. *Ruthless* was shelved on 16 October, with a recommendation that it should be tried again from Portsmouth, and that: 'Lieutenant Commander Fleming returns to Admiralty 1800 today Wednesday.'[3] Frank Birch, head of the naval section at GCHQ, wrote in a letter four days later that Alan Turing and Peter Twinn were 'all of a stew about the cancellation of *Ruthless*.'[4]

Fleming returned to working on Operation *Golden Eye* soon after. *Ruthless* must have seemed relatively straightforward in comparison. For a start, *Golden Eye* had to be sub-divided into two plans, Operation *Sprinkler* to assist the Spanish if they resisted a German invasion, and Operation *Sconce* if the Spanish cooperated with the Germans. Both would mean that Section H of

SOE would deploy sabotage teams using Spanish guerrillas to hit transport links and fuel stores.

One proposed leader for a five-man team to be parachuted in to Spain (or landed from a submarine) was Doctor Eduardo Martinez Alonso. He was born in Vigo, Galicia in 1903. His father was the Uruguayan consul there at the time. In 1912 his father was posted to Britain and six years later Eduardo entered Liverpool University to study medicine. In 1924 the tall handsome surgeon, who had a love of playing rugby from his university days, returned to Spain. His practice in Madrid grew to include members of the royal family.

Once Civil War broke out he was a marked man with his royalist associations in Republican Madrid, but his work through the Red Cross saved him from the firing squads. He observed at the start of the war: 'Everything was paralysed except murder, arson, and rape.'[5] He shared no political allegiances during the war, calling himself a humanitarian, and he used his Madrid flat to hide people and aid their escape.

The Republicans sent him to work at a prison near Aranjuez, south of Madrid, on the river Tagus. He was to all intents and purposes a prisoner himself. Once he learned that he was marked for execution he escaped in 1937 to Valencia, where with a fake passport he boarded an American ship to Marseilles. When he returned to Spain he worked in Nationalist hospitals and, at the end of the war, returned to Madrid.

With the coming of World War II, as physician to the British Embassy, he got to know Alan Hillgarth well and was recruited into his network as agent 055. His medical reputation and Nationalist Army service was ideal cover for his frequent visits to the embassy. He soon began helping escapees using the family home *La Portela* at Vigo as a safe house. From there local fishermen would take them out to British ships in the estuary. Poles and Jews, who were escaping Nazi persecution, also used the route, especially after the Vichy government in France made things more difficult by restricting the issue of visas, and the Spanish refusing entry into Spain without one. This resulted in a large increase of 'indocumentados' coming over the Pyrenees. Those arrested by the Spanish were interned in the notorious concentration camp *Miranda de Ebro* near Burgos, which was two hundred miles north of Madrid. Hastily constructed during the Civil War, it was surrounded by stone walls topped by barbed wire. It was hot in summer and freezing in winter.[6] The camp was soon overcrowded. Eduardo was an active member of the Red Cross and a former doctor in the Nationalist Army. The commandant welcomed his help, and was delighted to release the victim of typhus to hospital. This gave Eduardo an idea to invent a major outbreak of the disease. Thus large numbers of inmates would be whisked away in borrowed ambulances.

These inmates would find their way to the Embassy, or to Margarita Taylor's flat in Madrid, another of Hillgarth's agents, an Irish woman who ran a tea room on the Paseo de la Castellana. Once forged papers had been obtained they were moved on in embassy cars, usually concealed in the boot. They were moved to Gibraltar or north-west to Galicia crossing the river Mino into Portugal. With the help of countless people and many safe houses, this escape route was in operation from the end of 1939 until the end of 1941, with an average of ten people a week being smuggled out.

Vigo, in Galicia, was full of German agents and Dr Martinez Alonso came under increasing suspicion. Hillgarth felt that time had run out for him and therefore made arrangements for his friend to leave the country. However Eduardo was engaged to be married to Ramona, who was the daughter of a Galician doctor. The marriage went ahead on 3 January in Madrid, before the couple went into hiding while people thought they had gone on their honeymoon. Passports were obtained, then an Embassy car driven by David Barrington Smith, ostensibly on the staff of the embassy but in fact an early SOE arrival, took them to the border near Ciudad Rodrigo west of Salamanca. At the crossing, their passports received a cursory glance and then they were in Portugal. On 2 February their plane landed in Cardiff.[7]

Eduardo, from a grateful British Foreign Office, received a stipend of £20 a month in recognition of his service. Most of the escape routes he had built continued to operate without his presence. Later he would become a physician at Queen Mary's Hospital Roehampton. He continued to maintain links with Alan Hillgarth and the FO. He was seconded to SOE and began his training regime in Scotland for *Golden Eye*. At the converted farmhouse, Camusdarach near Inverness, he learnt the dark arts of sabotage and unarmed combat and how to: 'blow things up, kill the enemy from behind with knives and hand grenades, Tommy guns, traps, kicks in the most delicate parts of man's anatomy, and other disgusting manoeuvres.' There he was given the name of Lieutenant Marlin to be used on operations.[8] Spaniards for *Sprinkler/ Sconce* had been training in the Highlands since December 1940. One report commented that: 'The most striking thing about the Spanish troops is their pride in being members of the British army, and also their gratitude for the work that has been done in this country on their behalf.'[9]

Ian Fleming was no doubt glad to head for Spain in February 1941 to review *Golden Eye* on the ground. He would be happy to get away from his desk, and the bickering between the SIS and SOE over the operation, but also to get away from the Luftwaffe bombs. In the Blitz, he had several narrow escapes managing to survive in three buildings that were badly damaged, including in Dover during preparations for Operation *Ruthless*. On another occasion he was attending a dinner party given by Sefton Delmer and his wife Isobel in their Lincolns Inn flat with a 'small and select dinner party' when they were visited by a 'small and select bomb'.[10] The flat was badly damaged and the entrance hall was largely destroyed along with the staircase. The only way down was to be lowered twenty feet to the piece of staircase still intact.

In Fleming's flat at 22 Ebury Street, skylights could not easily be blacked out so he had to find temporary accommodation at the Lansdowne, the St James's Club or the Carlton Hotel. At the latter, his third-floor room was destroyed by a bomb. Ian helped rescue a waiter and maid who had been buried under the wreckage. Later he went to sleep with the other residents in the Grill room. He was woken there by what he thought was running water, only to find an old man relieving himself on the carpet. Later he found out that the old man was an eminent bishop.[11]

On 16 February 1941 Ian flew out to Lisbon and then to Madrid where he was issued with a courier's passport from the Madrid embassy dated the same day. It was issued in order to ease his travel between the Rock and Madrid. He was glad to travel in civilian clothing and wore a dark blue suit with an Etonian tie. He carried a commando fighting knife which he bought from Wilkinsons and carried on his foreign assignments. It was engraved with his name and rank on the blade.[12] His fascination with gadgets extended to a fountain pen that could be fitted with a cyanide or tear gas cartridge, which he carried as well. He was fully prepared to explore his fantasies of life as a secret agent.[13]

Arriving in Gibraltar, Fleming would have seen firsthand the amount of activity going on in the colony and the work which had already been done. Before the war, there were no land-based aircraft and only three Swordfish float planes. A runway had now been constructed, which though not full length, could take Bombays and Wellingtons carrying light loads. The decision was taken at the time not to antagonise Spain. It was not until October 1941 that the runway was realigned and extended out into the bay for nearly half a mile on reclaimed land, which would have been keenly observed by German agents from the balconies of the Hotel Reina Cristina in Algeciras. The runway would have a public road crossing it, which is still a feature today. In 1940 the decision was made to locate as many installations and support facilities underground as possible in order to expand on Gibraltar's limited space.

Accommodation, hospitals, storage caves, water and sanitary arrangements were built into a vast network of tunnels and chambers running the length of the Rock. In all there would be thirty-four miles of tunnels, most of which were finished by 1943. The work was carried out by four companies of Royal Engineers and a Canadian Tunnelling firm that had perfected a diamond drill blasting method, which was a new drilling technique that saved a lot of manual labour.[14]

It is possible that this had an influence on Fleming's later writings. In *Dr No* Bond and Honeychile Rider are imprisoned by Dr Julius No in a warren of rooms built into the 'side of the mountain' on Crab Key, the island that ended in a 'cliff-face'. The walls of the corridors were moisture free, and 'the air was cool and pure with a strongest breeze coming towards them. A lot of money and good engineering had gone into the job.'[15]

At Gibraltar Ian set up a *Golden Eye* liaison office with its own cipher link. It was to consist of a team of ten naval personnel led by a commander, and included demolition officers and a petty officer telegraphist.[16] But if Spain succumbed to German entreaties to join the war, or was invaded, it was unlikely that Britain would be able to hold Gibraltar. To be able to continue monitoring Allied shipping in the Mediterranean and the Atlantic another backup office was set up in Tangier and commanded by Henry Greenleaves.

On 14 June 1940 Spain had occupied the international zone of Tangier on the pretext of guaranteeing its neutrality. This, however, was a ploy as Franco dreamed of annexing the whole of Morocco. At the time, the city of Tangier was a hotbed of agents from both sides. The Abwehr had established offices there. It was only two and a half hours by boat across the straits to Spain, seven hours by road from Casablanca and three hours on a flight from Lisbon.

The old town with its Grand Soco market square was called the Medina, and was made up of narrow streets which no traffic could enter. The red-light district of Zoco-Chico was full of bars and brothels where all tastes in alcohol, drugs and sex were catered for. The Cafe de Paris was opened in 1920 by Madame Leotine, who was the first woman to run such an establishment in Tangier, and it soon became a meeting place for spies. Paul Bowles, the American writer who lived in the town for many years, wrote: 'During the war it was thought every fourth person was a spy, smuggler or refugee.' He preferred the Cafe Hafa where you could get a coffee at five in the morning and stayed open all night.[17]

Only a year later, the film *Casablanca* premiered, based on Murray Burnett and Joan Alison's unproduced play called *Everybody Comes to Rick's*. It was in some ways a fair depiction of what was going on in Tangier at the time. One line in particular rang true: 'That everybody in Tangier [Casablanca] has problems.'[18]

Ian Fleming enjoyed a night on the town with Henry Greenleaves there and the heady atmosphere for him was like a tonic. He would have felt, albeit briefly, that he was a real spy. Yet even in that short time they learned that General Erwin Rommel had arrived in Tripoli, Libya to command the newly formed Afrika Korps.

The British Consul to Tangier, the straight-laced former Guardsman Major Alvary Trench-Gascoigne, had been in the post for less than a year. He is likely not to have been too impressed with his new attaché, or the visiting NID officer, for carousing around the town. After all, he already had enough on his plate. Despite Trench-Gascoigne's protests, Franco allowed the German consulate, closed since 1914, to reopen. The consulate became a large legation on the site of the Mendoub's palace which was to run a serious espionage centre for the next three years.[19] In a report Commander G. H. Birley of NID Gibraltar noted: 'Although H. M. Consul-General [Trench-Gascoigne] and Greenleaves are on friendly terms, the former still cannot, think, rid himself of the feeling that Greenleaves is an interloper.' This state of affairs was not helped by 'the fact that Greenleaves and the SIS do not get on well together whereas H. M. Consul-General has implicit faith in SIS.'[20] In an earlier report by Greenleaves to Birley he had noted in regard to the SIS: 'On your instructions, I shall have no further contact with this Department.'[21]

Part of Fleming's remit from Godfrey was to meet Colonel William Donovan at Gibraltar. Donovan was reaching the end of his second journey to Europe on behalf of the US government, where he had investigated the economic, political, and military situation in the Mediterranean and Middle East. Colonel Vivian Dykes, Churchill's personal representative, escorted him.[22]

Donovan was a giant of a man, 50 years of age in 1940 and of Irish descent. His sobriquet was 'Wild Bill', and he had received a chest full of medals when he commanded 1st Battalion 165th Regiment, which was part of the New York's 69th (*Fighting Irish*) Division in World War I. His men had given him the nickname due to his impressive feats of endurance. He had met Admiral Godfrey in 1940 while on his first mission to Europe to find out if Britain would fight on as Churchill had promised. He returned from that mission convinced they would. He advised the President that the US should do everything possible to aid Britain, including full collaboration in intelligence.[23]

On the second journey, Donovan left the USA on 6 December and would not return until March 1941. He visited many countries around the Mediterranean basin and spoke with all sorts of people from common soldiers to dictators.

He lunched with Admiral Andrew Cunningham aboard the *Warspite* at Alexandria on Sunday 9 February and Cunningham found him to be a 'pleasant and interesting man, very much alive.' They talked about naval affairs in the Mediterranean: 'he offered to send a message to the United States saying we must have more fighter aircraft. I did nothing to discourage him.'[24]

On 24 February Donovan landed in Gibraltar harbour onboard an RAF Sunderland Flying Boat, which had dealt with a 40 mph headwind and touched down with only fifteen minutes of fuel left. They stayed at Government House that night. As Donovan had a problem with his eye resulting in a minor operation, he missed the dinner Dykes took with Hillgarth and Fleming, the Governor and several other guests.[25]

The next day the party set off for Madrid at 7.10am. Dykes recorded in his diary for Thursday 25 February 1941: 'I sat with Ian Fleming much of the way. He is the brother of Peter Fleming and was on Reuter's staff before the war. He told me some interesting experiences as a Reuter's man and was inclined to knock it [alcohol] back too much.'[26]

Donovan tried to secure a meeting with Franco by indirectly suggesting that the USA might be able to offer economic aid. He met with Serrano Suñer who he took to task about the shocking condition of Spain and the poor government which the people had to endure, leaving 'the minister almost speechless with fury'.[27] Donovan also conducted several meetings with Sir Samuel Hoare in which the Ambassador pointed out that American economic aid to Spain would help immensely to keep the Peninsula out of the Axis and 'frustrate Hitler's efforts to conquer all Europe'.[28] Donovan then flew on to Lisbon to try to get the same message across to the Portuguese dictator Salazar.

In Madrid, Hillgarth and Fleming held final discussions on *Golden Eye* before Ian returned to London. Likely, the two men did not agree with the best method of going forward with it. Hillgarth was beginning to sense that there were too many people involved, and was beginning to doubt the wisdom of sending so many SOE agents, then known as SO2 from the sabotage section of SIS, into the country where they were colluding with the Left in Spain. He referred to this as 'dangerous, amateurish activities'.[29] Fleming, on the other hand, had confided to Dykes that he believed SIS and SO2 were on course for a 'crash-out'.[30]

In April Fleming wrote a report on: 'Divisions of interests between SIS & SO2 (SOE)'. He observed that since the creation of SO2: 'as a separate entity, charged with sabotage in enemy countries, SO2 and SIS have been in keen competition.' In Spain he felt the attempts by SO2 to form a 'sabotage organisation' had left the naval attaché, trying to direct these operations, 'compromised to a certain degree'.[31]

Yet in January only a few weeks before, Hillgarth had been in London and met with Hugh Dalton, the Minister of Economic Warfare and head of SOE, who told the prime minister that Hillgarth 'has consented to supervise the whole of our activities in Spain.'[32] Godfrey was not happy with his star attaché being compromised and wrote to the chiefs of staff in April that 'intelligence is of primary importance' and SIS should be given precedence and have the right of a 'veto' over any SO2 projects.[33]

Hillgarth tried to smooth things over with Godfrey and even to persuade Hoare, who was dead set against any cloak and dagger business, that SOE could do important work in preparation for a German invasion 'provided they were rigidly controlled.'[34] He later wrote a report on 'The role of the Naval Attaché'. He felt that he had to create a sort of 'substitute SIS in Spain'. He explained that this would not cause trouble because: (a) my reports went to both DNI and CSS and (b) my relations with SIS in Madrid were first class.'[35] He went on further to explain:

> When SOE was formed as a separate entity from SIS, there was inevitably rivalry between them. Though their functions were different, there were unavoidable instances of trespass. You cannot carry out clandestine operations without intelligence to guide you, and you cannot help acquiring intelligence in the course of your proceedings.
>
> The natural desire of SOE to operate in the Iberian Peninsula and Spanish Morocco met, however, an even stronger opposition from the Foreign Office and the Ambassadors in Spain and Portugal who were all, very naturally, fearful of some stupid explosion or an ignominious capture of British agents, with consequent harm to our general policy. In this fear they were justified, although my Ambassador recognised that SOE could do important work in preparations against a possible German invasion of the peninsula, provided they were rigidly controlled. A compromise was eventually reached by which SOE were allowed to operate in the peninsula in a precautionary way only, and I was chosen to control them. That is to say, they could initiate nothing without my approval and the progress of what was approved had to be fully disclosed to me every day.
>
> On the whole this worked very well, but it was an unenviable task for the controller. I was continually berated by the Ambassador and by the Foreign Office whenever I went to London for allowing anything at all, while the chief of SOE on the other side was continually at me to allow more. Meanwhile the DNI was always fearful that I would slip from controlling into directing and get involved and compromised. So I was under fire from three sides.'[36]

Two incidents with SIS caused alarm within the British Embassy and created more work for Hillgarth. The first centred on Paul Lewis Claire, a French naval officer, who transferred to the Royal Navy after France fell. He was taken on by SIS O Section to land agents in France via the sea. By July 1941 he was in Spain, sent there by SIS, and arrested at the border while trying to get back into France. On 23 July he was in the Vichy Embassy in Madrid revealing SIS secrets to the naval attaché. This news reached Hoare who requested immediate instructions from SIS as Claire was expected at the British Embassy the next day to pick up his passport. Frank Slocum at SIS advised that Hillgarth should take 'what steps he can to intercept Claire'. He also suggested that SOE might 'liquidate Claire' and even thought about kidnapping Claire's wife in an attempt to bring him to heel. Colonel Stewart Menzies was in favour of capture.

Between them, Hamilton-Stokes and Hillgarth lured Claire to the Embassy where he was beaten up and drugged with morphine. He was then bundled into a car when they set off for Gibraltar, with instructions that under no circumstances should he be allowed to escape. On the long journey south, Claire began to regain consciousness and called for help in a Spanish village. To keep him quiet, he was hit over the head with a pistol, but the blow proved too hard and he died. The message from the SIS agent in Gibraltar read that the 'consignment arrived in this town completely destroyed owing to over attention in transit' and would be disposed of.[37] Hoare claimed 'once again we have had here to save SIS from catastrophe' rather ignoring that Hamilton-Stokes was an SIS officer.

There were protests from the Spanish Foreign Ministry after Vichy France broadcast on the radio about the affair. Two days later, the London *Daily Telegraph* hit back with the headline: 'Nazis invent kidnapping'.[38] Later Ian Fleming informed the Red Cross that Claire was 'missing believed drowned' while on board the SS *Empire Hurst* which had been sunk by enemy aircraft 11 August 1941. After the war, to protect SIS, Claire's widow was paid a pension.[39]

The second incident to cause alarm was that of Lieutenant Colonel Dudley Wrangel Clarke. In this case, Hillgarth had to retrieve him out of a Spanish jail after he had been arrested in drag.

He was the head of the deception unit in Cairo and should have been in Egypt. His presence in such garb, right down to a brassiere, came as a surprise to both the Spanish and British. First he told the police he was a novelist trying to get under the skin of a female character. Then, he told Hillgarth that he was taking the garments to a lady friend in Gibraltar, despite the fact that the garments all fitted him, including the high heels.[40]

Hillgarth sent photographs to the prime minister's office with a light-hearted note for the staff: 'Herewith some photographs of Mr Dudley Wrangel Clarke as he was when arrested and after he was allowed to change. I promised them to the Prime Minister and thought you might like to see them too.'[41]

Clarke later maintained it was a ploy to see if his cover could hold with the Spanish and Germans. He returned to Cairo and went on to have a fine career in deception.

Hillgarth might well have felt aggrieved that Fleming seemed to live his life with few cares, while he was swamped by work on all sides. He was instrumental in the bribery operation of top Spanish officials and military officers and had telegraphed Churchill in June 1940 that the idea was 'already showing results'.[42] Some were not so impressed, however, including Kim Philby who wrote after his defection to the Soviet Union in 1963, that Hillgarth was paying far too much for information they knew already from 'a high official of the Direccion General de Seguridad'. Philby was annoyed as he had 'to fight to get an extra £5 a month for agents who produced regular, if less spectacular, intelligence.' Philby noted with disdain that Hillgarth had picked the code name 'Armada' to feed his illusions of grandeur.'[43]

When the risk of German Invasion in the spring of 1941 seemed likely, Hillgarth visited Gibraltar to check all was in order. He found to his fury that when the mission moved to Spain, Brigadier Torr, the Military Attaché, would command it. He wrote to Godfrey in anger: 'I am not quite clear what I'm to be or do – either just a lackey to the Ambassador and separated from the Mission or a sort of glorified interpreter ... Please take me away out of it to another job where I can be of some use.'[44] Godfrey quickly intervened to promote Hillgarth to the dormant rank of commodore and designating him as the Chief British Naval Liaison Officer. Godfrey wrote to him that he had spoken to the prime minister about *Golden Eye* and that the operation was under review. He assured him that he had put forward proposals that were in 'accordance with your wishes and in accordance with the recommendations which Fleming brought back from Spain and of which I know you are aware.'[45]

Godfrey thought that Hillgarth had written his letter 'rather hastily' and assured Hillgarth that he had his 'best interests in mind and that I appreciate your services in Spain sufficiently to make every effort to protect your future status against incursions from whatever quarter.'[46]

With everything else he had on his plate, it hardly seems credible that Alan in November should start an affair with Jean Cobb, on an official visit to Lisbon, but such are the mysteries of the human heart. They met while he was staying at Estoril and the affair would lead to his divorce from Mary and marriage to Jean in 1947. Their marriage would last until Jean's death in 1975.[47]

Later that year Hillgarth wrote a report on *Golden Eye* to argue that the 'fact that no invasion has yet taken place does not justify any relaxation. I feel however that the original plan from the naval point of view was unnecessarily ambitious.'[48]

It was of course Fleming's original plan, but Admiral Godfrey was happy with his work. On his return to London, Ian was tight-lipped about the trip, though he did tell Maud Russell, who worked in NI, that 'he had enjoyed the spring almond blossom in Seville.' In a letter to Hillgarth, he commended him: 'It is lucky that we have such a team in our last European stronghold and results have already shown the great contribution you are all making towards winning the war.' He also promised Hillgarth some Henry Clay Cigars, which he begged him to smoke himself 'and not give them to [his] rascally friends.'[49]

CHAPTER 9

Operation *Tracer*

Gibraltar, according to ancient Greek myths, was the northern pillars of Hercules, while Jebel Musa, across the straits in Morocco, is said to have been the southern pillar. Mythology is not quite clear on what Hercules did to create the straits, but after his tenth labour fetching the cattle of Geryon from Erytheia, he celebrated by either setting up the mountains, or he pushed them apart to create the Mediterranean Sea.

There is another more plausible theory that the Rock was formed 200 million years ago. The earth's great drifting plates which later formed Africa and Europe collided and a colossal mass of limestone was forced up from the sea and somehow turned over. The top of the Rock consists of millions of compacted seashells. Far from being solid, the Rock is honeycombed by natural caves which man has added to.

For centuries Gibraltar was not a western gateway but a north-south axis between Europe and Africa. The Phoenicians, named it Gib Alube, while the Romans named it Mons Calpe and the southern pillar Mons Abila, which means 'beautiful mountain'. It appears the Barber, Tarik ibn Zeyael, called the Rock the 'Geb-el-Tarik' translated as the Hill of Tarik. He is credited as the author of the name Gibraltar, just as the Moors called southern Spain Al Andalus becoming Andalusia.

The British captured the Rock in 1704. Although the defence of Gibraltar over the next few decades was no easy task, with one siege ending in March 1783 after three years and seven months. During this siege, Sergeant Major Henry Ince and his band of tunnelling builders built a whole new system of communication galleries 659 foot long within the Rock, and placed four more gun positions on the north face. Food was always a problem during the sieges and the garrison often suffered from scurvy. Fortunately, water was never a problem as rain water collected into a natural reservoir within the Rock and was piped down to the seafront. With the water filtered by the rock, it was said to have an excellent quality.[1]

The highest point is on the eastern face, 1398ft high, and near the cable car station. To the west lies the Atlantic past the sprawl of Algeciras. To the north the low hills of San Roque, to the south Morocco and the Mediterranean Sea is east.

Lawrence Durrell has one of his characters in the novel *Balthazar* describe the Mediterranean as 'an absurdly small sea, the length and greatness of its history makes us dream it is longer than it is.' The sea is 2,000 miles long in places and 1,600 foot deep, salty and tideless.[2]

During his long career in the navy Admiral John Godfrey would have been to Gib many times and seen its labyrinth of caves and galleries. As

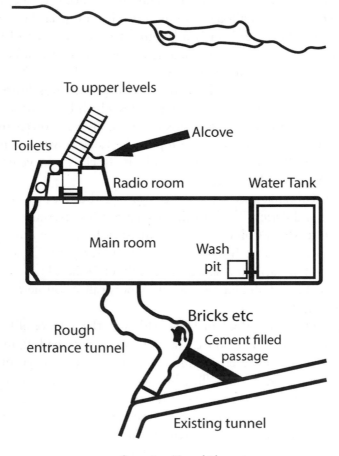

Operation *Tracer* hide.

the threat grew of the Germans occupying Gibraltar, the idea grew in his mind of a stay-behind team walled up within the Rock that could monitor shipping through the straits and relaying it through radio to the Allies. The idea originated in the late summer of 1941. Operation *Tracer* was so secret, and involved so few people, that meetings took place in Godfrey's flat at 36 Curzon Street in Mayfair rather than Whitehall.[3]

Commander Geoffrey Birley, the SOI of Gibraltar, with two engineer officers, Colonels H. M. Fordham and R. A. Hay, conducted a reconnaissance of the Rock to choose a site and start work on construction. The site chosen was in the existing tunnel system called Lord Airey's Shelter which was high up on the southern ridge of the Rock, and behind Lord Airey's Battery completed in 1891, just north of O'Hara's Battery. Lord Richard Airey was Governor of Gibraltar from 1865–70 but was more famous for issuing the fateful order for the Charge of the Light Brigade during the Crimean War in 1854.

The accommodation would be for six men with their wireless systems and stores, as well as a water tank with 10,000 gallons which could last a year. It was estimated that it would take the Germans twelve to eighteen months to find them. The camber would be 45 foot long, 16 foot wide and 8 foot high, with two narrow observation slits to overlook the Bay of Gibraltar to the west and the Mediterranean to the east.[4]

In December, the head of NID responsible for the Mediterranean, Colonel John Cordeaux RM, went out to view the work, and to tell Birley what the Admiralty signals experts wanted. He also had some questions from Lord Thomas Jeeves Horder who had been brought in by Godfrey along with Surgeon Commander George Murray Levick for advice on the men's welfare and survival.[5] Horder was a physician and advisor to the Ministry of Food during the war. Levick was a naval doctor and survival expert who had been part of Robert Falcon Scott's Terra Nova Expedition in 1911–1912. Due to pack ice, Levick and five other members of the expedition were forced to spend the winter on Inexpressible Island in Antarctica inside an ice cave that he called 'a dismal hole'.[6] After the winter ended, they walked two hundred miles to Hut Point and then on to Cape Evans where they were reunited with the Northern Party.

In 1940 he came back to the navy as a specialist in guerrilla warfare with the commandos who were training at Lochailort in Scotland. He taught fitness, diet and survival techniques, many of which found their way into Commando training manuals.

On 25 January Godfrey met with Cordeaux, Fleming, Horder, and Levick to consider the latter two's report, which had made recommendations for personnel, making sure they had exercise and recreation, clothing, ventilation, sanitation, food, alcohol, tobacco, and the disposal by embalmment and cementing-up of anyone who died. The team, it was agreed, would consist of six: one officer leader, two doctors and three telegraphist ratings. Horder would find the doctors, and DNI would find the rest. It is possible that Fleming had a part to play in *Tracer*, especially considering some of the details in his later novels.[7]

Ian Fleming's short story *From a View to a Kill* may have echoes of *Tracer* in it. In the story, NATO despatch riders from SHAPE headquarters in France are being ambushed and losing vital information to a Soviet GRU (Soviet Military Intelligence) 'left behind spy unit' which Bond uncovers. He finds the spy unit to be 'certainly the most professional that had ever been devised – far more brilliant than anything England prepared to operate in the wake of a successful German invasion, far better than what the Germans themselves had left behind in the Ardennes in 1944.' When it was published in 1962, *Tracer* was still classified as Top Secret along with the auxiliary units, who would have been concealed in elaborate underground hideouts to strike at the Germans if an invasion of the UK had taken place. Fleming would probably have been aware of the auxiliary units too. *Tracer* was strictly an intelligence gathering operation but, again in the same story, there is a hint of what would have taken place on the Rock when a 'pedal generator would get going deep down under the earth and off would go the high-speed cipher groups.'[8]

Work carried on at the site in secret, with the labourers unaware of the location. All of the workers had been brought out from the UK and were returned as soon as the work was complete. All did not go smoothly. The chamber became known as Braithwaite's Cave named after the commanding officer of the construction gang, Major J. A. Braithwaite, who died in an accidental explosion while tunnelling.[9]

The accommodation was laid out with toilets being placed beside the radio room. The main room had a large water tank at one end along with a wash pit. The radio room housed the standard MK3 transmitter and HRO receiver, which was an HF (shortwave) communications receiver manufactured by the National Radio Company of Massachusetts USA. Three 12 Volt 120 ampere hour batteries would be charged by one of two generators, one hand-propelled and one bicycle-propelled, which had a secondary role of aiding fitness. The bicycle would also be used to drive a ventilation system, while the chain was replaced by a leather drive to cut down on noise. A rod aerial, 18 feet long, would be thrust out through the observation apertures when required.[10]

Near the main chamber, a staircase led up to the east observation post, and it was decided that the aerial would be hidden in a pipe extending down the stairs when not in use. As originally conceived, the apertures would be slits of the same size. This was later changed so the eastern post aperture would be larger, overlooking a narrow ledge, so that a man could climb out for fresh air while being concealed from view. Part way up the main staircase, another set of stairs led up to the western post. This observation aperture could be sealed off with a wedge. The chamber was plastered and the floor was covered with cork tiles to reduce noise.[11]

Another meeting took place at Godfrey's flat on 17 February 1942. Recruits for the team were discussed and once chosen, it was decided that Levick would stay with them through their training. They hoped to have the 'expedition ready by the end of May, the period of rehearsal and training occupying two months.'[12]

Godfrey sent a memo, dated 13 April, to those involved. In it he said: 'Now that *Tracer* is fairly launched, I should like Cdr Scott to adopt it and take it over as soon as possible but he will certainly need help from Fleming and Merrett for some time to come.'[13] Edward Merrett was Godfrey's private secretary and a solicitor 'with a taste for drawing and a genius for friendliness and reducing tension.'[14] Once the Gibraltar team was in place, other *Tracer* teams would be considered for posts in places such as Aden, Malta, Colombo, and Trincomalee.

By the end of the month five members of the team had been assembled, including Surgeon-Lieutenant Bruce Cooper, twenty-eight years of age in 1942, and recruited by Levick while on shore-leave from his Plymouth based destroyer *Versatile*. In May 1940 his ship was bombed and damaged while helping evacuate the Dutch royal family. The destroyer lost all power and was dead in the water. Ten men were killed and a third of the crew were wounded many of which were treated by Cooper which earned him a mention in dispatches. Later *Versatile* was towed into Sheerness by the destroyer *Janus*.[15]

Cooper was asked to recommend another doctor and he suggested Arthur Milner, a civilian physician. The two had been friends since their student days studying medicine at Durham University. Milner was not keen to start with as he suffered from chronic seasickness. However, even though he was required to join the navy, he was assured he would never have to serve at sea.

Survival training took place in Scotland. The team leader here was replaced after he felt unable to share a meal with ratings. Once the training had been completed, the team moved onto Gibraltar, where they were established by August. There they were given 'cover' jobs. Cooper was a doctor aboard the docked HMS *Cormorant* but the drafting officer there felt Cooper might be better employed on a fighting ship. That officer was soon drafted back to the UK. Life on the Rock was pleasant as they waited. They conducted regular training stints in the chamber. Cooper recalled entering the Rock Hotel as an RNVR surgeon-lieutenant, and leaving covertly as an army sergeant to disappear into the Rock.[16]

By the end of August *Tracer* was largely ready to go. W/T had been fully tested and all stores were in place. A survival manual had been printed. There were even some games and a library in place, with a variety of books, one of which attributed *Anna Karenina* to Dostoyevsky.[17]

Yet *Tracer* had been made largely redundant by the German invasion of the Soviet Union in June 1941. However, the failure of the Wehrmacht to take Moscow in October – November and the success of the Russian counter-attack changed this view. As a result, the required conditions to bring Spain into the war no longer applied. OKW issued instructions that political and military relations with Spain would continue to be cultivated, but *Felix* would have to wait until the Russians had been dealt with. The operation was put on hold. Once resurrected, it would take longer to implement and the time was extended to six months. Hitler reluctantly agreed and OKW published orders to that effect in March 1942.[18] Although *Felix* would come up from time to time, it was doomed as Germany's position had weakened since 1940. They were heavily engaged in the Mediterranean and Russia and the enemies were closing in on Hitler's Germany.[19]

With *Felix* abandoned, Gibraltar's security was not seriously threatened again, though German and Italian aircraft bombed the city and harbour with little result. However, the security of the port and naval base would be tested by underwater attacks, particularly by the Italian Navy, which would come later in the war.

The story of *Tracer* ended on 20 August 1943 with a final W/T exercise, followed by the removal of the stores and the sealing of the chamber. Godfrey and the First Sea Lord felt 'that the principle of *Tracer* should be permanently recognised and that, in future wars, *Tracer* teams should be organised and *Tracer* locations prepared throughout the world.'[20]

CHAPTER 10

Portugal

In 1939 Portugal and Spain signed the Iberian Pact, a non-aggression treaty, which was mostly the work of Salazar. An add-on agreement to the treaty was signed in July 1940. Hoare wrote then: 'It was a definite sign that Spain wished to maintain her independence and to keep the Iberian Peninsula out of Hitler's continental system.'[1]

David Eccles wrote to his wife Sybil in May 1940: 'I saw Salazar yesterday and was immensely impressed. Nothing I had heard would have equalled the dignity, good sense and charm of the best-looking dictator in Europe.'[2]

Antonio de Oliveira Salazar, dictator of Portugal, was fifty-one at the time and had been in power since 1932. He founded *Estado Novo* (New State) the authoritarian right-wing party that ruled the country until 1974. His main aim with the coming of war in 1939 was to keep Portugal neutral. Britain and Portugal had the oldest mutual defence treaty, still in existence today, which dated back to 1373 with England. The treaty, the Portuguese government announced, would remain intact. However as Britain had not sought assistance, Portugal would remain neutral. Britain did not object. Portugal had fought on the side of the Allies in World War I when Germany declared war in 1916, as the Portuguese had refused to stop trading with Britain. Portugal lost 12,000 men during that conflict and many more civilians due to food shortages as a result of U-boat attacks on shipping.

During World War II Portugal was the only country where the Allies and Axis powers were able to operate without restrictions, provided they remained within the law. The Portuguese fiercely guarded their neutrality but were caught in the economic, naval, and espionage activities of both sides. Yet for all that 'Barely a shot was fired, or a bomb dropped.'[3] It was rather more about intrigue, and deals done in nightclubs and bars or even dark alleys. The locals were more than willing to lend a hand provided they were well paid.

Roger Makins of the British Foreign Office was tasked with keeping Spain neutral through trade and he was to broker a War Trade Agreement. He had no direct experience of the Iberian Peninsula so he sought the help of David Eccles who would become his man on the ground, as well as his 'ideas man'.[4] He joined the new Ministry of Economic Warfare in September 1939.

Eccles had been chairman of the Santander-Mediterraneo Railway, which Franco had used to move his troops in the Civil War. Eccles worked at the company's head office in Burgos. He was fluent in Spanish and so was sent to Madrid to push Hoare into action on the WTA. He wrote in November 1940: 'The Spaniards are up for sale and it is our job to see that the auctioneer knocks them down to our bid. I don't mind an inescapable blackmail.'[5]

First he had to sell the triple agreement to Salazar in Lisbon. He was enamoured with the city calling it the 'most adorable place. The combination of blue skies and sea, the colours and the gardens have gone straight to my heart.' Although the Embassy location he found to be 'sunk in a slum where dogs bark and cocks crow almost all night', he found the sound of ships from the docks to be 'romantic enough to be agreeable.'[6]

On 26 May he met with Salazar for 'three-quarter hours'.[7] During the meeting he explained the British proposal, which Salazar said he would put before the Spanish immediately. The British Ambassador Sir Walford Selby annoyed Eccles by 'wittering repeatedly the same idea about six times' but Salazar largely ignored the ambassador and spoke directly to Eccles. The note he gave Salazar outlined the Anglo-Spanish-Portuguese agreement on trade dated 22 May 1940:

Most Secret

1 The maintenance of neutrality in the Iberian Peninsula has been from the outbreak of the war, an interest vital both to Portugal and to the United Kingdom. On this point His Majesty's Government have from the first made their attitude perfectly clear, and have always recognised that the personal influence of the head of the Portuguese Government is the strongest factor for making peace in the Peninsula. They do not hesitate, therefore, to ask Dr Salazar to undertake the difficult and delicate task of securing from Spain certain practical assurances concerning her intention and ability to remain neutral.

2 Believing that the key to the Spanish situation is to be found in consolidating the regime of General Franco, and that the chief danger to this regime comes from the economic distress, exploited by foreign agents. His Majesty's Government are prepared to make available at Spanish ports, before the end of June, one hundred thousand tons of wheat. The precise sources from which this wheat will come have yet to be worked out but the bulk will probably be secured by diverting cargoes from the United Kingdom or other nearby destinations. Payment for the wheat may be made through the Anglo-Spanish Clearing. The French Government will co-operate in finding the quantity of wheat required.

3   His Majesty's Government are ready to assist Spain to buy Portuguese Colonial products, subject to a guarantee of non-re-export, by agreeing that payment for them should be made through the Sterling Area account of the Anglo-Spanish Clearing. This account has at present a large balance in favour of Spain, representing the unspent portion of the loan recently made by the United Kingdom to Spain. If further finance is required it will be sympathetically considered when the amounts involved are known.

    The list of the Colonial products to be acquired shall be agreed by the three governments, and it is hoped that all the goods can be transported to Spain in Portuguese ships.

4   His Majesty's Government desire that the sums received for Portuguese Colonial products, paid for through the Anglo-Spanish Clearing, shall not be converted into another currency, but spent within the Sterling Area.

5   The essential requirements of Portugal, of which provisional list was drawn up by Count Tovar, (Salazar's adviser on economic affairs) have been sympathetically studied in London, and certain assurances can be given.

6   Before communicating these proposals to the Spanish Government His Majesty's Government wish to discuss with the Portuguese Government the nature of the assurances which should be asked from Spain. HM Ambassador and Mr Eccles will refer to this question tomorrow. In the meantime they hope Dr Salazar will consider what steps he can ask General Franco to take to consolidate his position.

7   Dr Salazar will note that the proposals contained in this memorandum require considerable elaboration in detail, but it is hoped that the general outline is sufficiently clear to enable him to estimate the plan as a whole.[8]

It was very much a stick and carrot approach. On 24 July 1940 Britain signed the tripartite agreement on trade with Spain and Portugal, and the first shipments of wheat started heading for Spain in June. Hoare in Madrid advised going slow on the 'sweetener' as it was likely that Spain might 'be forced to abandon its neutrality'.[9] He advised this despite his observations on his travels that 'the country was on the verge of starvation.'[10]

Eccles's confidence in his role received a boost when Sir Ronald Campbell took the place of Selby as ambassador in Lisbon. Campbell, an experienced and skilled diplomat, was level-headed in a crisis, following in the best traditions of the Foreign Office. When Germany invaded Russia in 1941 its source of wolfram (tungsten), used in the armaments industry to harden steel, was cut off, as it was manufactured in the east. So Germany turned to Portugal and Spain, the biggest producers in Europe, to fulfil its needs.

As the 'Wolfram Wars' heated up and prices rocketed, Salazar realised that he had to act. Portuguese agricultural workers were being tempted away from the land to the mines and the promise of high wages. This was damaging the country's ability to produce food and wine. It was a situation he could not allow to continue. In February 1942 the Portuguese government started regulating the trade, setting limits on production, and the price that could be charged. Before the war it was selling at around £300 a ton, but by May 1942 in Spain it had reached £6,200 and by July £8,000 such was its importance to both sides.[11]

Portugal was the bigger producer of the two countries, with mines located in central and northeast areas. Portuguese production was now bought by the government at a set price including that of foreign owned mines. In effect Salazar had nationalised the industry and ended the free-for-all of the 'gold-rush era'.[12] He then performed a balancing act by selling to both sides. The Allies complained, but Salazar's defence was that by selling to the Germans he was protecting Portuguese neutrality, which after all was what Britain wanted too. Indeed Britain had been careful not to buy up the entire production for exactly the same reason.[13]

In October 1941 David Eccles visited the wolfram mines before Salazar's reforms and wrote to his wife:

> I am in the middle of the wolfram racket, it is most unpleasant, but we must somehow deny such precious stuff to the enemy. I can't exactly tell how badly the Germans want the metal which is now £5,000 per ton against £150 before the war. If we paid vast prices for something, you can be sure the price was a measure of our needs, the Germans on the other hand are very corrupt, and a big part of an inflated price may be due to Goering and other brigands making money for themselves.[14]

The Salazar reforms did not stop German smuggling which took many forms. It was taken across the border on the backs of donkeys far away from any official border crossings. It was hidden in other exports while customs were paid off with envelopes of escudos. Much was smuggled onto German 'ghost trains' running from the Spanish-Portuguese border area, on through Spain and into France. It was all paid for in cash or gold. Salazar denied any smuggling took place, but after being threatened with economic sanctions by the Allies, he placed a complete embargo on wolfram exports to both sides. The result was that 100,000 Portuguese miners were put out of work.[15]

Samuel Hoare said of it: 'The word wolfram will probably be written on my tombstone – a word that before the war was practically unknown for a mineral that was as worthless as dust in 1939'.[16]

Throughout the war years, 40 per cent of Spanish exports went to Germany. They consisted of mainly iron ore, wolfram, lead, zinc, hides, olive oil, fruits and textiles. In exchange Germany provided manufactured goods, metal, and chemicals and military equipment all in a much smaller volume. This trade balance in favour of Spain was repaid in part by reducing the Spanish Civil War debts owed to Germany. Portugal exported rather less to Germany, making up no more than 25 per cent in any one year of the war.[17] Unlike Spain, Portugal had the problem of Germany paying for goods in their trade imbalance with forged currency. The Bank of Portugal informed Salazar in April 1942 that this was the case.

The Germans had started forging bank notes in 1939 under Operation *Andreas* but the results were poor and only about £500,000 of notes were produced. Later under Operation *Bernhard* the notes were much better and millions in pounds and US dollars were produced. Perhaps the most famous case was the German agent, the Albanian Turk Elyesa Bazna code named 'Cicero', who was paid in forged currency for rolls of film he took when he was valet to the British Ambassador in Ankara of 'Top Secret' documents. He was paid a total of some £300,000 that was worthless. After the war he tried to sue the West German government for compensation but was unsuccessful.[18]

Operation *Kondor* involved two German agents, Johannes Eppler and Heinrich Sandstette, who were guided across the Sahara Desert by the explorer Laszlo Almasy. It was an attempt to infiltrate British Headquarters in Cairo in May-July 1942 to aid Rommel's drive to the Nile, and the venture was funded by counterfeit money. The Abwehr sent these agents out with forged money in far too big denominations which drew attention to them.[19] Also at the time they should have been aware that British troops in Cairo were paid in Egyptian currency, rather than sterling. These were elementary mistakes that led directly to their arrest.[20]

Another German agent, the double agent for the British, Eddie Chapman, was parachuted into England in December 1942 with £990 on him. The notes were contained in a moneybag and still had bands stamped with 'Reichsbank Berlin' and 'England' on them in pencil. Such a mistake would have led to the firing squad for a true German agent.[21]

In May 1942 the Portuguese demanded payment in gold for all of the wolfram going to Germany. The gold payments were to be deposited in the Swiss National Bank in Bern, so there was to be no direct payment between Berlin and Lisbon. Reichsbank gold would be used to buy escudos from Switzerland. After the sale of the gold, Swiss Francs were made available to Portugal, which could then be used to buy gold from Swiss commercial banks. Initially this did not require transportation of gold to Lisbon, which was a risky business in wartime. Later, because of the sheer amount accruing, it became unavoidable. In 1939 Portugal's gold reserves stood at 63.4 tons, and by the end of the war it amounted to over 350 tons, of which some 123 tons came directly from the Reichsbank.[22]

The Portuguese tried to keep these dealings secret, but in a few months the British had worked out what was happening by intercepting cable traffic and bribing a few officials. In 1943 the Allies warned Portugal that all gold leaving German banks was considered stolen. When the news got out, it was broadcast by the BBC for effect. The Lisbon gold dealers besieged the Bank of Portugal to try to exchange German gold for clean gold. When the Portuguese government refused, many melted the bars down and moved it off to other markets abroad.

As it became increasingly likely that Germany would lose the war, more gold and other valuables started arriving. The British MEW (Ministry of Economic Warfare) estimated some $550 million of gold had been looted by the Nazis from the occupied countries. By 1943 it was well established that gold was arriving from victims of the Holocaust. This included gold teeth, watches, rings and jewellery melted down into Reichsbank bars. So much was coming in that it was often smuggled back out again quickly to South America.

It came in largely by air, arriving at Lisbon's Portela airport on Lufthansa flights. Due to the sheer volume of cargo and lack of passengers, these were known as 'ghost flights'. Both sides bribed Portuguese customs – the Germans wanted them to turn a blind eye, and the Allies wanted to obtain cargo lists. Campbell wrote to Salazar to demand that the flights be suspended, as did the Americans, but with no result. Under the Allied Safehaven Protocol, neutral European countries were asked to freeze looted German assets until after the war. However Salazar left the request unanswered. Eventually, in May 1945, a Portuguese law was introduced that complied with most of the Allied demands which froze German assets in Portugal.

Gold crops up many times in Ian Fleming's James Bond books, often in the form of buried or lost treasure. As a boy he loved a treasure hunt, and he found his first loot in Cornwall aged nine, while on a family holiday at St Ives. Searching caves for amethyst quartz one afternoon, he thought he had found some 'as big as a child's football'. However, it turned out to be ambergris, a grey substance produced by the digestive system of a sperm whale, which at one time was used by perfumers as a fixative. He carried it back to the hotel in the lap of his jumper but it began to melt. When he showed it to his mother she was not impressed and said 'What a mess you have got your clothes into.' In spite of her scolding he was excited, convinced he was rich, and would never have to go 'back to school again.'[23] For the rest of his life he remained an avid treasure hunter.

The hunt for Rommel's treasure is mentioned in *On Her Majesty's Secret Service* where it is 'supposed to be hidden beneath the sea somewhere off Bastia [on the east coast of Corsica].'[24]

Goldfinger was about a SMERSH conspiracy thwarted by Bond to plunder the gold reserves of the United States from Fort Knox Kentucky. For research

Fleming went to Guy Wellby, a London goldsmith, to get the facts about smelting the metal and transporting it.

Octopussy, the short story published after his death, tells of Nazi gold bars obtained by Major Dexter Smythe RM whose greed led him to kill Hannes Oberhauser, who had taught Bond to ski and had been a father figure to him. Oberhauser had led Smythe to the two bars of gold, which 'glittered' in the sun. Both had the marks of 'the Swastika in a circle below an eagle' as well as 'the mint marks of the Reichsbank'.[25] After removing the Nazi markings, he tries to sell the gold through the Chinese Foo brothers in Jamaica. However, they still knew it was Nazi gold because the bars contain ten per cent lead which is a sure giveaway that they are from the Nazis, who always tried to rob and swindle. 'Very bad business, Major very stupid' says one of the Foos. Of course, with 90 per cent gold, the bars are still worth a fortune.[26]

Portugal, particularly Lisbon and Estoril which was ten miles away, was a hotbed of spies and informers in World War II. Early in the war the red-light district of Lisbon, the dock area of Alcantara fronting onto the river Tagus, was controlled by the Germans. Their agents were keen to find out the movements of Allied convoys.

Lisbon was given a low priority before the war. The SIS did not even have an office there, and only had one agent sharing a room at the Embassy. In June 1940, two more agents arrived and were given their own office. Eight months later, Ralph Jarvis, a section V counter-intelligence officer, took over as passport control officer. By 1942 he had succeeded in identifying the organisation of the German waterfront operation. This information was handed to Salazar who then suppressed the organisation.[27]

Despite the success of SIS Lisbon, Stewart Menzies was far from satisfied with it. He told Philip Johns, second to Jarvis, to stop the 'redundant Economic and counter-espionage stuff' and to switch their main efforts onto 'Armed Forces and Italy'. A month later the Assistant Chief of SIS Claude Dansey was telling them to recruit a group of agents to watch the ports in north-west Spain. Sir Ronald Campbell thought that Johns had become too close to anti-Salazar groups and replaced him in late 1942.[28]

Shortly after the attack on Pearl Harbor, the American OSS arrived in Lisbon. Kim Philby, overseeing the Iberian Peninsula for SIS, thought of them as 'a pain in the neck'. They shared information with the Americans which was largely ignored and resulted in a string of elementary mistakes, such as recruiting agents that were known to work for the Abwehr. As a result OSS rapidly went through two leaders of the Lisbon station.[29]

It was this espionage cauldron that Ian Fleming and Admiral Godfrey arrived into on 20 May 1941. By then SIS was into its stride, and by the end of the year the Lisbon station signal traffic was the highest of all SIS stations.[30] They were en route to the USA there to help develop collaboration on intelligence between the two countries. They would fly on the Pan Am Clipper service from Lisbon to New York via the Azores and Bermuda. The two days in Lisbon were scheduled in order to check the progress on *Golden Eye* with the heads of station. Fleming was not impressed by the service rivalry that was hindering headway.[31]

Dressed in civilian clothes they had checked into the Hotel Palacio in Estoril, with Fleming registering as a 'government official'.[32] The hotel was built in 1930, with an entirely white facade and extensive exotic gardens. In 1969 it would be featured in the Bond movie *On Her Majesty's Secret Service*. In 1941 the ballroom and casino nearby were favoured meeting places, and were often full of glamorous refugees or royal families on the run. The Palacio and Inglaterra hotels were regarded as Allied, while the Atlantico was German. All three were rife with rumour, intrigue and bribery. Most of the staff was on the payroll of one side or the other or both.

Watching all this activity was the PVDE, Policia de Vigilancia Defesa do Estado, Portugal's secret police, from their headquarters at Rua Victor Cordon in Lisbon. It was run by Captain Agostinho Lourenco, known as the 'Director', and an ardent fascist utterly loyal to Salazar. He had fought with the British in World War I and was considered to be a man not to be crossed. He was not overly concerned what the foreign intelligence services got up to as long as it did not affect Portugal.

The Lisbon *London Times* correspondent, Edward Lucas, found out what happened if you displeased Lourenco in December 1940. He had written articles for a US magazine insisting that the Portuguese people were pro-British while the government was pro-German, and that nothing much was done to curb Nazi espionage within Portugal. He was arrested by the PVDE on Christmas Eve and subjected to interrogation for six hours, before being deported in January. For good measure, and to appear even-handed, the Italian journalist Dr Cezare Rivelli was also expelled.[33]

On Fleming and Godfrey's second evening in Estoril they went to the casino. There Ian tried his hand at the table, playing a long, unsuccessful game until he was cleaned out of a modest amount by the Portuguese he played with. During the game he is supposed to have whispered to Godfrey: 'Just suppose these fellows were German agents. What a coup it would be if we cleaned them out entirely.'[34] Fleming's own experiences must have impacted the opening lines of *Casino Royale* in 1953. First he describes the atmosphere: 'The scent and smoke and sweat of a casino are nauseating at three in the morning. Then the soul-erosion produced by high gambling – a compost of greed and fear and nervous tension – becomes unbearable and the senses awake and revolt from it.'[35] The narrative moves on to the second paragraph to introduce James Bond and how tired he feels at three in the morning: '… when his body or his mind had had enough and he always acted on the knowledge.' This helped him to '… avoid staleness and the sensual bluntness that breeds mistakes.'[36]

Lieutenant-Commander J. A. C. Hugill met Ian Fleming for the first time early in 1942, when he had to report to NID. He was first interviewed by a Royal Marine Colonel, and then he saw Fleming who, after telling him he was going to Lisbon to be the assistant naval attaché, asked him: 'Do you gamble by the way?'

Hugill replied, to what he thought a strange question, 'not as a rule' because he seldom had the spare cash. He added that it would perhaps not be a good idea to gamble in a neutral country in case it started trouble. He was then taken in by Fleming to see Godfrey. The first thing Godfrey said to him was:

'Do you gamble?'

'Oh no sir' said Hugill.

'I do. I enjoy it.' Godfrey said laughing.[37]

Two weeks later Hugill was in Lisbon. He recalled seeing Ian in the city on more than one occasion and that he would always go to the casino at Estoril. But he is not sure about this as he wrote about it many years later. 'Perhaps all that talk of gambling had embedded itself in my mind or perhaps a mention of Estoril in one of the Bond sagas has aroused this unworthy suspicion.'[38]

The Pan Am Clipper service terminal was located on the Tagus river, a purpose-built port for the huge Boeing 314 Clipper flying boats. They had the range to cross the Atlantic or Pacific at a cruising speed of 188mph. It could reach New York from Lisbon by refuelling at the Azores. The plane provided the passengers with the height of luxury, with a bar, dining room and even a turn down bed service.

Fleming and Godfrey took the service to New York aboard the Dixie Clipper NC 18605, arriving at the La Guardia flying boat dock on the afternoon of 25 May. Their cover story for going to America was to inspect the ports, but their real mission was to help William Stephenson who had just arrived to take over the British Passport Control Office. He would coordinate intelligence operations in America. President Roosevelt followed Godfrey's advice and made Bill Donovan head of the new US Intelligence department, the Office of Strategic Services (OSS).

The blueprint for the new service was drawn up with the help of Fleming. David Eccles had briefed Donovan on much of what was going on in Spain and how they were keeping Franco on a short lead. Fleming wrote a seventy-two page memo on what kind of design the US Intelligence agency could take. Another Fleming memo to Donovan dated 27 June dealt with the possibility of America entering the war, advising them to implement part of the first memo urgently they join the conflict 'in a month's time'.[39]

By 29 July Ian was back in Lisbon to check on the progress of *Golden Eye*. This time he stayed with David Eccles who would go on to arrange passage for him to Tangier. In their talks, Eccles despaired of the petty squabbles between the various British agencies. 'The FO are all right.' But 'The others, the amateurs and the minor departments there has been and will be trouble without end.[40]

In Tangier, Ian found the NID *Golden Eye* agent, Henry Greenleaves, was doing good work, but found the SIS man Toby Ellis to be 'an undesirable individual'.[41] Greenleaves had written to Commander Geoffrey Birley of NID Gibraltar to say that he would avoid further contact with SIS in Tangier:

> In the past I have given any information that I possessed, if this were asked for and have occasionally been handed information which E. (Ellis) thought to be of interest to me. I have not found the latter to be very reliable and, in addition, have found the open criticism of this Department by members of the supposedly uninstructed public to be most disconcerting.[42]

However, he found the SO2 man Robert Schelee with which he shared an office: 'useful to me in many ways, particularly through his existing business contacts in the French Zone ...' He was happy to continue on alone providing Gibraltar did not fall.[43]

In a letter to Godfrey, Menzies argued that Greenleaves lacked training in intelligence operations and, in view of what happened next, he may have had a point.[44]

Greenleaves would be arrested after a drunken night spent with Fleming in which they had broken into the bullring and drawn a large 'V' sign in the sand. Ian apologised to Commander Birley because he might 'have received something of a shock on hearing of my escapade with Greenleaves, of which I admit I was thoroughly ashamed, but it appears to have created nothing but the most ribald mirth in London and so perhaps it was not such a shameful affair as I thought it was.'[45] To get back to England as soon as possible to report to Godfrey, he chartered a special plane from Tangier to Lisbon at a cost of £110 to the Admiralty.[46] Fleming wrote to Greenleaves: 'Operation "Catastrophe" has been greeted with the most unseemly mirth in the Foreign

Office and Admiralty, and there will certainly be no reactions whatsoever from London. I hope there has been no backwash with you locally.'[47]

The SOE was put in charge of Operation *Panicle* (a similar sub scheme to *Golden Eye* like Operation *Sconce* in Spain), which aimed to destroy key installations in the event of a German invasion of Portugal. Whereas espionage activity was tightly controlled in Spain, with Samuel Hoare banning covert operations, there were no such reins in Portugal and so *Panicle* developed much further.[48]

After only three weeks of training and with little knowledge of Portugal and Spain, Jack Beevor arrived in Lisbon in January 1941. His cover was as assistant military attaché, but he was actually there to develop SOE and Operation *Panicle*. It had two stages: when the invasion happened, and after the invasion had taken place. Sabotage of the oil and gas installations and the Lisbon docks were especially important. Roads and railways leading to Spain were to be blown up along with electricity stations as well. These plans had been drawn up largely with Portuguese knowledge. However in 1942 PVDE was tipped off by the Germans that the British were planning far more extensive damage of the infrastructure than they had been told about, which was correct.[49]

It came to a head in February 1942, when Beevor, in an attempt to foster better relations with SIS, agreed to their use of his flat in Lisbon. The flat was used by SOE for meetings and to hide people for short periods. SIS wanted to interview a local informant who was too sensitive to see at the Embassy. Shortly afterwards, that informant was picked up by the PVDE who told them about the flat and what went on there. They soon found out that Beevor was the lease holder. The subsequent PVDE investigation suggested that SOE were orchestrating anti-government unrest via the communists. This, however, was not the case, other than the fact that several agents in Beevor's network were communists and would sometimes meet in the flat.

Destabilising government was a line none of the warring parties were to cross. In early March, Salazar summoned Campbell to his office behind the Palace of Sao Bento. There he calmly expressed his concerns. He pointed out that British plans for Operation *Panicle* went much further than what had been agreed. He then announced, much to Campbell's shock, that he wanted SOE to be dismantled in Portugal. In the days after the meeting, the PVDE conducted a series of arrests and interrogations against British interests, and some 300 people were picked up.[50]

The FO advised Campbell to try and stall, hoping that the affair might blow over. In another meeting with Salazar, the Ambassador tried another tack by going on the offensive against the PVDE, accusing them of Gestapo tactics and that they had been infiltrated by the Germans. Salazar was unimpressed. Campbell then tried to assure him that SOE had been dismantled. Afterwards he wrote to London to ask if they were going to stop the SOE activities.[51]

Salazar did not call off the PVDE who carried on their relentless pursuit of the anti-government factions. In a later meeting with Campbell, the ambassador laid the blame for the crisis on Beevor. He advised that it might be better if the British removed Beevor before Salazar asked them to.

The FO and SOE were furious with Campbell that Beevor had been sacrificed in such a manner.[52] MEW even weighed in with support for Beevor but to no avail. Again, Campbell turned his fire on the German penetration of Portuguese government departments. He supplied Salazar with a detailed report prepared by SIS of their activities, but it did not save Beevor who was sent home in June.

Jack Beevor may have been apprehensive about flying home when he learnt the fate of the KLM Royal Dutch Airlines/BOAC Flight 777A only a few days before he was due to fly. The Douglas DC-3 'G-AGBB' had been shot down by German fighters. the worldwide press covered it. Salazar was shocked, Churchill was upset, and the reason why was that the highly regarded British actor Leslie Howard had died on that flight along with everyone else on the plane.

The London born Leslie Howard Steiner came from a Jewish family. He was a stage and film actor, producer and director, and is best known for playing Ashley Wilkes in the film of Margaret Mitchell's book *Gone with the Wind*. He was visiting the Iberian Peninsula on a propaganda tour for the British Council. An elegant man, always well dressed, he was a great asset to Britain for his roles in the propaganda war films he had starred in.

After visiting Spain for the British Council, along with his travelling companion Alfred Chenhalls, the film director and Howard's agent, they returned to Lisbon to take a flight home. They had tried to get an earlier flight on 31 May on the BOAC flight from Lisbon to Whitchurch airport near Bristol. These flights were in high demand and usually full. They hoped that some passengers might not turn up or that they might persuade others to give up their seats, but no such luck.

The airport was watched by German spies, who noted that Howard would be flying on the next flight. Some theories purport that a German agent may have mistaken the large, bald headed Chenhalls for Churchill and the slim, tall Howard for Chief Inspector Walter Thompson, the prime minister's bodyguard. This is unlikely to be the case as Churchill would have never flown on a civilian flight during wartime and he would not have tried to obtain a ticket. It is more likely that Howard was recognised and viewed as a prime target in his own right. He was considered by some Nazis to be the most dangerous British propagandist.

There were thirteen passengers on Flight 777A, most being British businessmen and civil servants, along with four crew. Aircraft on the Lisbon-Whitchurch run had been attacked before, with one being attacked only weeks earlier before escaping.

'G-AGBB' came under attack by a flight of Junkers 88c6 maritime fighters over the Bay of Biscay. The last radio message from the Douglas DC-3 said they were being followed and then that they were under attack.[53]

The Luftwaffe pilots were angry afterwards upon learning who was onboard, as the aircraft could easily have been captured and forced to land at Bordeaux. The day after the plane was shot down, a Sunderland Flying boat was sent to search the area for survivors. That aircraft was also attacked, but managed to shoot down three of the attacking JU 88's. Crippled, the Sunderland limped home and crash landed at Praa Sands near Penzance in Cornwall. After this event, all the Lisbon BOAC flights were re-routed and only flew at night.[54]

Luftwaffe Enigma messages were being read at the time by GCHQ under the Ultra intelligence. They did not warn the aircraft of the likely German attack, for this could compromise the secret existence of Ultra, which at the time was decoding thousands of messages. It is just as likely, given the sheer volume of messages, that the one relating to Flight 777A was not decoded in time.

The attack and destruction of Flight 777A shocked Salazar so much that he decided to clamp down on espionage activities. A few days later he introduced a law that made espionage a criminal offence by both foreigners and Portuguese citizens. The PVDE was charged with implementing the law. This, however, did not end the spying game and merely resulted in more bribery of the PVDE officers who grew richer as a result.[55]

CHAPTER 11

Isabella-Ilona

The summer of 1941 marked the high point of the political and military rapport between Nazi Germany and Fascist Spain. Franco was enthused with the Nazi crusade against the Soviet Union which he thought of as a 'just war'.[1] After all, it was Stalin and his communist lackeys whom he blamed for the tragedy of the Civil War. Like Hitler in this case, he saw the attack on Russia as a great holy war. Even a division of Spanish volunteers, the Blue Division, was raised to take part. On 14 February he gave a speech in Seville in which he condemned the Anglo-American alliance with the Soviets:

> Europe is being offered as a possible prey to communism. We have no fear that will actually happen; we are absolutely sure that things will not end thus, but if there should be a moment of danger, if the road to Berlin were left undefended, it would not be merely a division of Spanish volunteers who would go, but a million Spaniards who would offer themselves.[2]

The Blue Division was the largest force raised by a non-belligerent country to fight on a major front in World War II. On 27 June the 'Legion of Falangists Volunteers' was announced. Samuel Hoare tried to convince Serrano Suñer of the risk involved in fighting against an allied army 'but he and Franco would not listen to any of my arguments.' Franco assured Hoare that Spain could take part in the crusade against Russia without becoming embroiled with the Western Allies.[3]

The Blue Division was Serrano Suñer's child. He believed that it would be the first of many Spanish Divisions that would fight with the Axis. It was called the Blue Division after the colour of the shirts worn by the Falangists who made up the bulk of the first recruits. In some parts of Spain more volunteers came forward than were needed, with most coming from the middle classes and universities rather than the working classes.[4]

The Division was made up of three regiments of infantry, three battalions each, and one mobile battalion. The officers and most of the NCOs came from the regular army. They were paid by the Germans at the same rate as their own soldiers, as well as by the Spanish government. In July, the division began training in Bavaria under German instructors and the first troops left for the front on 19 August. They were sent to the north of the line away from the drive on Moscow. It took them fifty-three days to reach the front line at Novgorod by train and on foot where they came under Russian fire for the first time on 7 October.[5]

It was not only the members of the Blue Division who were keen to get to Russia. Back in London in August 1941, Ian Fleming was looking for a new challenge and had applied to join the British Military Mission to Moscow as naval representative. The leader of the mission known as 'Mac' was Major-General Noel Mason-MacFarlane. He had known Ian from Berlin in the late 1930s and had come across him again while second in command of the Gibraltar garrison up to March 1941. At the time, Mac was also head of the joint intelligence centre on the Rock and the combined forces group ready to activate *Golden Eye*. He was not impressed by Ian thinking he was 'gullible and of poor unbalanced judgement.'[6] He told Major General Francis Davidson, the Director of Military intelligence, that he did not want Fleming 'foisted' upon them. He felt that he was likely to harm the 'so far very cooperative and matey family' he had so far assembled. Mason-MacFarlane was far from the only detractor of Ian Fleming. Patrick Dalzel-Job who served in 30 AU also found Fleming to be 'cold and austere'.[7]

However the question never really came up as Godfrey would not release his key assistant. Ian was disappointed, telling Peter Smithers RNVR that he had 'hoped to lose myself there for protracted winter sports, but I dare say skiing with a Panzer Division behind is less fun than the old-fashioned kind.'[8]

The creation and deployment of the Blue Division removed many of the most ardent Falangists from the army which made Franco's position more secure. Francisco Franco Bahamonde, the 'Caudillo', was forty-nine in 1941. He was born at the naval base at El Ferrol in Galicia, the son of a corrupt naval paymaster, from a family with a tradition of naval service. Franco was intended for the navy, but the loss of ships in the Spanish American war put paid to that. Instead, he was enrolled in the Infantry Academy in 1907. Posted to Morocco in 1912, and into the Rif Wars, his rise through the ranks was spectacular. By 1923, he commanded the Foreign Legion, which famously, under his command, relieved the Spanish enclave of Melilla after a three-day forced march. He was a dedicated soldier and became the youngest general in the army in 1926. In 1929 he married Maria del Carmen Polo.

Franco was short in height and by early middle age had become portly with a paunch and had a high-pitched tone to his voice.[9] Samuel Hoare, in his first interview with him, found it 'difficult to draw him into a discussion that involved the interplay of question and answer.' He did not shriek like Hitler and was not a great actor like Mussolini but he had the 'voice of a doctor with a good bedside manner.' On first sight, Hoare wondered 'how he could ever have been the brilliant young officer in Morocco and the commander-in-chief in a savage civil war.'[10] The American journalist John Whitaker met Franco in 1936 and said of him: 'a less straight forward man I never met.'[11]

Although Franco shared the enthusiasm of the Falangists for the crusade against the Soviet Union, at heart he was not a radical politician. He had no wish to transform society, but instead was a conservative traditionalist. The historian Stanley Payne wrote that few 'historians and analysts of Franco consider him to have been a core fascist'.[12]

The Blue Division was disbanded in October 1943. By the end of the unit's first year in Russia, 1,400 men had been killed. SS General Sepp Dietrich was full of praise for his Spanish troops who he said may have been 'ragamuffins' but were 'fearless fellows'. The total volunteers that fought with the division was around 45,000, with casualties amounting to some 50 per cent including serious cases of frostbite and illness.[13]

As the Blue Division volunteers gathered in Spain, Chief of the German General Staff, Franz Halder, asked for a plan to be drawn up to check any British invasion of the Iberian Peninsula while German forces were heavily engaged in Russia. He set 15 May as the date on which the preliminary plan should be ready.[14] The Seventh Army were based at Bordeaux, as they had been involved with *Felix*, and they would draw up the plan, which would be code-named *Isabella*. Seven divisions and one armoured brigade would be needed for the operation. However it soon became apparent there were serious flaws with *Isabella*, which had been identified with *Felix*. The problems were centred around transport. Due to the poor railways and roads in Spain, any response to an enemy invasion would be too slow. A preventative operation also presented political problems. Just before the attack on Russia, Adolf Hitler studied *Isabella* and was unhappy with it. *Isabella* was re-drawn again to allow for three alternatives, *Isabella* with warning, *Isabella* to include Felix, and *Isabella* without warning. With no British movement against the Peninsula, and the eastern front consuming troops at an alarming rate, *Isabella* was in a precarious state. Admiral Canaris was sent to Spain in November to review the situation.

In Madrid he spoke twice with General Vigon, Minister of War, who Samuel Hoare felt was completely 'dominated by Admiral Canaris.'[15] Canaris asked for support to establish new shipping observation and radar posts, nine of which were to be constructed on the north shore of the straits of Gibraltar and five on the southern, all equipped with the new infrared system. Vigon got the approval of Franco and the building of the new network began in March 1942. It was referred to as Operation *Bodden* and it was hoped that it would be in operation the following month. General Gerhard Matzky from Halder's staff, one of the *Isabella* planning team, arrived a few days after Canaris. They set off together along with Spanish Colonel Pardo to visit Algeciras. They returned home via Portugal and were back in Germany by December. The conclusion reached was that the lack of enemy activity made *Isabella* redundant. Only a few days later, they stripped the operation's allotted troops and sent them to the eastern front, which eliminated *Isabella* as a practical operation.[16]

It was about this time that the British code-breaking operation Ultra broke the Abwehr enigma radio code and learnt about Operation *Bodden*. There were twenty messages a day going to the German Admiralty from the station at Algeciras alone. All Ultra intercepts relating to naval matters went to NID Room 13 where section 17M was housed. As Bletchley Park improved, the secret messages arriving numbered as many as 200 a day. Section 17M was run by the forty-two-year-old Lieutenant-Commander Ewen Montagu, a barrister and workaholic, who came from a wealthy banking family, the second of three sons to Baron Swaythling. Godfrey had found another gem, and saw him as one of his 'men with first class brains'.[17]

When Operation *Bodden* crossed his desk, Montagu realised these new radar stations were a dangerous development: 'These had very elaborate equipment based on something they called a bolometer which worked, in so far as I could understand it, by infra-red rays, and had sufficient accuracy to detect the size of any ship passing by measuring the heat of her funnels. Their range extended clear across the straits and they would be unaffected by weather conditions.'[18]

The problem then was how to deal with them without compromising Ultra. The RAF photographed the locations, bombing raids were considered and a Commando raid, but any such action on Spanish soil was full of risk. So this hot potato, via the Foreign Office, was handed to 'our ever-reluctant Ambassador to protest to the Spanish government.'[19]

Kim Philby, in his book *My Silent War*, says that he wrote a dossier which Hoare took to Franco on Operation *Bodden*, after first convincing his boss at Section V SIS, Felix Cowgill, 'that the operation was both worthwhile and feasible.' The draft of the document was passed by Menzies. Instructions were sent to Hoare who, despite Philby's low opinion of him, 'rose to the occasion magnificently.'[20]

Operation *Ilona* plan 1941–42.

On 27 May Hoare, dressed in full regalia, went to see Franco at his residence El Pardo. There, he presented a large dossier on the German installations. He also suggested that Allied-supplied petrol had been used in their construction. Franco understood the veiled economic threat. Franco denied any wrongdoing and claimed that the sites were merely artillery positions, and that the Germans were there only for technical assistance. Hoare was soon told, having investigated the matter, that they had found only 'sea-side villa's' with no incriminating radar.[21]

Soon 17M knew the real story and so the Spanish warned the Germans that: 'The Bodden operation must be stopped in its entirety.' The cost to the Germans was great, including two Mercedes cars given to the Spaniards for their prompt warning to remove the radar. Montagu observed: 'the steady increase in my knowledge of the Spanish readiness to lie to us officially was of great use in the later planning of Operation *Mincemeat*.'[22]

In the spring of 1942 Hitler returned to the question of Spain and the possibility of Allied intervention there. He had been badly shaken by the British raid on St. Nazaire although not disastrous to the German war effort. Under the Fuhrer Directive Number 42, *Ilona* was born, in which he outlined that if the Allies were to move against the Peninsula, they would immediately seize

Ian Fleming at Room 39 in the Admiralty London, wearing the uniform of a RNVR commander. (Sidney Beadell/ *The Times*/News International Syndication)

Naval attaché for Madrid, Alan Hillgarth, in the uniform of a Royal Navy captain. (Tristan Hillgarth Private Collection)

Admiral John Godfrey, Director of Naval Intelligence, 1939–42. (IWM A 20777)

Admiral Wilhelm Canaris, later Head of the Abwehr, here as *KorvettenKaptain*. (Thede Palm)

Adolf Hitler and Francisco Franco shaking hands during the meeting at Hendaye Station, one of the great turning points of World War II. (IWM MH 11546)

Adolf Hitler in Paris, 23 June 1940, shortly before he would have to make the decision on *Sealion*, *Felix* or *Barbarossa*. (US National Archives No 540179)

Pan Am Clipper Flying Boat No 314 passengers arriving at Lisbon landing stage on the Tagus River. (US Library of Congress)

Dictator of Portugal, Antonio Oliveira de Salazar.

Sir Samuel Hoare, British Ambassador to Madrid, 1940–45. (US Library of Congress 36841)

A 1940s photograph of Estoril, a popular seaside resort to this day. Hotel Palacio is on the left.

Estoril Casino, a hotbed of spies in the 1940s.

Lisbon, city of light. The lights burned in the city throughout World War II. (Estudio Horacio Novais, C. G. F. Art Library)

Dusko Popov British double agent code-named 'Tricycle'. (US National Archives and Records Administration)

Leslie Howard, British film and stage actor, who died when BOAC Flight 777 was shot down by the Luftwaffe over the Bay of Biscay in 1943 as he was returning from an anti-German propaganda mission to Spain and Portugal. It has been suggested that he was involved with British Intelligence. (*Gone with the Wind* publicity photo)

Cartoon featuring Franco being welcomed by Juan March in the presence of Spanish grandees. March supported Franco in the Spanish Civil War but the Allied cause in both world wars. (Album de Photos)

Lord Airey's Battery located at the highest point on the Rock of Gibraltar at 1,383ft built on the site of O'Hara's Tower. The entrance to Operation *Tracer*'s hide was close to this point. (Author's collection)

Operation *Tracer* room, note the cork floor to reduce noise. (Author's collection)

HMS *Seraph* submarine 219. The boat took General Giraud and his son to Gibraltar though he flatly refused to have anything to do with the British, so on this mission the boat flew the Stars and Stripes and had a joint American commander. Later she delivered Major William Martin on his mission. (Royal Navy)

Italian two-man *Maiale* pig, so-called because it was difficult to steer, here inside its carrying pod, which was strapped to a conventional submarine for transportation. As used by the *Decima Mas* to attack shipping in Gibraltar. (Author's collection)

The diving and power controls of an Italian two-man *Maiale*. (Author's collection)

Rommel's failure to reach the Suez Canal was the last factor to convince Franco to stay out of World War II. He is pictured here with 15th Panzer Division near Tobruk in November 1941. (US National Archives No 540147)

the passes in the Pyrenees and occupy the northern Spanish coastal region. Four divisions, two armoured and two infantry, would be committed with a further three in reserve.[23]

A few weeks later, a dramatic change took place within the Spanish government with the fall of Serrano Suñer, which brought into question the Spanish resolve for fighting with the Nazis. The pro-Axis Foreign Minister, Franco's brother-in-law, known by many as the derisory 'Cuñadisimo' (supreme-brother-in-law), was ousted after the Basilica of Begoña incident, which took place in August 1942. A Carlist traditional right wing group had been attending a memorial mass in the church near Bilbao, for their troops fallen during the Civil War. It was attended by two government figures in General Jose Varela and Antonio Iturmendi of the Interior Ministry. As the congregation began to leave the church they were attacked by a group of Falangists with hand grenades. Varela sent telegrams out all over the country warning of revolution.

Franco thought that Varela had overreacted, but felt unable to intervene in the cases of the six Falangists arrested, some of whom were veterans of the Blue Division. They sought a more radical regime along with immediate entry into the war beside Germany. All were convicted, with two given the death sentence and one executed. However the moderate right were out for retribution against the FET (Falange Española Tradicionalista), the radical wing of the Falange party. Franco dismissed some rather minor government officials in an attempt to appease them but he was advised by his undersecretary Luis Carrero Blanco that someone with a bigger stature should go. Otherwise, the moderates would feel that the FET had got away with it and Franco was merely a puppet. Serrano was an ideal candidate as a once president of the Falange party. He had also begun to irritate Franco with his constant criticism, and the fact that he had been conducting a rather too public affair with the wife of an army officer, which was frowned on by the staid Caudillo. On 3 September, Serrano Suñer was sacked and would never return to government. Franco also took the opportunity to dismiss Varela, whom he blamed largely for the whole affair, promoting in his place Carlos Asensio to the General Staff, a pro-German who would appease the FET.[24]

Although in London at the time, Hoare was delighted upon hearing the news and felt that: 'Providence had certainly intervened in our favour.' A dangerous situation had been averted between the army and the party. Hoare added: 'To avoid a crisis, Franco acted true to type. He simultaneously dismissed Serrano Suñer to satisfy the army, and General Varela to draw the teeth of the Falange.'[25]

Even better for the Allied cause was that General Francisco Gomez-Jordana took over Foreign Affairs. He was conservative and practical and a man they could do business with. On 21 September the new government released a statement to pacify the Germans declaring continued devotion to 'our crusade, with the anti-communist character of our Movement and with the imperatives of the European New Order.'[26]

Canaris was sent post-haste to Madrid to assess the new government. He reported that the appointment of Asensio was a step in the right direction and would likely bring about a more pro-German stance in the army, while Jordana was a more balanced foreign minister. Many Germans who had had to deal with Serrano were glad he was gone. Suñer was even detested by Hitler. The fall of Serrano Suñer resulted in Stohrer, the German ambassador in Madrid, losing his job. He had been reassuring Berlin that Suñer was in a strong position only weeks before he was replaced. Samuel Hoare wrote with some obvious relish about Stohrer's attempt to save Serrano Suñer:

> The Ambassador was at Biarritz when he heard the news. As his own car was in dock, he took a German military car, and hurried off to Madrid. But the military car had no papers, and he was held up at the frontier with the result that he did not arrive in Madrid until thirty-six hours after the event. It was then too late for an effective protest. It was also too late for Von Stohrer himself. He was never forgiven by Ribbentrop for this double lapse of knowledge and energy. His days were numbered, and it was no surprise when soon afterwards he was recalled from Madrid.[27]

Hitler had been grooming Agustin Munoz Grandes, commander of the Blue Division, and once secretary of the FET, to lead a new pro-German movement in Spain. After the government changes in Madrid, Munoz Grandes voiced his willingness to return home to champion this more radical pro-German leadership. If German troops were to move into Spain, he would make sure that they were welcome and would then force Franco into joining the Axis.

In July Rommel had reached El Alamein, and one more push would mean that the Suez Canal would fall, which was one of the parameters Franco had given for joining the Axis. In August, on the eastern front, Sevastopol and Rostov had fallen. In the Atlantic, Allied shipping losses in June reached 800,000 tons. Hitler had no intention at this stage to intervene in the Spanish labyrinth, and Munoz Grandes's theories were mere 'fantasies'.[28]

On 25 September, a panic at OKW had *Ilona* dusted off. A junior officer of the SS 'Langemark' Regiment reported the loss of his briefcase, and inside this briefcase were documents relating to *Ilona*. The staff at OKW quickly switched the code-name to *Gisela*.[29]

It was just as well that they took another look at *Ilona-Gisela* for the balance of power was about to shift in the Allies favour. Samuel Hoare had been called to London in August, and held 'in-numerable meetings' in which: 'It was clear

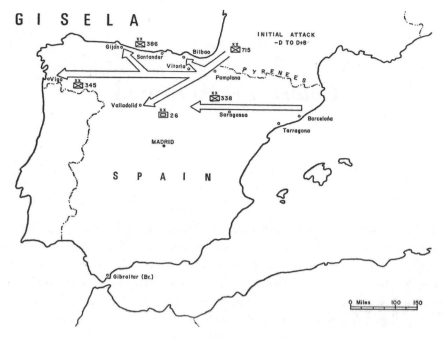

Operation *Gisela* plan 1943.

Spain had become more, rather than less, important to the plan of campaign.'
One of the questions he was asked was what the likely Spanish reaction might
be to an Allied landing in North Africa, to be called Operation *Torch*.[30]

CHAPTER 12

Golden Eye Activated

Brigadier Vivian Dykes wrote in his diary on Sunday 8 November 1942: 'Heard on the radio that Algeria had asked for an armistice. We are in possession of Algiers and Oran. Some scrapping on the Casablanca front. Spain seems quiet. It looks a big success. Thank God!'[1] He was then British secretary of the combined chiefs of staff committee in Washington, which was at the heart of policy making. He had spent the day with Bill Donovan, who had come up with the idea for the US to occupy North Africa. Both men likely had their minds on the time they had spent with Alan Hillgarth and Ian Fleming in Gibraltar and Spain and were wondering what the reaction there might be. *Golden Eye* was activated, and its agents were in position.[2]

A prolonged debate had taken place over several months during 1941-42 over the merits of a cross-channel invasion that year. Churchill favoured a Mediterranean strategy, because of his *'soft underbelly'* of Europe theory. Operation *Sledgehammer* was put forward by the Americans, which would involve a landing to seize the French port of either Brest or Cherbourg during the autumn of 1942. They would then hold on to it while building up troops before a breakout the following year. The original Allied concept, Operation *Roundup*, was for a full-scale invasion of Europe in 1943. *Sledgehammer* was seen as far too risky to the British so the invasion of French North Africa, Operation *Torch*, was agreed as the Allied strategy in July 1942. Two subsequent events would reinforce that this decision was correct.[3]

The Dieppe Raid of August 1942, Operation *Jubilee*, where some 6,000 men were put ashore to gather intelligence, destroy port facilities and radar installations as well as boost morale back in Britain, was a disaster. Near 60 per cent of the landing force was killed or captured. The RAF lost double the amount of aircraft compared to the Luftwaffe, and the Navy lost thirty-three landing craft and a destroyer.

Ian Fleming, through the smoke and chaos from the pitching deck of HMS *Fernie*, watched the action as the destroyer steamed in circles near the town. Back in March he had come up with the idea, one of his better ones, to form a specialist Commando unit to capture intelligence material from enemy bases. He had learned how the Germans had done a similar thing during the battle for Crete. He put it to Godfrey in a memo with the heading 'Most Secret' before outlining his proposal. He argued that commandos should be sent with the forward troops during a raid, and if successful: 'Their duty is to capture documents, ciphers, etc before they can be destroyed by the enemy.'[4] Godfrey approved of the concept.

In July, the Intelligence Assault Unit was formed. It became 30 Assault Unit in 1943 made up largely of Royal Marine Commandos, along with naval men and some specialist army and RAF ranks from time-to-time. They were first bloodied at Dieppe. The unit became known as 'Red Indians' within NID, and later as 'Fleming's Red Indians'.[5] During the raid they were tasked with entering the Kriegsmarine HQ, which was housed in a dockside hotel, to seize any secret documents and cipher machines there. Fleming's men were on board the old China Station Yangtze River gunboat *Locust* for the voyage there. They were under the wing of 40 Royal Marine Commando, as 10 Platoon X Company, led by Lieutenant H. O. Huntington-Whiteley. They went over the side via scrambling nets into landing craft 2,000 yards from the main beach. Covered by a smoke screen before hitting the shore, they entered into a brutal maelstrom of noise and confusion.

From the *Fernie* with her 4-inch guns blazing away Fleming could see little of what was going on. The destroyer was hit near the funnel, killing one man and wounding several others. The raid began at 3am, and by 11am a withdrawal was ordered, and the destroyer was berthed at Newhaven sixteen hours later. In his report, Fleming wrote: 'The machinery for producing further raids is there, tried and found good. Dieppe was an essential preliminary for operations ahead.'[6] The raid confirmed that in order to land on a well-defended shore, a larger force with better coordination was required.

Out of the 370 men of 40 Commando that sailed to Dieppe, twenty-three had been killed and seventy-six wounded. Two of the dead marines, Samuel Bernard Northern, known as Ginger, and John Moir Alexander were from the Intelligence Assault Unit.[7] The unit would land at night during Operation *Torch* on Sunday 8 November which would be a far more fruitful enterprise than Dieppe had been.

The second event to prove that *Sledgehammer* would be unlikely to work was the battle of Alam el Halfa on the Libyan-Egyptian border. During the

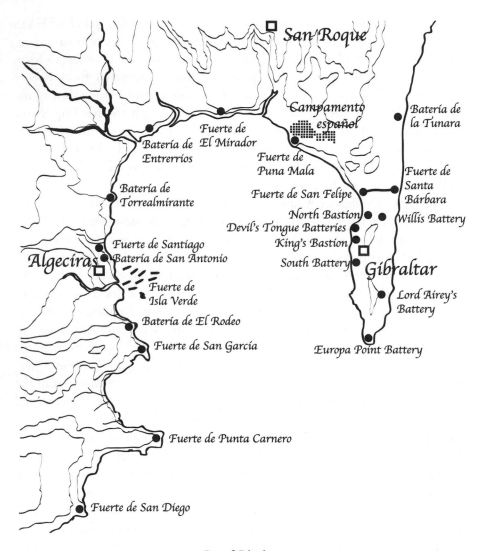

Bay of Gibraltar.

first few days of September General Bernard Montgomery, the new 8th Army commander, won the defensive battle on Alam el Halfa ridge. The battle forced Erwin Rommel, the 'Desert Fox', to abandon his drive for the Suez Canal. With his supply lines precarious, he was forced to withdraw to his start lines. Montgomery waited to build up his strength for the second battle of El Alamein.

★

The Germans had managed to blow up a merchant ship and a small warship at Gibraltar with limpet mines. This was before Room 17M at NID, through Ultra, began reading their messages and the threat was defeated. British divers were sent down into the harbour area to watch the ships on the days of expected action. The Italians were to prove an altogether different proposition, and not just because the British could not read their radio messages.[8]

The Decima Flottiglia MAS, Tenth Light Flotilla of the Italian Navy, known for short as X MAS, was one of the best units of naval commandos to come out of World War II. During World War I, the Italian Navy had sunk an Austrian dreadnought battleship in the naval base at Pulo. Two frogmen had ridden a slow speed torpedo with a detachable warhead into the harbour, before placing it under the keel and sinking the 20,000-ton ship. In 1935 the Italians began to update the torpedo, resulting in the famous Maiale (pig) two-man human torpedo. During the course of the war, X MAS led by Commander J. Valerio Borghese, would sink over 200,000 tons of Allied shipping with pigs and limpet mines.

From October 1940 to August 1943, X MAS launched a series of attacks against Allied shipping in Gibraltar. The first attack was launched from the submarine *Scire* with the target being the battleship *Barham*. All three pigs broke down and two of the frogmen were captured, with the other four swimming to the Spanish Coast.[9]

They tried again in May 1941 using the *Scire* again. The submarine had been waiting at Cadiz for an opportunity. The pig crews had flown to Spain with forged passports on a civilian flight to help maintain their fitness rather than being cooped up on the submarine. However, once again, all the pigs broke down and the crews had to swim for the Spanish shore. The next mission in September was a success, sinking three British merchant ships, one of which was the *Denbydale*, a tanker inside the naval base. The pig in that case had avoided the small boat patrols and got through the nets to the target.[10]

In December X MAS achieved its most spectacular success in Alexandria by sinking the battleships *Queen Elizabeth* and *Valiant* in the harbour. Both ships settled on the bottom and were eventually refloated but the attack put them out of action for many months.

In 1942 X MAS sent a frogman team to Algeciras, where they hid in a villa. Using limpet mines on 14 July and 15 September they swam across to Gibraltar and sank five merchant ships. They used the Italian ship *Olterra* as a base. This ship was damaged and lying on the bottom near the breakwater at Algeciras, with parts of the superstructure visible above the surface.

Later an underwater exit was constructed to use pigs brought in by submarines. It was kept secret from the Spanish and although there were many

British agents in the town, none knew anything about it. X MAS, operating from the *Olterra*, sank fourteen Allied ships totalling 75,578 tons.[11]

Although the captured Italian nuotatori (frogmen) had revealed nothing under interrogation, British intelligence in Gibraltar suspected that there was a ship or land base on the Spanish side of the bay, from where the raids were being staged. Alan Hillgarth was sent to investigate and suspicion fell on the *Olterra*. He protested to the Spanish authorities, which led to the Spanish Navy searching the ship but finding nothing. After Italy collapsed in 1943, Hillgarth found out from a contact in the Italian Embassy that there had indeed been a special compartment on the *Olterra* from which the frogmen operated. The ship had been interned originally with her crew, but over the months her crew had been slowly swapped with members of X MAS. The ship was finally towed to Cadiz where she was taken apart and the compartment found below the waterline.[12]

A keen swimmer and diver, Ian Fleming was intrigued by the exploits of X MAS, and has Bond refer to them in *Thunderball,* when he tells Felix Leiter of the CIA that the *Olterra* affair was 'one of the blackest marks against Intelligence during the whole war'.[13] Emilio Largo, an Italian and Bond's enemy in the book, is a lieutenant of Ernst Stavro Blofeld the 'founder and chairman' of SPECTRE, 'The Special Executive for Counter-Intelligence, Terrorism, Revenge and Extortion'. Their plan is to hijack a Vindicator Bomber carrying two nuclear bombs, so they can hold the world to ransom. Largo uses his luxury motor yacht, the *Disco Volante*, to recover and move the bombs, which has its own below the waterline compartment.[14]

In *Live and Let Die*, Fleming has Bond destroy Mr Big's motor yacht *Secatur* with a limpet mine he attaches when the boat is anchored off Jamaica. The mine explodes at just the right time as Bond and Solitaire are being towed at speed toward a reef by the *Secatur* where they will be torn to shreds by the razor-sharp coral.[15]

William Stephenson claims that Fleming did an agent's sabotage course in Canada and was taught about limpet mines which gave him the background for this scene, but there is some dispute whether Ian Fleming ever attended a course for OSS and SOE agents at Oshawa on the shores of Lake Ontario. According to Stephenson he is supposed to have emerged from the course with top marks. The course would have included him completing a long underwater swim, at night, and placing a limpet mine on an old tanker without being detected. However there is no evidence he was ever there on a course, though it is possible that he visited the establishment during a conference he attended at Quebec in 1943.[16] John Pearson, the Fleming biographer, argued that the school at Oshawa 'provided him [Fleming] with a lot of the tricks he would pass on to James Bond' and in the long run it helped him decide 'just what kind of an agent Bond must be'. Stephenson told Pearson that Fleming 'was an outstanding trainee' but that he lacked the temperament to make a good agent. He did not lack for 'courage' but had 'far too much imagination'.[17]

In September 1942, Fleming and Godfrey were due to go to Washington when they received in the news that Godfrey was to be promoted to Vice Admiral. They were told this on the same day that Pound told him his appointment as DNI was over. Godfrey could be bad-tempered and impatient, which had made him enemies within the Joint Intelligence Committee. He also had a difficult relationship with Churchill, who he felt interfered too much in things he had little knowledge of. He left in December 1942 having held the post for three and a half years. At that time, only Blinker Hall had held the role for longer.

It remains ambiguous as to why Godfrey was sacked in September. Pound sent him a note the next day which said that the JIC could no longer function 'as long as you were a member'.[18] It seems that the trigger was Godfrey sending Admiral Andrew Cunningham intelligence summaries, which contained information on all three services. This had been approved when Cunningham was commander-in-chief of the Mediterranean, but not when he went to Washington. The summaries continued whereas Field Marshal Dill, on the same mission, was only getting assessments rather than full intelligence. It never occurred to Godfrey that this would upset the other services. It is possible that Dill complained, but the significant factor was that the Vice Chief of the Naval Staff VCNS Admiral Henry Moore and Pound would not support Godfrey. Pound might well have had more pressing matters on his mind. He was extremely ill and in a little over a year would be dead. He suffered from a brain tumour, which seriously affected his concentration. He died on 21 October 1943, Trafalgar day.[19]

The trip to the USA still went ahead but it had lost some of its sparkle. In New York they visited the NID office before moving onto Washington, where closer relations with the US Navy were being formed. German U-boats had enjoyed dominance off the eastern seaboard of the United States and in the Caribbean. In the early months of 1942, they sank twenty-five ships in ten days. In February of that year, the Kriegsmarine had introduced a new four-rotor Enigma machine. This meant that it took longer for Bletchley Park to break the messages, and so the Allies were unable to stop many of the attacks in early 1942 during the Battle of the Atlantic. Godfrey had sent some of his best people to America to improve intelligence and direction-finding, which is the art of listening to high frequency radio messages to obtain a fix on a submarine's position. Captain Rodger Winn, an expert on submarine tracking, managed to convince Admiral Ernest King USN to adopt the tactic. This was not an easy task given that the US Fleet commander could be notoriously difficult to please.[20] Godfrey was thrilled when direction-finding was adopted, and it was possibly his greatest contribution to the war.

Later Godfrey went to Canada while Fleming went to Jamaica for an Anglo-American conference to discuss further naval cooperation in the Caribbean where over 300 ships had been sunk. The SIS agent Ivar Bryce, a life-long friend since he had met Ian and his brothers on a Cornish beach when they were boys, went with him. Bryce had been working for Stephenson in Washington and North America in the 'dirty tricks' department, encouraging anti-German feeling wherever he could. They took the Silver Meteor train to Miami, which had started running in 1939 from New York. The train is *The Silver Phantom* in *Live and Let Die*, which runs from New York, Washington, Richmond, Savannah, Jacksonville and Tampa. On board compartment H, in car 245, a space is reserved for Bond under the cover name Bryce.[21]

In Jamaica they stayed at Bellevue, a 200-year-old plantation house where Nelson once stayed, owned by Bryce's wife. It is close to Kingston where the conference took place at the Myrtle Bank Hotel. Bryce hoped that Ian would come and stay when the war was over, but the island had not been at its best, and the weather had been 'really dreadful'. Yet Ian had loved the island, and told Bryce on the plane leaving Jamaica that one day 'I am going to live on Jamaica' and 'swim in the sea and write books'.[22]

By the end of September, Ian had arrived back in London to concentrate on Operation *Torch*. He had to make sure *Golden Eye* was in place and ready and that his 'Red Indians' of the Intelligence Assault Unit would soon be storming ashore in Africa. Godfrey was still on hand, but had received a new job offer as flag officer commanding the Royal Indian Navy in Bombay, leaving his desk at NI in November. He thought about it for a day and sought advice from his old friend Cunningham and came to the conclusion 'that in war time you must do what you are told'. He had also wanted to see the East and the Pacific and so 'India appealed to me strongly'.[23] He would be replaced as DNI in the New Year by Captain Edmund Rushbrooke, who was not keen on the job. Joan Saunders, who worked at NID, felt that Godfrey was 'too good' for the job while 'Old Rushbrooke was no good, and if it hadn't been for Ian Fleming the whole thing would have run down.'[24]

In Spain, Alan Hillgarth was ready and waiting to supervise and direct the agents of H section of the SOE. Alan had a portable wireless transmitter and two cars in case his staff had to take to the road. One was a Humber Super Snipe 'with huge tyres'. He loathed that car, after the steering broke on it one day at 40mph and nearly killed him.[25] It had cost £196.18.2d to restore it.[26]

He had recommended for a lorry to be ready at Madrid to carry the transmitter along with a petty officer telegraphist. In a report from Birley to Hillgarth, he outlined the staff needed on the 'outbreak of hostilities' as two officers, two telegraphists, and three Royal Marines to join him by road. He noted that: 'Petty Officer Telegraphist Bowling is a wizard and all his W/T routines are accurately taped with Admiralty, Gibraltar, and the Army set at Spanish Military G.H.Q. (if required).'[27] Hillgarth wrote in his *Golden Eye* report in November 1941 that he wanted three officers in Gibraltar to be 'under my orders. I reckon that with this personnel and this means of communication and transport, I shall be in a position to maintain efficient liaison between the Spanish minister of Marine, wherever he may be, and Gibraltar.' It is clear that he thought they would be dealing with the Spanish against the Germans.[28]

Ambassador Hoare was in Madrid on the day of the *Torch* landings and spent the afternoon 'shooting wood pigeons' to give the impression of unconcern amid all the rumours swirling around:

> I had several hours to think of the convoys that were already on their way and the Spanish reaction that the operation would excite. When I finally received the telegram that the expedition had begun to land, I was for the same reason careful not to ask for a melodramatic interview in the middle of the night. I accordingly arranged to see Jordana at 11am on Sunday Morning.[29]

The US Ambassador to Madrid, Carlton Hayes, telephoned Foreign Minister Jordana at one o'clock in the morning of Sunday 8 November to tell him about Operation *Torch*. As the invasion was mainly made up of American forces and under American command, Hoare was happy for Hayes to take the lead. If anything Jordana was relieved, as he had become aware in the weeks before that the Allies would open up a new front which could involve Spain.[30]

Franco met with his ministers the next day, where they considered calling up the army reserves. General Asensio and other ministers argued for a pro-German stance, but Jordana wanted strict neutrality. That same day Franco received a cordial letter from President Roosevelt in which he stated that these moves are in no shape, manner or form directed against the government or people of Spain.'[31]

With the agreement of his ministers Franco decided to wait before calling up any troops, for fear that the Allies would interpret this as an act of aggression. Three days later, rumours of a German move through Spain were rife and that Hitler would seek passage for his troops. The government agreed they must refuse any request and that they would begin a partial mobilisation to increase Spain's Army to 700,000 men to cover the passes in the Pyrenees. Jordana continued to try and gauge German intentions.[32]

On 23 October Montgomery's artillery had opened fire and begun the final battle of El Alamein. By 6 November the Africa Korps was in full retreat. Rommel had lost half his army and nearly all his tanks and could not recover the losses. On 19 November the Red Army launched its powerful counter-attack at Stalingrad. Hitler's response was to occupy the whole of France and to seize control of Tunisia to pour troops in to gain a final foothold in North Africa at the expense of the Eastern Front. The German troop movement near the Pyrenees caused concern in Madrid and Lisbon. Salazar sent a press release to say that the German ambassador to Madrid had assured Spanish neutrality, which forced the German government to make a similar statement.[33]

The Abwehr and Admiral Canaris got much of the blame for the intelligence failure in not predicting the Allied invasion of North Africa. Jodl commented: 'Once again, Canaris has let us down through his irrationality and instability.' Hitler said to Keitel that 'Canaris is a fool' and that the 'Abwehr reports were always defeatist and always wrong.'[34]

Yet there had been warnings. The British had not woven together an elaborate deception plan for *Torch*, but they had produced a lot of 'noise' about various possibilities including, Norway, Dakar and Sicily as well as a large relief effort for Malta.

Some fairly accurate Abwehr reports came in, including one from the Vatican in October which indicated that while the Americans would land in Dakar, the British would land in Algiers. Captain Herbert Wichmann of the Abwehr sent a detailed report which indicated that an Allied landing in French North Africa was possible. Canaris had also been supplied by the pro-German Muslim leader Hadji Amin Mohammed al-Husseini, the Grand Mufti of Jerusalem, who the Admiral had known since 1938, with a detailed report on an Allied landing in North Africa for early November between the 5th and 10th of the month. Nine American Divisions would be shipped direct from the USA and a further five from Britain. This report appears to have come direct from Muhammad V, the Sultan of Morocco, who changed sides in the war frequently, depending on which side seemed to have the upper hand. Canaris took it to Keitel who dismissed it, insisting that the Allies did not have enough ships or landing craft for such an undertaking. Canaris did not press the point. Colonel Friedrich Heinz, who served under Canaris, said after the war that the Admiral had been intentionally vague with the facts about the North African landings.[35]

A trait existed in the German high command, emanating from Hitler and infecting OKW, that intelligence which contradicted his own view was not to be investigated. It did not matter where that intelligence came from, for he had the same approach with the 'Cicero' documents from Ankara that were supplied by an agent of the SD. These documents revealed that Germany was facing an overwhelming coalition that would not fall apart, yet he chose not to listen.[36]

The *Torch* landings marked the start of a string of events that would lead to the demise of the Abwehr and Canaris. *Torch* was followed by the invasion of Sicily and the fall of Mussolini, both of which the Abwehr failed to predict. In January the Abwehr agent Erich Vermehren and his wife in Istanbul chose to defect to the British. The Vermehrens were not a particularly great coup for the British, but their propaganda machine went into overdrive to overplay their importance. However, their defection had an effect which went beyond intelligence. It caused consternation in Germany and marked the virtual demise of the Abwehr as an effective service, before being taken over by the SD. Hitler was furious and summoned Canaris to a meeting which would prove to be the Admiral's last with the Fuhrer. The defection seemed to indicate that 'the crew was abandoning ship' and Hitler told Canaris that his service was falling apart. The Admiral responded that it was 'hardly surprising given that Germany was losing the war.' As a result, Hitler decided to put the Abwehr under the control of Himmler and Ernst Kaltenbrunner, head of the SD and RSHA.[37]

The two World War I vintage destroyers HMS *Broke* and HMS *Malcolm* brought Ian Fleming's commandos, along with American Rangers, towards the port city of Algiers on the moonless night of 8 November. Commander Henry Fancourt commanded the two ships of Operation *Terminal*, and their mission was to seize the harbour and prevent damage to its facilities. The commandos for this operation were known as the 'Special Engineering Unit' and came under Mountbatten's Combined Operations. Despite this, Fleming still kept a good eye on his protégés and their development. They were now commanded by Commander Robert (Red) Ryder VC, one of the heroes of the St. Nazaire raid. He built his unit around three sections from the Royal Marines Commandos who came from both the army and navy. The navy troop initially only had five naval officers in it who had a 'technical' role. Their job was to instruct the men from the other troops in which loot to grab. The two other troops also had a fighting role with two officers and twenty men each.

The bow of the *Malcolm* was reinforced with concrete to crash through the Algiers harbour boom. The American troops were to take and hold the port area, while other troops landing on beaches to either side of the town would soon relieve them. The commandos' job was to get into the French Admiralty building on the Mole and grab intelligence material.

Due to the dark night, *Malcolm* and *Broke* could not find the narrow entrance into the harbour. Both ships ran in close to the harbour wall on repeated sweeps. As *Malcolm* was about to finish an abortive run, she was lit up by searchlights and came under heavy fire from French shore batteries. The ship was hit several times, with three out of four boilers put out of action, and ten men were killed and twenty-five wounded. The ship lost speed and listed to starboard whilst heading back out to sea. *Broke* was instructed to lay a smoke-screen to cover the *Malcolm.* On her fourth attempt, *Broke* sliced through the boom and came alongside the mole. By then it was 5.30am and getting light, when the American troops landed and took the commercial port area. At roughly 8.00am, the Vichy French started firing again. The *Broke* was hit and was forced to leave at 10.30am. The ship was hit again when sailing out to sea, and had to be taken in tow by the *Hunt* class destroyer *Zetland* before sinking two days later.

The American troops were now holding the harbour under Lieutenant-Colonel Edwin T. Swenson. They were heavily outnumbered and, when faced with tanks, they surrendered.

The 30AU Commandos managed to transfer from the crippled *Malcolm* to HMS *Bulolo*, the HQ ship, from which they got ashore twelve miles west of Algiers. From there they set off towards the city and the secondary target of the Italian Armistice Commission HQ. Lieutenant Dunstan Curtis RNVR, commanding the naval troops, praised Fleming's detailed briefings and: 'how much thought he had given to our whole show. He had organised air pictures, models, and given an expert account of what we were to look for when we got to the enemy HQ.'[38]

The next day the commandos took the Italian HQ, capturing seven Italians. Admiral Darlan surrendered Algiers to the Americans, but the wily sailor said that he lacked the authority to do the same with the rest of the country. In the German Armistice Commission, from where the Abwehr ran a cell, Curtis found an Enigma machine. It was 'a "KK" rewired multi-turnover Abwehr machine' along with six weeks worth of traffic. The machine was flown back to England via Gibraltar and two tons of documents followed by sea. The 'back traffic was soon broken', and from it a detailed picture emerged of Spanish collaboration with the Abwehr.[39]

Many regard *From Russia with Love* as the best Bond novel. In it, SMERSH (Death to Spies), the Soviet counter-intelligence department, attempt to take revenge on the British Secret Service by luring James Bond to Istanbul to meet the beautiful Tatiana Romanova, who apparently wants to defect. She would bring with her a 'Specktor' machine that could decipher Soviet radio traffic. Bond thinks this would be a 'priceless victory' and for the Russians, 'a major disaster'.[40] The 'Specktor' described is similar to an Engima machine. It is 'case size' and has 'three rows of squat keys rather like a typewriter'.[41] What happened next in Algiers unfolded like the plot of a spy novel. Two days after Darlan surrendered Algiers, he called for a ceasefire in the rest of the country despite saying that he did not have the authority only two days before. The US Commander General Dwight D. Eisenhower gave him the authority by confirming him as the political head of French North Africa. This was a move which infuriated the Free French under General de Gaulle, as well as Churchill who saw Darlan as a 'dangerous, bitter, ambitious man'.[42]

The SIS had smuggled General Henri Giraud out of France by submarine to take over in French North Africa. He had been taken prisoner at the fall of France, but had escaped from Konigstein Castle, which his German prison guards regarded as escape-proof. The castle was situated near Dresden on the left bank of the River Elbe, and he escaped with a rope which was smuggled to him in cans of ham. It was quite the achievement for a man of sixty. He got back to France in the spring of 1942.

An American officer watched Giraud approach the submarine *Seraph* in a fishing boat from the conning tower. He wrote: 'His gloved hands were folded over a walking stick and a raincoat was thrown over his shoulders like a cloak. It was the first time I had ever seen him and he looked rather like an old-time monarch visiting his fleet.'[43]

He arrived in Algiers on 9 November to take over. The scheme was codenamed *Orange*. Three days later, Sir Stewart Menzies 'C' head of the SIS was asking about Giraud's relationship with Eisenhower.[44]

Churchill, meanwhile, warned Roosevelt that 'deep currents of feeling are stirred by the arrangements with Darlan' and that he had 'an odious record'. Menzies had told Sir Alexander Cadogan, permanent head of the Foreign Office, that Churchill's call for the French Resistance to set 'Europe Ablaze' had little hope of success if they dealt with fascists like Darlan. On 22 November Darlan announced that he was taking control of the French Empire. The British cabinet then met in a secret session. Three days later, Darlan's assurance that he would bring the French Fleet over to the Allies proved false, as French officers in Toulon scuttled seventy-three ships as the Germans were arriving.

Cadogan began to wonder if they should eliminate Darlan. He wrote in his diary that the Americans had let 'us in for a pot of trouble' and that 'We shall do no good until we've killed Darlan.'[45]

Fernand Bonnier de la Chapelle was born in Algiers and was an ardent monarchist who detested the Vichy regime. He was a youthful 20-year-old with the hint of humour in his face. He was taking training at a joint OSS/SOE base at Ain Taya, near Algiers, waiting to be parachuted into France. Fernand was with a group of resistance members that had seized control of Vichy buildings on 8 November. On Christmas Eve, after he and two friends drew lots, he was chosen to shoot Darlan. He entered the Palace of State and waited for Darlan. As the Admiral returned from lunch, he shot him twice. One bullet entered his head and the other his chest. It is said that Darlan's last words were: 'The British have finally done for me.'[46]

Fernand was arrested and questioned. He admitted that he belonged to the Corps Francs d'Afrique, a resistance force formed by Giraud. Rumours swirled around Algiers that it had been a plot orchestrated by the SIS. Fernand was convicted, condemned and executed. Right up until the end, he did not believe the firing squad would shoot him, and assured the priest that they would be using 'blank cartridges'.[47] The court martial was organised by Giraud and conducted in secret with no Allied officers present.

Within hours, Giraud was appointed high commissioner of French North Africa as Menzies had intended. Menzies happened to be in Algiers at the time. On the day Darlan was shot, he was having lunch with Squadron Leader Frederick Winterbotham, who was in North Africa on Ultra business. The news came in that Darlan had been shot dead only a few hundred yards away. Winterbotham thought that the murder came as no surprise and it was as if 'they could not have cared less'.[48]

The pistol said to have been used to kill Darlan was a .22 semi-automatic Colt Woodsman issued to the assassin from the SOE stores. The officers in SOE all denied having any role in the assassination.

Weeks after the *Torch* landings, Operation *Golden Eye* was stood down, along with the contingency plans, Operations *Backbone* and *Backbone II*. *Backbone* had been set up to counter any move by the Germans into Spain. The plan was to seize control of Spanish Morocco where there were 100,000 'poorly equipped' Spanish troops, and the area around Gibraltar.[49]

On 22 December Hitler invited Admiral Raeder to dinner. Most of the time was spent discussing the Iberian question. Raeder made a strong case for an Allied invasion of Spain as a 'strategic necessity'. This impressed Hitler who ordered *Gisela* to be reactivated. Admiral Canaris was sent to Spain on

26 December to try and find out if the Spanish would resist an Allied landing. As a result, even with the deteriorating situation at Stalingrad, Hitler cancelled all troop transfers between the eastern and western fronts, and ordered three mobile units, including one armoured division, transferred to the west.[50]

The Allied concerns were similar, and within the first few weeks of 1943, *Backbone II* was drawn up to deal with (a) Spain starting hostilities or (b) a German invasion of Spain. The plan would include a three-pronged invasion of Spanish Morocco and also to establish a bridgehead into southern Spain around Gibraltar. An invasion force would arrive directly from the UK. However, like many other contingency plans of both the Allies and Axis, they were never used.[51]

CHAPTER 13

The Canaris Factor

The greatest factor in keeping Spain out of World War II was the will of Franco. He came to power in the dark days of the Civil War in July 1936 when the rebel Nationalist Commanders set up a Junta of National Defence in Burgos. As Franco was the most experienced soldier, he became the commander-in-chief. It was but a short step to becoming dictator. Franco's rule of Spain would go through many phases, some of which were extremely brutal, but he bent to the winds of change and survived. He had basic convictions that did not change the unity of Spain. A traditional Catholic, Franco believed in the Spanish Empire and retaining what was left of it.

On 19 April 1937 the decree was published announcing that: '… The Caudillo will exercise absolute authority' and he would be '… responsible to God and to History.'[1] He soon became convinced that Spain needed to adopt the Italian Fascist model to become a strong country. But at the end of the Civil War, Spain lay exhausted. By the time the Second World War had started, Franco was frustrated in his enthusiastic wish to join the Axis. He was impressed by the German war machine, which he thought invincible, and believed that Spain owed the Axis for their support during the Civil War. This is clear from his message to Sir Samuel Hoare in 1940: 'Why do you not end the war? You can never win it.'[2]

The Allied economic approach of carrot and stick did have a restraining effect. He needed British, and later Anglo-American, wheat and oil to feed and run the country. He was fully aware that joining the Axis would result in the loss of parts of the Spanish Empire. Winston Churchill wrote:

> So great was the danger that for nearly two years we kept constantly at a few days' notice an expedition of over five thousand men and their ships, ready to seize the Canary Islands, by which we could maintain air and sea control over the U-boats, and contact with Australasia round the Cape, if ever the harbour of Gibraltar was denied to us by the Spaniards.[3]

As the war progressed, Franco would have been aware of Allied plans like *Golden Eye* and *Backbone* if Spain were to join the Axis. Despite this, Spain was the only neutral country to send a fully equipped Division to fight with the Germans in Russia. Unlike Portugal and Turkey, Spain never supported the Allies. Turkey joined the war in February 1945, albeit too late to make a difference, and Portugal allowed the Allies to use her Atlantic islands as bases during the battle against the U-boats from October 1943.

Franco's key personal link to the Third Reich, forged through the bloody years of the Civil War, was with Wilhelm Canaris. The Admiral had been the catalyst for German support and had remained at the centre of German-Spanish relations. Both men shared a conservative and Catholic background. Canaris had tried to restrain Franco at the end of the Civil War when he took revenge against the communists, warning him 'that summary justice and mass executions were not consonant with Christian ethics.'[4] His attempts to curb Franco's 'investments in terror' had little effect and their friendship cooled as a result. The Civil War was won in April 1939 but conflict went on in the military courts, in the prisons, the concentration camps and the slavery of the labour battalions.[5]

Count Ciano visited Spain for ten days in July 1939. On his return he described Franco as a 'queer fish', who sat in the 'Ayete palace, in the midst of his Moorish Guard, surrounded by mountains of files of prisoners condemned to death with his work schedule, he will see about three a day, because the fellow always has siesta.'[6]

The 'White Terror', as it became known, was estimated by Gabriel Jackson in his *The Spanish Republic and the Civil War 1931–1939* to have cost the lives of 200,000 Spaniards who were executed or died in prison camps.[7] Others estimate the death toll to have been between 150,000–400,000.[8]

While Franco warned Samuel Hoare of the hopeless British position, he was listening to Canaris in private who warned him that Germany under Hitler would lose the war. None of these meetings were recorded yet several people knew of the caution he advised. Samuel Hoare was not one of them for he was surprised to learn after the war ended that Canaris had been one of the leaders of the German resistance movement.[9]

Franco, with the Admiral's cautionary words on his mind, made the most 'outrageous demands' of Germany to join the war. After one of his many emissary trips to see Franco on behalf of Hitler, General Franz Halder was told that Spain would do nothing because they had too many 'economic problems'.[10] At the Hendaye meeting, Canaris was not present, yet through his Vatican agent he sent a message to Franco delivered by Serrano Suñer: 'to hold Spain out of the game at all costs.'[11]

In 1942, when Giraud escaped from Konigstein Castle, Canaris was ordered by Hitler to track him down and kill him. The hunt was code named Operation *Gustov*, but despite a reward of 100,000 marks for information leading to his capture, the general escaped. The Abwehr did little to try and apprehend Giraud. Canaris told General Keitel that the Abwehr were not assassins like the SD. Instead, he tried to find out through double agents where Giraud was going and whether he knew anything about the Anglo-American invasion plans. However Bletchley Park, reading Abwehr signals, were able to warn Giraud to be extremely careful with whom he was speaking. Canaris was playing a dangerous game by disobeying Hitler. When he told Keitel he had handed the matter over to the SD, he was in fact using the recent death of its leader Reinhard Heydrich as cover.[12]

When Hitler sent Canaris to see Franco in December 1942 to gauge the Spanish reaction to a possible Allied landing in Spain, nothing was said to him about the Ilona / Gisela operation being activated. These operations would mean a pre-emptive occupation of Spain. However, it is likely that Canaris knew about it and saw another Hitler blunder looming.[13] Canaris's friend Erwin von Lahousen, an Abwehr man, went with him. In Madrid, Canaris drafted a telegram stating that the Spanish Foreign Minister Gomez Jordana had claimed that Spain would be willing to accept a German Army on her soil only if the Eastern Front held firm. As the relief of the trapped sixth army at Stalingrad had already failed, conditions were getting more remote by the minute. Lahousen said that Canaris saw Gomez Jordana a few hours later where he showed him the draft for approval. He agreed with it without changing a word. It was duly sent to Hitler by telegram.[14]

The assassination of Reinhard Heydrich by SOE agents in May 1942 is considered by Paul Thummel, British agent in Prague, to be an act to protect Canaris.[15] The relationship of the head of the Abwehr with the British SIS is full of blurred suggestions, but few hard facts. Two weeks before Heydrich was killed, Canaris and his wife went to stay with the Heydrich's family in Prague. By then he was not only head of the RSHA, but had also been appointed the Reichsprotektor of Bohemia and Moravia in September 1941. They were trying to reach agreement on the roles of the various branches of German Intelligence services. Heydrich was trying to restrict the Abwehr. Canaris remained calm and friendly toward the man he had helped in the early years of his naval career when they had served together on the *Berlin*. He had told Canaris that he would replace 'inept, politically unreliable' Abwehr officers with better SS men, which may have been a reference to Canaris himself.

In the early spring of 1942 an SOE team of Czech commandos, trained in Britain, parachuted into Czechoslovakia with orders to kill Heydrich. The assassination team, code named *Anthropoid*, had been in Prague for some time when a heated meeting took place with local resistance leaders. A message was sent to London to request that the mission be called off, as it was likely to provoke harsh reprisals. In London there was a delay, but the mission was not cancelled. According to Colonel František Moravec, the Czech head of military intelligence, the SIS insisted that the operation go ahead without consulting him and he only learnt this was the case after the war. It was felt within the Czech resistance that Heydrich died because he was close to uncovering British agents and sympathisers within the German High Command and Canaris was known to have had links to the SIS.[16] Menzies must have known of Canaris's dilemma and he was known for not shirking from ruthless action when needed to protect his service and friends. Although *Anthropoid* was an SOE mission, Moravec believed it was Menzies who had insisted that the mission must go ahead.[17]

Whatever the motive was for Heydrich's death, it became the only assassination of a high-ranking German official in the war. He was attacked on 27 May in his car on the way to his headquarters at Prague Castle when he was struck by grenade fragments and died of his wounds on 4 June. German reprisals were brutal, with the village of Lidice liquidated on 9 June. 198 adult males were shot, and all the women were deported to Ravensbruck concentration camp, and the children taken to Germany for adoption. Following Heydrich's death, Himmler became chief of the RSHA and day-to-day operations became the responsibility of Ernst Kaltenbrunner.

In December 1940 Menzies had the opportunity to see Duško Popov, code named 'Tricycle', who was in London having flown in from Lisbon. His cover for the trip was that he was representing some Yugoslav Banks. Popov had started off as an Abwehr agent, but never had any intention of spying for the Germans. Rather he became a double agent when he was approached and recruited by the SIS in Belgrade. His control was passed to the XX Double Cross system run by MI5. He had told his Abwehr masters that he was in London to collect some intelligence from a friend at the Yugoslav legation. He even got the Germans to pay for the trip. His code name 'Tricycle' was apparently because of his 'fondness for three-in-a-bed sex'.[18] He would become the centre of a large network of false agents. By establishing an espionage ring in England, it enhanced Popov's standing in the Abwehr and led to what Menzies wanted, which was information on Canaris.

Menzies invited Popov to spend the New Year weekend at Dassett near Woking. Popov described the house as: 'a Victorian mansion set in a large park, the lawns perfectly manicured.'[19]

Over that New Year's weekend Popov spent several hours speaking with Menzies in his study with: 'Deep armchairs, a fireplace where the flames were miraculously steady, book lined walls – it was the traditional and perfect setting. What followed was not commonplace.' Menzies said it was a regret to him that Popov was no longer an MI6 man. He thought he had the makings of a good spy, although he needed to curb his tendency to ignore orders. He told him he 'had better learn or you will be a very dead spy'. Menzies explained that Churchill had met Canaris in 1938, and had come to the conclusion that the Admiral was a catalyst for the German resistance against Hitler. Menzies went on: 'Eventually I may want to resume the conversation that Churchill initiated. In that event, I must be in a position to evaluate the strength of those around Canaris.' He went on to tell Popov that any information pertaining to Canaris and his inner circle was 'to come directly to him and not through any intermediary'.[20] There is no evidence that Canaris ever met Churchill, although before he was in power in 1938 he met with one of the admiral's trusted lieutenants Fabian von Schlabrendorff at Chartwell.[21]

Many writers and commentaries have said that Fleming based his character James Bond on Duško Popov. Popov also said that the 007 number came from his Uncle Milivoj Popov's apartment phone number 26–007.[22]

Menzies would also protect Canaris from direct attack. In 1943 an Abwehr decrypt crossed Kim Philby's desk that Canaris was to visit Spain: 'He was going to drive from Madrid to Seville stopping overnight at a town called Manzanares.' The town is about 110 miles south of Madrid. Philby knew the town from his time in Spain during the Civil War, and knew that Canaris would stay at the Parador.

> So I sent Cowgill (his superior) a memo suggesting that we let SOE know about it in case they wanted to mount an operation against Canaris. From what I knew about the Parador, it would not have been difficult to have tossed a couple of grenades into his bedroom.
>
> Cowgill approved and sent my memo on up to 'C'. Cowgill showed me a reply a couple of days later. Menzies had written in his official green ink: 'I want no action whatsoever taken against the admiral.'[23]

At the funeral of Heydrich, Schellenberg saw Canaris weep at the graveside before telling him in a voice choked with emotion: 'After all, he was a great man. I have lost a friend in him.'[24] Later, Canaris tried to obtain a meeting with Menzies with Portugal as a possible destination.

'C' had a good reason to go to the Iberian Peninsula with the Allied invasion of North Africa looming. Here was an opportunity to perhaps shorten the war through the German Resistance. He was willing to go but Anthony Eden, the Foreign Secretary, vetoed the idea. Eden felt that it could endanger the pact with Stalin if he heard about the meeting. Stalin might suspect the West of trying to do a deal with Germany. Unknown to them all at that time, double agent Kim Philby would have informed his masters at the NKVD if he had found out.

Hugh Trevor-Roper, who worked at MI6 in 1942, had written a study on Canaris, which concluded that a meeting with the Admiral 'should be attempted'.[25] Philby, after reading the document, wrote it was 'speculative'.[26] We now know that the real reason that the Soviets did not want the resistance to topple Hitler was because it would interfere with their plans to spread communism through central Europe.[27]

With Menzies in Algiers during December 1942, Eden had gone to Moscow on 7 December until the end of the month. Canaris had been sent to Madrid in December by Hitler and he was in Algeciras around New Year's Eve. There he cooked a Turkey for his staff whilst wearing a chef's hat and apron. He was skilled in the kitchen and was assisted by a Spanish cook he knew well, and went to some lengths to make it a party to remember.[28]

Frederick Winterbotham shared lunch with Menzies in Algiers on Christmas Eve. 'C's personal assistant Patrick Reilly told Anthony Cave Brown an odd story that at the beginning of December in 1942, 'C' had asked him if he would like to take some leave: 'I was surprised at this suggestion for it was the only time he made such a suggestion. I was rather tired and I accepted gratefully.' When Reilly left, Menzies was at his desk, and when he returned he was still there.[29] Forty years later Reilly learnt that 'C' had been away from Winterbotham too, who wrote to him and asked him if he knew why 'C' had gone to Algiers. Reilly doubted 'C's journey to Algiers had anything to do with Darlan's murder, although it was a coincidence that he had been there at the time. In the end, he concluded that he had been given leave so that he would not know where Menzies had been.[30]

The truth was that the SIS had not been involved in the murder of Darlan, and if any British service was involved it would be the SOE. Both Canaris and Menzies were in close proximity at the same time. A clandestine meeting would certainly have had its appeal. Churchill a year earlier told the SIS to test the validity of German opposition to the Nazis' peace attempts. There were also some alarming reports which had surfaced of a possible German accommodation with Stalin. Hitler would tell the Japanese ambassador Baron

Oshima confidentially that this would only happen once Germany had made a serious 'peace proposal to Russia toward the end of 1942.'[31]

Eden's visit to Moscow to find common ground with the Soviets achieved little due to the air of mutual suspicion between the nations. With Eden out of the way it is possible that Churchill endorsed a Menzies-Canaris meeting. He would likely have been eager to know about possible peace talks between Berlin and Moscow, and Canaris would have been able to shed light on the matter.

It is definitely possible that these two heads of opposing intelligence services met in Algeciras. It was only a short boat trip across the bay from Gibraltar and the Spanish town was often visited by British officers. Dances at the Hotel Reina Maria Cristina were popular and frequented by both sides, looking for a dark-eyed Spanish beauty. Would Menzies have risked such a meeting? Later in the war he paid a visit to a SIS safe house in occupied France to try and approach the British after all.[32] Ian Colvin records that the SIS in Gibraltar knew Canaris was across the bay and suggested a scheme to kidnap him, which they put to higher authority. London, however, said no as 'he was far more valuable where he was'.[33]

Roosevelt's press conference at Casablanca in January 1943 scuppered any hope that Canaris had harboured of a peace deal. Roosevelt announced that peace could only come with the 'unconditional surrender by Germany, Italy, and Japan'. He thought the Casablanca declaration was a mistake that would prolong the war. He confided to von Lahousen that Germany was guilty of starting the war but that the Allies were guilty of prolonging it: 'I believe the other side have now disarmed us of the last weapon with which we could have ended it. Unconditional surrender, no, our generals will not swallow that. Now I cannot see any solution.'[34]

It was Walter Schellenberg who reluctantly went to arrest Canaris three days after the July 1944 plot to kill Hitler had failed. He knew exactly where he would be as he was under house arrest. Canaris's fall from power after the Vermehren affair meant he had come under suspicion.

> I received a telephone call from SS Gruppenfuhrer Mueller [Heinrich Mueller head of the Gestapo]. He and his chief Kaltenbrunner had been assigned to carry out the investigation into the plot of July 20. In a sharp voice Mueller ordered me to drive to Canaris's home and inform him that he was under arrest – this was an official order from Kaltenbrunner. I was to take Canaris to Fuerstenberg in Mecklenburg, and not to return him to Berlin until everything had been cleared up.[35]

Schellenberg tried to refuse but Mueller warned him that if he did not comply he would also be arrested. After agonising for a while he came to the conclusion: 'I might be able to be of some help to Canaris.'[36]

At the admiral's house in Berlin-Schlachtensee, he found Canaris to be as calm as usual. He was to be arrested for involvement in the July plot to kill Hitler, although no evidence was ever found against him. He asked Schellenberg to arrange a meeting for him with Himmler, which Schellenberg agreed to. Schellenberg claimed that he gave Canaris the opportunity to escape but he refused: 'No dear Schellenberg, flight is out of the question for me. And I won't kill myself either. I am sure of my case, and have faith in the promise you have given me.' Schellenberg says he talked to Himmler, who assured him he would speak to Canaris.[37]

Heinrich Himmler was Reichsfuhrer SS in 1943. He had developed the SS into an army, expanding from three regiments to thirty-eight divisions. The July plot led to an increase in his powers and authority. It was Himmler who by early 1944 felt that he had enough evidence to accuse Canaris of not having Germany's best interests at heart and went to Hitler, who dismissed the admiral. A short time later he was put under house arrest which prevented him taking part in the July plot. Himmler kept Canaris alive, with the hope of using him in future contacts with the British. When it became clear that this was unlikely to arise, Canaris was court-martialled by the SS and sentenced to death. He was executed on 9 April 1945 in Flossenburg concentration camp. When he was led to the gallows, he was forced to be naked in order to inflict a final humiliation.[38]

At the Nuremberg Trials many testified to his courage in opposing Hitler. During the war he went out of his way to help those persecuted by the Nazis, and saved many Jews by getting them out of Europe via Spain, passing them off as Abwehr agents. The Chabad-Lubavitch organisation campaigned for his recognition as a Righteous Gentile. This organisation is a philosophical movement, which was started in the 19th century in Russia named after the town of Lubavitch, and is the most dynamic force in Jewish life today.

The CIA sponsored monograph *The Intelligence War in 1941* held the view that, as a consequence of, the 'Canaris Factor', 'Franco decided that Spain should remain, in effect, neutral.[39]

After Admiral Canaris's death, his widow Erika was left destitute. With the end of the war, there came little improvement in her circumstances under the Allies, and the bank accounts of general staff officers were frozen and pensions stopped. Early in 1948, Erika Canaris was taken to Switzerland by two Spanish diplomats. From there she went to Spain, where the Spanish government gave her a generous pension for life and a villa in Barcelona. The *Caudillo* was paying a debt as best as he could through his friend's widow. Canaris was the man who, more than any other, had saved Spain from the calamity of involvement in World War II.

CHAPTER 14

Body at Huelva

In 1964 John Godfrey reminded Ewen Montagu by letter that it was from one of Ian Fleming's schemes that the basic idea that would kindle into Operation *Mincemeat* was gleaned: '… of the dead airman washed up on a beach.' Godfrey gave the ideas to Montagu when 17M was formed, after the latter was placed in charge of naval deception. Montagu, however could not recall Godfrey passing it to him.[1] He liked Fleming even though he felt that he 'would sell his own grandmother'.[2]

After the *Torch* landings and defeat of the Afrika Korps, there were questions of what the Allies would do next. The obvious move was to invade Sicily and try to knock Italy out of the war. However, this move would be equally obvious to Hitler and his generals with Sicily being the natural next step to take. Thus the deception plan Operation *Mincemeat* was born, where the body of a dead Royal Marine Major would be washed ashore in Spain from a supposed crashed aircraft. The body was named Major Martin, and he had documents on his person which indicated that the Allies would land not in Sicily but in the Eastern Mediterranean. It was hoped that the Spanish would photograph the papers and hand them to the Germans, while the originals would find their way back to the British.

In 1953, Montagu's book *The Man Who Never Was* came out, where he states: 'It all really started through a wild idea of George's. He and I were members of a small inter-service and interdepartmental committee which used to meet weekly to deal with questions of the security of intended operations.'[3] Montagu in a later work identified George as Flight Lieutenant Charles Christopher Cholmondeley and the committee as the 'Twenty XX'. The XX Committee was a group formed to exploit double agents. The XX stood for double-cross.[4]

Cholmondeley's idea came from the 'Trout Memo' which had 51 ideas in it mostly penned by Fleming. 'Trout' referred to fishing, because they were trying to lure the enemy to bite. Number twenty-eight on the list was one Fleming had come across in a novel by Basil Thomson, *The Milliner's Hat Mystery* published in 1937. In this story a body is found in a barn and every document on its person is found to have been forged. Fleming, influenced by this, came up with *Mincemeat*: 'a corpse dressed as an airman with dispatches in his pockets could be dropped on the coast, supposedly from a parachute that had failed.'[5]

With Fleming's idea and the fate of the RAF's Catalina flying boat FP119, Cholmondeley began to form a plan. The incident in September 1942 caused some alarm in Allied intelligence when it looked as if the invasion of French North Africa might have been revealed. The Catalina en route from Plymouth to Gibraltar on 25 September crashed into the sea during a violent electrical storm over the Bay of Cadiz. All ten people on board were killed. One of whom was Lieutenant James Hadden Turner RN, a courier carrying letters for the Governor of Gibraltar, informing him that American General Dwight Eisenhower would arrive on the rock just before the landings set for 4 November, while another letter contained more details of the invasion.

The bodies were washed ashore south of Cadiz near La Barrosa, and were recovered by the Spanish authorities. A day later they were turned over to the British consul. Turner's corpse still had the letters in his pockets. The consul was informed that the bodies had not been tampered with, which immediately aroused suspicion. Experts were flown out to Gibraltar, and the body and the letters still in his coat pocket were minutely examined. The envelope flaps had been opened by the immersion in salt water, but the writing was 'quite legible'. The question was whether the Spanish or Germans could have read them in the limited time available. They are unlikely to have done so as the examiners noted while 'unbuttoning the jacket that sand had fallen from the buttonhole.' Sand had accumulated there while the body was rolled by the tide on the beach. It was thought that the sand would not have been replaced after reading the letters and buttoning the jacket. This meant that the date of the *Torch* landings had probably not been compromised.[6]

Another passenger on the Catalina had been Louis Danielou, an intelligence officer with the Free French forces who was codenamed 'Clamorgan', who had been on a mission for SOE. His notebook, written in French, was recovered from the aircraft, and it mentioned the British landings in North Africa. An Italian agent procured a copy from the Spanish authorities which he handed to the Germans. They treated it with little value, even suspecting that it could have 'been planted as a deception'.[7] This affair revealed 'that the Spanish could be relied on to pass on what they found, and that this unneutral habit might be turned to account.'[8]

The main problem for the XX Committee was how to convince the Germans that the Allies might strike somewhere other than Sicily. Montagu thought that they 'had little hope to persuade the Germans that we were not going to attack Sicily', but that they might convince 'the professional German High Command to believe that we were going to be rash enough both to try that and begin a Balkan invasion almost simultaneously.'[9]

The eccentric Cholmondeley had come up with a method to deliver false information that could work. He had read Fleming's memo which suggested the use of a dead body carrying documents. The crash of the Catalina could also be used to improve the chances of success. On 31 October he submitted his plan codenamed 'Trojan Horse' to the committee. A body could easily be found, dressed in a uniform of 'suitable rank' and given a background. The body would carry revealing documents including letters between high ranking commanders hinting at targets other than Sicily. The body would be dropped into the sea 'where the set of the currents' would carry it ashore. The method had one great advantage over the live courier in that a dead man could not talk.[10]

Montagu was assigned to work on the plan as it would fall under naval control: 'Charles and I worked very happily together, always thinking on the same lines and easily resolving any differences of opinion.' The two men carried out the tasks which they were best suited to.[11]

The story of Operation *Mincemeat* has been well covered by several authors but not in the context of keeping Spain out of the war.

The body used was that of a Welsh tramp called Glyndwr Michael, who died in London after eating rat poison. He was transformed into Major William Martin of the Royal Marines and given a detailed background. A member of combined operations and an expert in landing craft, he would carry correspondence between high ranking commanders, along with personal letters. The team even invented a fictional fiancée for Martin 'Pam', who was based on the image of Jean Leslie, a secretary at MI5. The body would carry a picture of her on a beach in a bathing suit. Letters from 'Pam' were penned by Hester Leggett, a senior woman in the department. She was a spinster who 'poured every ounce of pathos and emotion she could muster' into the job.[12] One dated Sunday 18th ends: 'Bill darling, do let me know as soon as you get fixed & can make some more plans & don't please let them send you off into the blue the horrible way they do nowadays–now that we've found each other out of the whole world, I don't think I could bear it. All my love, Pam'.[13]

There was another letter from his bank, dated 14 April which enquired as to when he was going to clear his overdraft of '£79.19s.2d' signed by 'E. Whitley

Jones Joint General Manager'.[14] It was even sent to the wrong address at the Army and Navy Club, Pall Mall. There the hall porter marked the envelope 'not known at this address. Try Naval and Military Club, 94 Piccadilly'.[15] It was such a convincing looking postal 'cock-up' that the envelope and letter were included on the body.[16]

Ian Fleming had little direct involvement with *Mincemeat*, but Hillgarth did. Lieutenant-Commander Gomez-Beare, or the 'Don' as he was referred to, went to London during the spring of 1943 to be brought into the plan to prevent things going wrong in Spain. He returned to Spain via Gibraltar to make sure that the British consuls along the Gulf of Cadiz would contact him straight away if a body was washed ashore. Huelva, a fishing port, was chosen for the drop off, with the body being thrown from a submarine rather than an aircraft. With a busy fishing community it had a good chance of soon being discovered. There was also a strong German presence in the town with close links to the local police which offered another advantage. Huelva was also the home of a particularly 'active and influential' German spy Adolf Clauss.[17]

He was the son of a wealthy industrialist who had moved to Spain in the nineteenth century from Leipzig. Clauss had fought with the Condor Legion on the Nationalist side during the Civil War. When World War II broke out he offered his services to the Abwehr, and by 1943 ran a large spy ring on the Atlantic coast from his farm at La Rabida.

The body of Glyndwr Michael was kept refrigerated until ready for use. The chiefs of staff had given approval in principle, as a change of strategy might have made the operation redundant. In the end, the final approval was given by Churchill who was told there was a risk that it might have the opposite effect and pinpoint Sicily. His reply was: 'I don't see that matters. Anybody but a damn fool would know it was Sicily.'[18]

When the body was dressed, it was provided with all those odds and ends that people carry such as matches, cigarettes, bunch of keys, change, bus tickets etc. The briefcase containing the important documents was attached to the body by a chain similar to those sometimes used by couriers. The body was placed in a canister of dry ice which was then bolted down to make it airtight which would reduce decomposition on the sea journey south. They then set off for the Holy Loch in Scotland where the submarine *Seraph* was waiting. They had to travel quickly as the body needed to arrive in May. The transport was a souped-up Fordson BBE Van fitted with a V8 engine. It was driven by the racing driver St. John 'Jock' Horsfall, well known before the war on the racing circuits, who then worked for MI5.

With Martin, Montagu and Cholmondeley on board, they raced north setting off at 2am. It was a hair-raising experience with Horsfall doing most of the driving reduced to using masked headlights in the blackout. They arrived early in the morning of 18 April at Greenock. There were some scares getting the 400lb container onto a launch to take it out to the submarine depot ship HMS *Forth*. It was then lowered by crane onto the *Seraph* and stowed below through the torpedo hatch. The submarine sailed 'at 1800 British double summer time 19 April from the Holy Loch.'[19]

At 4am on 30 April, the *Seraph* surfaced a mile off the Spanish coast in the eerie light of dawn. The canister was moved out onto the casing. The crewmen were then sent below having been told it contained 'secret' instruments. Four officers and Lieutenant Bill Jewell, the submarine commander, were left to deal with the body. Two kept watch while the bolts were released and Martin was lifted out: 'The body was placed in the water at 0430 in a position 1480 Portil Pillar 1.3 miles approximately eight cables from the beach and started to drift ashore. This was aided by the wash of the screws going full speed astern.'[20] At 0733 Seraph signalled: 'Operation *Mincemeat* completed. Request onward route.'[21]

Madrid and London both waited anxiously for news. Not until 0500 on 2 May was Hillgarth able to signal to DNI that the consul at Huelva had reported a body washed up. Jose Antonio Rey Maria, a local fisherman out after sardines, spotted the body and brought it in after dragging it aboard his boat. Later that day, Francis Haselden, the Vice-Consul, sent a further message which he knew the Germans would read – the body was that of Major Martin RM. Haselden suggested that he had died of drowning and that the: 'Spanish naval authorities have possession of papers found. Consul at Huelva have arranged funeral today.'[22]

At one point a Spanish lieutenant asked Haselden to take the briefcase. Thinking quickly, Haselden told him that it would be better if the Spanish Authorities examined the contents first as he might be reprimanded. This action saved the whole operation. By this time 'Don' Gomez-Beare was hurrying to Huelva. He had already telephoned Haselden to ask if anything had been washed ashore with the body, obviously referring to important documents, because he knew the lines at the Madrid Embassy were bugged. The communications were being passed onto Karl-Erich Kuhlenthal, the head of the Abwehr in Madrid. At the same time Hillgarth was keeping London informed by a secure cipher.

The Spanish postmortem found that the British officer had entered the water still alive, but had then drowned and had remained in the water for eight to ten days. On 2 May, in blistering heat, Major Martin was buried in

Huelva's Nuestra Senora de la Soledad Cemetery with full military honours. Adolf Clauss watched the ceremony. He did not sign the mourner's book, but rather slipped away when it was over. From the shade of a Cyprus tree 'Don' Gomez-Beare watched him walk off toward the town and followed at a discreet distance.

Several messages went back and forth between Montagu and Hillgarth. The Germans would have read some of the messages in which the NID gave the impression of increasing alarm. Alan was urged to get the 'documents back at all costs' but he was not to show 'undue anxiety' and alert the 'Spaniards to the importance of the documents and encourage them to open or "lose" them.'[23]

The Spanish opened the documents with great skill and then took them to Wilhelm Leissner of the Abwehr who had them photographed. They were then replaced in the envelopes and returned to the British. On 12 May Hillgarth reported to the DNI that he had the documents and briefcase. That same day, an Enigma intercept at Bletchley Park brought confirmation that the Germans had produced copies of the documents, which told of a 'source' which was 'absolutely reliable' indicating an attack on Greece.[24] Keeping the deception going, Alan returned the documents to London in the Embassy's diplomatic bags on 14 May. While London harangued him with messages over the whereabouts of the Martin papers, the documents arrived back at the Admiralty on 21 May and were quickly examined by experts. They knew instantly that the letters had been opened as eye lashes left inside were missing and it was clear that the letters had been unfolded. Alan was told to spread rumours that the British were confident that the letters had not been tampered with.[25]

Alan Hillgarth put the final touch to the deception by writing a letter to John G. Martin Esq, care of the Admiralty, which he hoped the Germans would read:

> Sir, In accordance with instructions from the Admiralty I have now arranged for a gravestone for your son's grave. It will be a simple white marble slab with the inscription which you sent me through the Admiralty, and the cost will be 900 pesetas. The grave itself cost 500 pesetas, and, as I think you know, it is in a Roman Catholic cemetery.
>
> A wreath with a card on it, with the message you asked for, has been laid on the grave. The flowers came from the garden of an English mining company in Huelva.
>
> I have taken the liberty of thanking the Vice Consul Huelva on your behalf for all he has done.
>
> May I express my deep sympathy with you and your son's fiancée in your great sorrow. I am, Sir, your obedient servant. Alan Hillgarth.[26]

Hitler at first doubted the documents, but came around to think of them as genuine. Subsequently, units were moved from Sicily to Crete, mainland

Greece and Sardinia. Operation *Mincemeat* was a clear success and in more ways than one. The loss of Sicily led to the invasion of Italy and the fall of Mussolini which meant that there was no chance of the Spanish ever joining the Axis. Alan Hillgarth's skilful role in Spain had been widely recognised, and in October he left Madrid to take up a new post in the intelligence department under Admiral Sir James Somerville, Commander-in-Chief Eastern Fleet.[27]

CHAPTER 15

The Ideas Man and 007

Granted 56 days of resettlement leave, Fleming was demobbed from the navy on 10 November 1945. He had spent six and a half years at the Admiralty in a job he loved at NID which had stretched his talents to the fullest. Life would never be the same again. As he walked away from the role, his memory was full of a wealth of events and colourful characters to draw upon with his writing. He considered whether to stay in the navy or alternatively transfer to MI5 or MI6. He discussed his options with Stephenson, but decided that the world of the peacetime secret services were not for him after 'the wartime variety-show of Room 39'.[1]

After Operation *Golden Eye* was stood down in 1943, his 'Red Indians' 30 Commando came to dominate his remaining time with NID. With the change of DNI to the more staid and bureaucratic Captain Edmund Rushbrooke, there were no exciting trips to Lisbon, Tangier and the USA. Fleming became more desk bound and Room 39 was no longer the hive of ideas it had been. Edward Merrett said of Ian: 'He wasn't James Bond. He was a pen-pusher like the rest of us.'[2]

After the *Torch* landings, part of Fleming's unit remained in North Africa to drive east with the Anglo-American forces, while Montgomery's 8th Army was advancing from the west. In Bone (now called Annaba), Sousse and Sfax, Royal Marine Bon Royle wrote: 'We got into Sfax well ahead of everyone and found the usual groups of disconsolate I-ties. Again a busy time in various HQ's' and 'Curtis (Lieutenant-Commander) seemed pretty pleased with what we picked up.'[3] They had captured a set of maps which detailed the enemy's minefields and defences of Sicily. They would prove invaluable to the Allied invasion.

30 Commando were one of the advance units to land in Operation *Husky*, the invasion of Sicily. Dunstan Curtis suffered from eczema, which was aggravated

by the heat of the African sun and so was sent home. He was replaced as CO in Algiers by Lieutenant Commander Quintin Riley. The Commando landed near Cape Passero with the 8th Army's XXX Corps. The unit's first targets were coastal radar. In a German manned station, they found many valuable documents including the handbook of the Telefunken T39 series of radar sets, which were used to direct fighter aircraft and anti-aircraft guns onto targets. This was sent to the RAF in Malta who began aiding their bombing missions.

In another radar station captured virtually intact, a complete set of Italian Air Force ciphers were obtained. Other notable finds took place at Syracuse, Augusta, and Messina. For Ian Fleming, success on this scale meant that he might lose control of the unit. This happened to an extent with the Italian detachment, which became virtually independent when they continued with the invasion forces of the mainland of Italy. Back in the UK, however, Fleming was kept heavily involved with 30AU's activities.[4]

Personal tragedy struck Fleming when his long-term girlfriend Muriel Wright, who he had known since 1935, was killed during one of the last V-1 raids in Britain. Her flat at Eaton Terrace Mews was undamaged, but some debris from the bomb blast flew through the window and struck her head killing her instantly. She had been doing her bit as a dispatch rider, and the evening before she had gone to get cigarettes for Ian, 200 Morland Specials, while he played cards at the Dorchester. He was called by the police to identify the body, rather than her elderly parents, and was shocked to find her still in her nightdress. Ian kept Muriel's bracelet on his key ring, and later wrote: 'Nostalgia is dangerous, unless you are certain of never seeing the subject of your nostalgia again.'[5] He refused to visit places they had frequented. Dunstan Curtis questioned his grief: 'The trouble with Ian is that you have to get yourself killed before he feels anything.'[6]

Robert Harling was more sympathetic as he saw Ian was 'utterly shattered' and that: 'Everyone in Room 39 was clearly depressed by Muriel's death.' The popular dispatch rider had been regarded by all the officers 'as an enchanting and beloved mascot.'[7]

Bond never succeeds at any long-term relationship. The American heroine Tiffany Case who appears in *Diamonds are Forever* lasts the longest, living with Bond 'for so many happy months'. But we are told in *From Russia with Love* that she has left him: 'He missed her badly and his mind still sheered away from the thought of her.'[8] James Bond does say 'I do' at the end of *On Her Majesty's Secret Service,* but Teresa di Vicenzo, Tracy, only lasts for hours after the wedding. They are on their way to honeymoon in Austria when Ernst Stavro Blofeld from a red Maserati shoots up the Lancia the couple are travelling in. All Bond sees is a 'snarling mouth under a syphilitic nose.' The

Lancia leaves the road and hits a tree. Bond survives, but Tracy dies: 'her face buried in the ruins of the steering-wheel.'[9]

Does Bond's loss reflect Fleming's loss of Muriel? There are comparisons as Tracy's death at the wheel of the Lancia is unlucky, being hit by a stray shot, similar to Muriel being struck in the head from fragments of the V-1 while the house she was in remained almost undamaged.

Fleming, after the death of Muriel, was able to absorb himself in the work to build up 30AU for D-Day and was often seen at the training grounds. Glanville argued at the time that they should operate as small sections of up to ten men, who would be 'self sufficient in transport and the men concerned qualified drivers. For special operations a number of such sections would be brought together with such larger formations as might be required.'[10] Curtis agreed with Glanville but Fleming did not, and was willing to ignore the lessons learned in the Mediterranean. There they had found that a section of two officers and six to eight men was the best size, as such units could easily be self sufficient and could handle the transport of documents. It seems that Ian was preoccupied with losing control if the unit operated with other larger ones. He was not overly impressed by the disastrous Leros Campaign where 30 Commando came in for some criticism after which there had been 'a good deal of witch hunting'. Sometimes referred to as 'Churchill's Folly', Operation *Accolade* in September 1943 was planned to capture the Dodeconese Islands in the Aegean, which was largely garrisoned by Italian troops at the time. This it was hoped would induce Turkey to join the Allies.[11] With the Italian Armistice coming in the same month, Churchill wanted to seize the opportunity of a new front, and ordered troops in Egypt to launch an immediate invasion. The American's opposed the operation. General Eisenhower was far from happy and thought that the operation was a distraction writing: 'If the decision to undertake *Accolade* depends upon a firm commitment for the diverson from our own operations of a material portion of our air force, then, *Accolade* will have to be postponed.'[12] The Germans pre-empted the British planning by taking Rhodes and they were able to operate aircraft from Crete to hold the upper hand. The British landings on Kos and Leros were a fiasco, with a lot of the forces involved being captured and several Royal Navy ships being sunk. The 30AU element taking part achieved none of their aims during the landings. Glanville wrote:

> Thus ended a singularly ill-conceived and largely unplanned operation and, although men had conducted themselves extremely well, had achieved no results respecting the basic objectives of the Commando. Moreover, it had incurred the loss of five valuable men, including an outstanding officer in Tom Belcher, and one severely wounded NCO who was unfit for further active service.[13]

It seemed to Glanville when preparing for D-Day as if 'we had to start afresh'. The unit engaged in the usual commando training of speed marches, field craft, weapon training and section drills.[14]

Marine Bon Royle, by now promoted to corporal, joined the intelligence section of 30AU at the new HQ in Littlehampton. He was issued with a Zeiss Contax II camera and given training in photography. There were many new recruits and the 'old hands were split up between troops' while: 'Somewhere above us, still on cloud nine sat Fleming, now a full Commander RNVR.'[15]

The strength of 30AU grew to over 300 men. A week before D-Day, Curtis held a dinner at the Gargoyle Club for 30AU's naval officers, and Fleming was invited. Harling says that the party 'went with a swing' straight away. There Harling learnt from Pamela Tiarks, who worked at Room 39 and came with Fleming, about the elusive nature of Ian. She said that he was like water running 'right through one's fingers and past as smoothly'.[16]

On 6 June 1944, D-Day, one section of 30AU landed at Arromanches in Normandy with the Canadians. The rest landed with the Americans and moved on Cherbourg but the results were disappointing with the Germans having destroyed most of the valuable materials. 'Curtforce', as the group was known, left Arromanches and moved west toward Port-en-Bessin and overran a radar station at Pointe-du-Raz de la Percee. The station was taken intact along with all its documents, including a top-secret list of all German radar stations in NW Europe. The Admiralty rated it to be the most valuable operational radar find to date in the war. As a result, all German radar in the area was jammed within 36 hours.[17]

Back at the Admiralty, Fleming felt he was losing control as 30AU began to act more like a standard commando unit. Robert Harling returned from Normandy to report to Fleming on D+3 at the Citadel, the 30AU HQ in the basement deep below the Admiralty, to find Fleming shaken by the losses the unit had suffered, for which he held himself responsible.[18]

By July 30AU had assembled at Carteret, south of Cherbourg, on the Normandy coast to await its next task. Fleming flew over with the DNI to visit them. He took them to task over a lack of discipline – Admiral Cunningham had labelled them 30 Indecent Assault Unit. Harling came to know some of the Marines well and found: 'They were merry, courageous, amoral, loyal, lying toughs, hugely disinclined to take no for an answer from foe or fraulein. Fleming always enjoyed anecdotes concerning their wayward ways.'[19] They did not take kindly to Fleming, though he had their best interests at heart, engaging in a stand-up row with Colonel A. R. Woolley, the unit CO, over the casualties. The argument was heard by a batman and relayed to the rank and file.[20]

After Fleming and Admiral Rushbrooke visited 30AU, the two went on a tour of V-2 Rocket sights and installations. It was a visit in which Ian must have drawn upon for one of his most accomplished Bond books, *Moonraker*: 'The shimmering projectile rested on a blunt cone of latticed steel which rose from the floor between the tips of three severely back-swept delta fins that looked as sharp as a surgeon's scalpel. But afterwise nothing marred the silken sheen of the fifty feet of polished chrome …'[21]

Rushbrooke and Fleming were later taken to see US General George Patton, who greeted the Admiral personally and conducted him into his canvas HQ. Harling and Fleming followed and inside they met Patton's senior officers. The General was on form with his flamboyant style, and Harling saw him standing 'tall, the impressive warrior, duly dressed for his heroic part in heroic garb' right down to the pearl-handled revolvers on his hip.[22] The Admiral and his aide were invited to take lunch, but Fleming feigned that important naval matters needed his attention. Harling had a jeep waiting and the two set off with his Marine driver Gordon Hudson, who had a secluded spot picked out where the two officers would not be disturbed only a few minutes away. Like all good marines, Hudson had scrounged some American K-rations and a bottle of local Calvados apple brandy. On arrival Hudson laid out a ground sheet, saluted, and left them with a promise to return in an hour.

The two men, easy in each other's company, ranged widely over many subjects including 30AU and Patton. Towards the end they discussed what they might do after the war. Harling thought he would return to: 'designing books, magazines, and advertisements'. He asked Fleming what he had in mind to which he replied that he was going to 'write the spy story to end all spy stories'. After all he had the 'background' and he hoped that he had 'the talent to tell a tale and a publisher to make it all public'. Harling almost choked on his food at the audacity of it much to Fleming's amusement, but he never forgot it.[23]

After Paris fell, most of 30AU returned to England to hone their skills for the final push into Germany. With the bulk of the naval war switching to the Far East, Fleming set off on a new mission to assess the Intelligence arm of the Pacific Fleet for the DNI. In Ceylon he found his old friend Alan Hillgarth, who had left Madrid in October 1943 and taken up the post as Chief of British Naval Intelligence Eastern Theatre. Admiral Godfrey had written to Hillgarth at the time praising him for his: 'exceptional work at a most difficult time in Anglo-Spanish relations'.[24]

Ian arrived in Ceylon two days before Christmas. He soon became a close friend of Claire Blanshard, the Wren assistant of Hillgarth. She was taken with Fleming, confiding to her brother that she liked 'him very very very much indeed'. He liked the heat of Ceylon and told her that he never wanted to spend another winter in England again.[25] He caught up with his brother Peter in Delhi, who was on the staff of General Archibald Wavell, and ran a small deception team which had managed to convince the Japanese that Allied strength in India was far greater than it was. Shortly after, he flew to Australia with Hillgarth and Claire where the war seemed far away. They stayed in Sydney's Petty's Hotel, and spent their time swimming at nearby Whale Beach and in the evenings they would sample the city's nightclubs. Via Pearl Harbor, Ian was back at Room 39 by February 1945.

Colonel Humphrey Quill RM now commanded 30AU, and by March the unit was following the Allied Armies across the border into Germany. The main targets on Fleming's blacklist were the advanced U-boats built and designed at Kiel. 30AU was the first Allied force to enter the town. Ian kept them busy with constant requests from his shopping list, of which some items were openly questioned to even exist. Much evidence was found about the fast type XVII U-boats, or 'Walterboats' as they were known, named after the Walter drive system powered by hydrogen peroxide and designed by Doctor Hellmuth Walter.

I. G. Aylen, known as 'Jan', then a commander serving with 30AU, came across two of the 'Walterboats' in Hamburg. *U-1408* and *U-1410* had been, 'heavily damaged by bombs' lying on the jetty. They resembled 'a gigantic fish rather than a conventional submarine … It was clear that certain parts, mainly the "boiler" unit of the turbine drive, had been cut away with a blow torch and removed.'[26]

In Kiel, 30AU caught up with Doctor Walter: 'a rather heavy, flabby-cheeked man'.[27] He talked freely but only about generalities. He would reveal nothing about using the liquid hydrogen peroxide in the combustion chambers, and confessed to being a loyal Nazi.

Colonel Quill rushed off to Admiral Karl Dönitz's HQ on the Danish border, where he obtained written orders from the admiral, the last leader of the Third Reich, that nothing was to be withheld from 30AU. Dönitz also sent one of his aides to see Walter with the same message. Walter then cooperated fully, ensuring that submarine test units, various torpedoes, aircraft jet engines and V-1 launch ramps were ready to demonstrate for Allied VIPs.[28]

The German one-man submarine was also on Ian's list. Admiral Bertram Ramsay, who by then had 30AU within his overall command, doubted such a vessel existed. Commander Ralph Izzard found one washed up near Walcheren off the Netherlands. He telephoned Admiral Ramsay about the find but he would still not believe such a thing existed. Not put off, Izzard commandeered a tank transporter, had the submarine loaded onto it, and set off for Ramsay's HQ, arriving as the Admiral was finishing breakfast. Ramsay still doubted it would ever be used as it was just 'a toy'. Izzard suggested he take a look down the periscope which he did, only to be met by the gaze of the dead German's eyes, whose bloated corpse was at the other end.[29]

With the items on Fleming's Black List near fulfilled by 30AU, he got in on the hunt himself. Commander Jim Glanville in Bad Sulza in the Weimarer region came across evidence of the German Naval Intelligence archives. Some had been destroyed, but other parts had been sent to 25KL/KA. It took Glanville some time to discover that they had been sent to Tambach. The only problem was that there were several places of that name in southern Germany. After a false start to the wrong Tambach, they finally settled on the castle of Tambach near the village of Ingolstadt in the Bavarian Alps, where there was a small naval base used to service mines and torpedoes.

The journey was difficult because of downed bridges and wrecked roads: 'The whole area was in a state of chaos, with SS units fighting it out, the Wehrmacht fighting or surrendering and with bands of escaped POW's, mainly Russian and Poles, roaming the countryside, or deserters from the German Army.' They reached the castle at sunset, and found their way in only to be confronted by a German naval rating who immediately surrendered when challenged by a Marine's Tommy Gun. When asked who was in command he replied 'Kontradmiral Gladisch'. Admiral Walter Gladisch was a veteran of World War I.[30]

The admiral by that time had served in the German Navy for forty-seven years and now had charge of the entire German naval archives since 1870. The old admiral confessed that he was delighted by the arrival of Glanville and his men. Admiral Dönitz had ordered him to hand over the records to the Allies. But he had doubted his ability to comply as some of his staff, notably the 'Kriegsmarine Helferinnen' similar to the Wrens, some of whom were ardent Nazis, wanted him to burn them, led by the 'formidable' Fraulein Androde who had been trying to contact the SS.

Lieutenant Jim Besant had to confront the Helferinnen. After meeting Androde, he thought she should 'have been drafted to Ravensbruck as the wardress in charge.' He had to keep them all confined and only had a few marines to do so. He decided to arm some of the German sailors loyal to Admiral Dönitz, and unite them on watch with a Marine Commando: 'They had strict instructions to make sure the women did not leave their quarters and that nobody from outside got in.'[31]

Concerned about the fate of the records, Ian Fleming set off for Tambach Castle. He told Harling after landing at Hamburg that 'For so chair-bound an officer, such an excursion promised to be an unusual tail-end bonus to his personal war.'[32] Fleming described the castle as: 'Cold. Dismal. Comfortless. Ghastly. Count Dracula stuff.'[33] He found the old admiral to be 'quite helpful' and that the possible destruction of 'those priceless naval records had been causing him quite a few sleepless nights.' The entire archives were brought to Hamburg in a convoy of three ton trucks, where they were loaded onto a fishery protection trawler for the voyage to London. Harling observes that Fleming only spent four days at Tambach, which rather proved his own theory 'that the somewhat basic and carefree life of 30AU in the field' was not for Fleming.[34]

Later Ian admitted to having enjoyed the trip to Germany and seeing a part of the country he had not seen before. Regarding the 30AU he felt, compared to others serving at the front, his 'Red Indians' had 'enjoyed a far more light-hearted war' Although the unit in its 'sharper moments' had lost too many men, he told the group that 'the rest of you got away with far more than a fair share of unadulterated entertainment.'[35]

For Ian Fleming the war was winding down. He had little to do with the German Naval Archives once they arrived in London. The end must be near in the Far East. After some mopping up operations in Norway, the end came for Fleming. After six years in Naval Intelligence, Ian Fleming had emerged as a far more mature man with a wealth of experience, though it had been exhausting. An established pattern to his life was gone. What to do next was the question.

He thought about returning to the city stockbrokers where his job had been kept open, but Lord James Kemsley had offered him a job far more to his liking at his newspaper group. With an attractive salary of £4,500 a year plus £500 in expenses and two months leave a year, he was made foreign manager at Kemsley Newspapers.[36]

He had contacted Bryce to find him a place in Jamaica of about fifteen acres, with cliffs and a secluded bay, and no road between house and sea. Bryce got the local land agent Reggie Aquart on the job who soon came up with a likely spot for £2,000. Bryce and Aquart went together to view the house near the village and harbour of Oracabessa on the north coast of the island. There was a small bay which was protected by a reef some twenty yards out. The land rose high above the water. Bryce and Aquart crawled out to the cliff edge to take a look. There was a strip of white sand below, and about ten feet out to sea was a small rock covered with a single white Portlandia. Bryce knew this was the place for Fleming. He cabled London and received a prompt reply from Fleming, who transferred £2,000 to the land-owner, an Irish Jamaican named Christie Cousins, and the land was his.

When Fleming arrived in early January 1946, the weather was much better than during his first visit. He was thrilled with the site Bryce had chosen for him. Eagerly he set in motion the building of his home. Reggie Aquart was to manage the project and local architects Scovell and Barber were engaged to work on the sketches Ian had brought with him, which had started life on an Admiralty blotter. The building was to be basic with shutters instead of glass in the windows. He wanted to feel those warm tropical breezes and had visions of birds flying in and out. The building work would cost £2,000 and would include a garage and staff quarters. A local carpenter was brought in to construct stout chairs and tables, again to Ian's own design, which Bryce thought were 'extremely uncomfortable'.[37]

The naming of the dwelling, according to various accounts, went through several choices before settling on 'Goldeneye'. It had been called 'Rock Edge' or 'Rotten Egg Bay' before but those were never in the running. Friends suggested 'Shame Lady' and 'Rum Cove' but Fleming called it Goldeneye, and probably intended to do so before he ever set eyes on it, after what he had done in Spain and Portugal. It has suggested that it could have been a play-on-words, as Oracabessa was Golden Head in Spanish. Aquart was of the opinion that it did not matter much what Fleming called the place as it would always be known as 'Rock Edge' by the locals. Little did he know that one day Goldeneye would become the most famous dwelling on the island.[38]

A little over six years later, Ian Fleming was married and had created the character James Bond, to which he became shackled, and through him would reveal his undercover autobiography.[39]

He married Ann, who he had known as Lady O'Neill since November 1934. They had met at Stanway in the Cotswolds. It was her childhood home when she had been Ann Charteris. At twenty-one years of age, she was newly married to Shane, the third Baron O'Neill. By 1936 the union had produced two children. She met Fleming again in the French resort of Le Touquet, which was used as the setting for Royale-les-Eaux in *Casino Royale*. Robert Harling described her as 'slim, dark-haired, fine-features, with a mildly imperious presence.' She was also a woman of 'vivacity, wit, vitality, charm, and brains'.[40] Ann found Ian to be 'immensely attractive' yet 'there was something defensive and untamed about him, like a wild animal.'[41]

After Major Shane O'Neill set off for active service in 1941 with the North Irish Horse Guards in Africa, Ann and Ian began going out together, soon becoming lovers. While staying with Esmond Rothermere, another of Ann's lovers, in his house at Ascot in October 1944 news came that Shane had been killed in Italy. Despite her affairs, Ann was distraught at her husband's death, and whilst full of guilt, she turned to Ian for support. Harling met Ian and Ann for lunch at the Etoile only a week after the news of Shane's death. He observed them closely for half an hour and found: 'Her gift for prompting gaiety in others was unquenched.' As time passed, he could not help surmising what 'this loss would really mean to herself and her two admirers. Would Rothermere's wealth prove too enticing, or Fleming's more puzzling personality prove too tempting.'[42]

Ann had expected Ian to propose marriage, but when this did not happen she accepted Esmond's proposal. Rothermere was the owner of the *Daily Mail* at the time. She told Ian, while they walked together in Hyde Park at the end of June 1945, that she had decided to marry Esmond. She wrote later that if Fleming had proposed marriage: 'I would have accepted.'[43] She moved into Warwick House, Viscount Rothermere's London Mansion, where she would become one of the city's leading society hostesses. Yet the affair with Ian went on first through secret assignations and later more openly.

In January 1948 she arrived at Goldeneye accompanied by Loelia, Duchess of Westminster for propriety's sake, and another member of the close-knit group. At first she was not impressed with Goldeneye, as during the night there were lots of animal noises from frogs and crickets.

Breakfast was prepared by the housekeeper Violet Cummings, a local woman of thirty-one, who was as Bryce put it the 'mainspring' of Goldeneye. The meal consisted of paw paw, the local mango-like tropical fruit, Blue Mountain coffee, scrambled eggs and bacon. Violet became devoted to Fleming and remained with him until his death.[44]

Ann recorded that her first day at Goldeneye was a 'wonderful day of birds, flowers and fish.' In the evenings before dinner they would watch moths and beetles which were attracted by the lamps. There were cocktails before the dinner of lobster and curried goat. Then there was Ian's after-dinner ritual. He would take his guests out to the cliff overlooking the sea where they would gaze over the sea. Ann wrote that they 'watched the spray of the reef and the high bright large stars of the region.' The two women left Ian 'smoking and wallowing in the melancholy'.[45]

On her return to England, Ann discovered that she was pregnant, and she knew the baby was Ian's. The baby girl was born prematurely in Scotland, named Mary, but she lived only a few hours. Their affair continued into 1949, though Esmond warned Ann on her return from Jamaica that she must stop seeing Fleming or face divorce. Yet their tempestuous relationship continued. She wrote to Fleming the following year after a short visit to Goldeneye that he was 'a selfish thoughtless bastard, but we love each other.'[46]

By now Esmond had had enough and the couple agreed to divorce. She was soon pregnant again by Ian. This time he married her. The wedding took place in Jamaica. On 24 March 1952 Ian married Ann at the magistrate's office in the town hall at Port Maria. Noël Coward and his secretary Cole Lesley were the witnesses. Ian Fleming's closely guarded bachelor life was over. He had told Ann during their talks about marriage that he could promise her nothing: 'I have not an admirable character. I have no money. I have no title. Marriage will be entirely what you make of it', which was hardly an enthusiastic proposal. As to money, they would not be destitute, since Rothermere, as part of the divorce settlement, had given Ann £100,000, which equates to over two million pounds today.[47]

They had been living together at Goldeneye since January. It was a quiet time, although with an undercurrent of tension. To amuse herself, she took up painting. According to Ann, she suggested that Ian should write something to amuse himself rather than getting bored. He agreed and said to her that he could not be idle 'while I screw up my face trying to draw fish.'[48]

Fleming must have had his thriller firmly in his mind before this. He had brought his trusty twenty-year-old Imperial Typewriter with him, and purchased a ream of good folio typing paper in a shop just off Madison Avenue on the journey over. He already had the name of his hero, which he had taken from the author of the book *Birds of the West Indies*, which was on his shelf at Goldeneye and often looked upon. He wanted a plain dull name and 'James Bond seemed perfect.'

His biographers disagree as to when Ian started writing *Casino Royale*. Pearson is precise, claiming it was after breakfast 'of the third Tuesday of January 1952' which would have been the 15th. It was just a month before King George VI died heralding the start of a new Elizabethan age. Fleming had swum in the morning before settling down at his roll-top desk with a good supply of cigarettes.[49]

However, Lycett points out Ann's statement about Ian starting work after Noël Coward came to dinner. Significantly, Coward did not arrive on the island until 16 February. Given the fact that Ian produced 62,000 words of *Casino Royale* it took him either eight weeks or four, the latter equating to 2,000 words a day, as the book was finished on the 18 March.[50] He started with no notes and no plan. He just started typing. Ann was glad to hear the clattering of the typewriter. Clearly it was all in his mind already, though perhaps within his subconscious. He worked from nine to twelve, while Ann was in the garden wearing a straw hat against the sun, trying to catch the vibrant flowers in paint. After lunch he slept for an hour and then at five returned to his desk, read what he had written, before putting the manuscript away in the bottom left-hand drawer of the desk. Around 90 minutes later, he began thinking about cocktails.

One question often asked is who Bond was based upon. Harling quizzed Fleming over the various men who claimed that they were the model as the fame of 007 began to grow. The first he cites was the RNVR officer Merlin Minshall, who was an amateur racing driver before the war. He took part in one of Ian's more hare-brained schemes, which Minshall had suggested, to disrupt the traffic on the river Danube by sinking cement barges on the river's narrow points. The plan was betrayed, but in true Bond style Minshall escaped in a high-speed chase.[51]

The next in Harling's discussion with Fleming was Fitzroy Maclean, who was another man who carried out covert operations behind enemy lines in North Africa, as part of the then newly formed SAS. Fleming had first met him in Moscow in 1939 when he was working for *The Times*. He was the author of *Eastern Approaches*, published in 1949, which was a fictional autobiographical account of his career as a junior diplomat in North Africa, and then with the partisans in Yugoslavia. The US edition was titled *Escape to Adventure*.

Fleming considered the book for serialisation in the *Sunday Times* but rejected it as he felt that the author claimed far too much credit for himself. These claimants for the Bond blueprint rather amused Fleming who was guilty at times of stoking the controversy. He said to Harling that he was amazed at 'the number of characters who want to leave something akin to a legend after they snuff it.'[52]

There have been many other candidates put forward. Fleming's father Valentine killed in World War I is one of the more unlikely ones because he barely knew him. His brother Peter is more likely, as he worked in intelligence, often in the field, and was a renowned travel writer. Patrick Dalzel-Job, the RNVR officer who served in 30AU, was an all action man, a marksman, parachutist and diver, but he ruled himself out as 'unlikely'.[53]

The double agent Duško Popov, code named 'Tricycle' by the British, certainly had many of Bond's traits in that he liked fast cars and fast women, as well as gambling. Fleming had knowledge of his casino exploits at Estoril, including slapping $30,000 onto a table.[54] There was Wilfred Dunderdale in Paris, chief of the SIS in the city, whom Fleming had come across in 1940. Even Fleming's friend William Stephenson, the Canadian spy chief codenamed 'Intrepid', has been suggested. He felt that Ian would never have made it as a spy as he did not have 'the temperament for an agent or [was] a genuine man of action.'[55]

Perhaps nearer to the truth was the person suggested by Leonard Mosley, foreign correspondent and espionage writer, who recalled chatting to Ian Fleming in April 1953 at the *Sunday Times*. Fleming had told him he had been inspired to create James Bond after reading about the exploits of Sidney Reilly, which he had found in the archives of British Intelligence during the war. Reilly was not so well known then as he is now. Mosley had written *The Cat and the Mice*, which was the story of the German spy John Eppler and Operation *Kondor*, the plan to infiltrate 8th Army HQ during the desert war.[56]

All these men no doubt influenced Fleming, but the main input to 007 was probably the man himself. John le Carre outlined when writing about his character George Smiley: 'All fictional characters are amalgams. All spring from much deeper wells than their apparent counterparts in real life. All in the end, like the poor suspects in my files, are remoulded in the writer's imagination until they are probably closer to his own nature than to anyone else's.'[57]

As John Pearson says, Bond had many of Ian's traits: he smoked the 'same number of cigarettes as Fleming did. He wears the same clothes.' He likes the same cars, is the same height and has 'the same love of scrambled eggs'. Of course, the gambling habit 'is entirely Fleming's'.[58]

The inspiration for 'M' is much easier to identify, with the many similarities to Ian's old boss at NID, Admiral John Godfrey. Both were crusty and bad tempered and the allusion to Godfrey is made clear in *On Her Majesty's Secret Service* with the reference to the battlecruiser *Repulse,* the ship Godfrey had commanded in the Mediterranean during the 1930s. 'M' is identified in *The Man with the Golden Gun* as Admiral Sir Miles Messervy.[59] Bond uses 'the clapper of the brass ships-bell of some former HMS *Repulse*' to gain admittance to 'M's' house and that '*Repulse* had been his last sea-going command.' Chief Petty Officer Hammond still looks after the Admiral as he had in the service. Admiral Sir Miles 'M' Messervy is a bachelor, however, unlike Godfrey who was married. *Repulse* was sunk off Malaya with the battleship *Prince of Wales* on 10 December 1941.[60]

Godfrey was not happy at being so clearly depicted as 'M' complaining after Fleming died that he had turned him into 'that unsavoury character M' who in *For Your Eyes Only* uses Bond to exact revenge on some crooks who have killed the Havelocks. Messervy had been the 'best man at their Malta wedding in 1925.'[61]

Six days before his marriage, Ian had finished his 62,000 words. There would be many later corrections, with paragraphs re-written and pages re-typed. But the bone of the story was there in that first draft, so the editing as such was only a tidy up. The plot was influenced by that night in the Estoril Casino but moved to the Casino at Le Touquet in the Pas-de-Calais region of northern France. He may also have been influenced by the story that Ralph Izzard told him when he had been working for NID in South America and had played against Nazi agents in the casino at Pernambuco on Brazil's Atlantic coast. Izzard's report had crossed his desk. This prompted Ian to take him out for dinner during which he quizzed him about the incident right down to the smallest details.

Another event he would embellish from the past was the killing of the Japanese cipher expert in New York, mentioned in chapter 9 *The Game Is Baccarat*. It explains how Bond got his double 0 number, his licence to kill, which was another invention of Fleming's, taken from the double 0 numbers used in Top Secret documents. The idea of the assassination came from the visit he made with Godfrey to the USA in 1941. There Stephenson let Ian observe the operation to break into the Japanese Consul-General's office in New York, which was housed in the Rockefeller center on the floor below Stephenson's office. First they watched the movements of the cipher expert before duplicating the keys, entering the office where a safe-cracker opened the safe, and removing the cipher books which were microfilmed then replaced. It was a fairly straightforward affair for Stephenson but Fleming was delighted to have been involved in a field operation that would later provide great scope for his fiction.

Later in *Casino Royale*, Bond explains in more detail the killing in New York. First he booked a room in an adjacent skyscraper from which he could observe the 'cipher expert'. Then with a colleague from the New York branch, 'and a couple of Remington thirty-thirty's with telescopic sights and silencers', they waited for days while watching the room. Then their chance came: 'He shot at the man a second before me. His job was to blast a hole through the windows so that I could shoot the Jap through it. They have tough windows at the Rockefeller center to keep the noise out. It worked very well.' Bond's shot comes a split-second after the first: 'I got the Jap in the mouth as he turned to gape at the broken window.'[62]

The blowing up of the Bulgarians in the book is thought to have been inspired by the bungled attempt by the Russians to kill Franz von Papen, the German Ambassador to Turkey and chancellor of Germany before Adolf Hitler. At about ten in the morning, in Ankara on 24 February 1942, von Papen and his wife had been walking from their house to the embassy along the tree-lined Ataturk Boulevard, which was deserted when: 'Suddenly we were both hurled to the ground by a violent explosion.' His wife was unhurt, but he had cuts and bruises and a temporary loss of hearing. Both were covered in blood. The Turkish Security Police soon got to the bottom of the mysterious explosion. Human remains were found over a wide area including a shoe and a foot hanging in a tree. Two Macedonian students recruited by the Russians had failed in the attempt, with the bomb going off before it was thrown. One got away but he was later found hiding in the Russian Embassy. First suspicions fell on the British SIS, and then the Gestapo, but finally the attempt was laid at the Russians' door.[63] Bond endures a similar attack against him in chapter 6 *Two Men in Straw Hats* in *Casino Royale*. In this case both Bulgarians manage to blow themselves up by mistake, and Bond is thrown to the ground by the blast: 'a ghastly rain of pieces of flesh and shreds of blood-soaked clothing fell on him and around him.'[64]

On Monday 13 April 1953 *Casino Royale* was published by Jonathan Cape. Like the following thirteen Bond books penned by Ian Fleming, and published by Cape, they were set in the Cold War era, but firmly rooted in World War II. In *Thunderball* Bond reflects with Felix Leiter: 'The war just doesn't seem to have ended for us ...'[65]

SMERSH was another organisation from the war. In *Casino Royale* we soon come across it and find: 'SMERSH is on the scent.'[66] SMERSH was a counter-intelligence agency of the Red Army formed in 1942, on the orders of Joseph Stalin, with a remit to fight anti-Soviet elements and penetrations by foreign agents. In 1946 its duties were taken over by the NKGB. SMERSH meant Smert Shpionam, which roughly translated to 'Death to Spies.'

The real SMERSH had been held responsible for the arrest, torture and execution of thousands of Russian soldiers, few of which were guilty. They were even said to have assassinated Leon Trotsky in Mexico in 1940, although this would make SMERSH older than officially admitted.

Ian Fleming claimed that he started writing *Casino Royale* to take his mind off his looming marriage, as if he was doomed, which naturally annoyed Ann, even more so as he would often peddle out the anecdote in company. However another motive was that the situation of the country in the early 1950s depressed him. Winston Churchill had returned to power in 1951, but his government was weak with a majority of only sixteen. His policy of strengthening the Empire was outdated. There was trouble in Egypt and Cyprus. Even worse for Fleming, British Intelligence had been rocked to the core by the defection of Guy Burgess and Donald Maclean to Moscow, tipped off by the third man Kim Philby, who had been a Soviet spy since the Spanish Civil War. This could explain why he uses Vesper Lynd as a double agent to reflect the times. Bond is suitably betrayed and telephones MI6 in London to tell them: '3030 was a double, working for Redland.'[67] British Intelligence was a laughing stock and not trusted by Britain's American allies. His brother Peter had written *The Sixth Column, A singular Tale of our Times* published in the summer of 1952. The novel was dedicated to Ian. It was the story of an attempt by the Soviets to undermine what was left of the British national character with a subtle propaganda campaign organised by their agents to infiltrate the highest places of the establishment. It was a call-to-arms for Ian to unleash James Bond 007 into the world and restore some national pride.[68]

Even then Ian looked on his creation as 'a mere entertainment'. He inscribed one of his later books, given to his friend Paul Gallico the American thriller writer, with: 'To Paul who has always seen the joke.'[69] Yet Gallico was full of praise for *Casino Royale* after reading the manuscript: 'The book is a knockout. I thought I had written a couple of pretty fair torture scenes in my day, but yours beats anything I ever read. Wow!'[70]

The Bond books are high adventure, and served as escapism from the drab face of Britain in the 1950s when they were first written, rather than an accurate depiction of the Cold War.

The *Listener* described Fleming's work as 'supersonic John Buchan'. Others thought that the Bond stories were a cross between Eric Ambler and Mickey Spillane.

In 1964, a decade or so after *Casino Royale* was published, John le Carre's *The Spy who came in from the Cold* was released. It replaced *On Her Majesty's Secret Service* at the top of the *New York Times* bestsellers list, and stayed there for thirty-five weeks. The dark, gritty novel tells the story of the anti-hero Alec Leamas, who inhabits a grey world of mistrust and devoid of heroes. He describes himself and spies to his girlfriend Liz Gold as: 'a squalid procession of vain fools, traitors too, yes; pansies, sadists and drunkards, people who play cowboys and Indians to brighten their rotten lives.'[71] Leamas would never order champagne, or drive a four and a half litre Bentley with an Amherst Villiers supercharger, which Bond had bought almost new in 1933.[72] For Bond and Fleming, who was living out his fantasies through his hero, are steeped in the world of World War II, a more glamorous age, when Britain was basking in its 'Finest Hour'.

Felix Leiter's rescue of Bond at the baccarat table where he stares defeat in the face while playing against the villain Le Chiffre, is with the supply of an envelope of money 'as thick as a dictionary' along with a note that explains it is: 'Marshall Aid. Thirty-two million francs. With the compliments of the USA.'[73] Perhaps Fleming, when he wrote these words, imagined that he was back in

Portugal. He could have remembered Duško Popov at the Estoril Casino take $38,000 from the inside pocket of his Savile Row dinner jacket and lay it on the green baize of the baccarat table, in effect gambling the entire bundle on the single turn of a card. Popov wanted to cut the short, fat Lithuanian down to size. The Lithuanian irritates everyone by showing off when he has the bank, calling 'Banque ouvente' which means that the bank has no limit. He likes to bully people and make the other players squirm. Yet he is stunned speechless at the sight of so much money. Popov asks the croupier if the casino is backing the Lithuanian who is still staring into space knowing full well that they would not. He picks up the money and says in a loud voice that such players should be banned from playing, and leaves the Lithuanian to enjoy his humiliation. Popov had used money given to him by the Germans to open an account in New York, which was set up to fund the Abwehr operation in Britain and would find its way to the British. His handlers on both sides would have been horrified to learn what Popov did on a whim at that baccarat table.[74] Fleming likely witnessed this while he was working on Operation *Golden Eye* and it gave him the taste of what being a secret agent could entail. Is it any wonder that he called his home in Jamaica *Golden Eye* after his greatest triumph.

John Pearson wrote: 'In his contract with the secret service during the war Fleming had been the man behind the desk. In Bond he got his own back, slipped his Beretta with the skeleton grip into his chamois leather shoulder-holster and went off to face death on his own account.'[75]

Ian Fleming died of a massive haemorrhage at 1.30am on 12 August 1964 at Canterbury Hospital – he was only fifty-six. He was buried in the cemetery of the Parish church of St. James, Sevenhampton near Highworth in Wiltshire only three days later. He wrote fourteen Bond books and numerous short stories about 007, two non-fiction books and the children's book *Chitty-Chitty-Bang-Bang*, which in its own right became a classic. At the time of his death these books had sold thirty million copies. The films based on his books have taken over five billion dollars at the box office. Bond has gone marching on without his creator with ten other authors having written 007 novels. Some of these authors have passed away too but Bond remains.

Former Royal Marine Commando John Gardner wrote sixteen good Bond books from 1981–1996. The 15th, *GoldenEye*, which in this case refers to a satellite weapon named *GoldenEye* was made into the 17th Bond film starring Pierce Brosnan as 007 in 1995.

And what of the others: Francisco Franco and Antonio Salazar remained in power, dictators of their respective countries for life. Salazar died in 1968,

Franco in 1975. Both have been justifiably maligned for the brutality of their regimes. However, by accident or design, they did help the Iberian Peninsula escape the horrors of World War II, and for that at least, the people of Spain and Portugal should be grateful.

Alan Hillgarth left the Royal Navy in July 1946, highly respected by his peers for the role he had fulfilled in Spain. He married Jean the following year after a protracted divorce from Mary. Son Torrella became Mary's home, with Alan only returning once to collect his books. Gurthalougha on Lough Derg, County Tipperary, became his home with Jean. He maintained close links with Spain through his numerous friends and business interests. He was a consultant on several of Juan March's companies. He was a prolific writer on many subjects for many publications but he never published another novel. His death in 1978 was mourned in many parts of Spain. His friend March, once a smuggler, became the sixth richest man in the world. In 1955 he set up the Juan March Foundation to support the arts. He died in 1962 aged eighty-one.

The double agent Duško Popov kept silent for many years about his exploits in the war, but after the publication of John Masterman's *The Double Cross System* he decided to tell his own story. In 1974 his autobiography *Spy/Counterspy* was published, a book that John Miller, his biographer, wrote which 'read like a James Bond novel' but was 'fundamentally accurate'.[76] A life of heavy smoking and drinking took its toll and he died aged sixty-nine in 1981.

Wilhelm Canaris paid with his life for the game he played with the Nazi high command. Many Germans at the Nuremberg trials testified to his courage in opposing Hitler. He once wrote: 'A war waged in defiance of every ethical consideration can never be won. There is still a divine justice made manifest on this earth.'

In 1945 Walter Schellenberg surrendered to the British and was subjected to a lengthy interrogation by MI5/MI6. He testified at the Nuremberg trials, but faced no charges himself. He was convicted by the West German denazification court and sentenced to six years imprisonment. During this time he wrote his memoirs which were published in 1956. He was released in 1951 due to ill health and moved to Switzerland, and then to Lake Garda in Italy. He died of liver cancer in 1952 aged forty-two.

In December 1944 Sir Samuel Hoare's ambassadorship in Madrid came to an end. He was created Viscount Templewood for a lifetime of service. His memoir *Ambassador on a Special Mission*, published in 1946, is an excellent account of the day-to-day running of an embassy office during a difficult time, even if he is guilty of over-playing his role occasionally. Later he sat on various committees in the House of Lords. He was president of the Lawn Tennis association from 1932–56. He died of a heart-attack on 7 May 1959 aged seventy-nine.

Admiral John Godfrey served in the Royal Navy for forty-three years. He was placed on the retired list in 1945 as a full Admiral. He was the only officer of his rank in World War II to receive no official recognition for his immense contribution to Allied victory. This was partly due to his role in the Royal Indian Navy mutiny at the end of the war, for which no blame was attached to him. Rather he was the victim of political expediency at the time with Indian Independence looming. Lord Mountbatten felt that he would have gone higher in the navy if he had been able to get on with his superiors.[77] Yet Godfrey showed no resentment or bitterness. He was pleased to be asked to edit the secret history of NID in 1947. He had an active retirement serving on the boards of several hospitals. In 1976 his memoirs were given to Churchill College, Cambridge. He died of a heart attack in 1970.

Ewen Montagu during 1945–1973 was the Judge Advocate to the Fleet. He wrote *The Man who Never Was* in 1953, which was made into a film in 1956 where he was played by Clifton Webb. Montagu himself made a cameo appearance as an Air vice-marshal. He also wrote *Beyond Top Secret Ultra* which concentrated on the technical aspects of espionage during the war. He passed away in July 1985 aged eighty-four.

In 1997 the Commonwealth War Graves Commission took over grave number 1886 in Huelva's Roman Catholic Cemetery. The original inscription reads: 'William Martin, born 29 March 1907, died 24 April 1943, beloved son of John Glyndwyr Martin and the late Antonia Martin of Cardiff Wales, Dulce et Decorum est pro Patria Mori, RIP. (It is sweet and fitting to die for one's country.)'

Later in the year, the British government added a postscript to the marble slab:
Glyndwr Michael
Served as Major William Martin, RM.[78]

Endnotes

The following abbreviations have been used:
The Avalon Project/Lillian Goldman Law Library APLG
Bundesarchiv (Germany) Bun
Central Intelligence Agency Library/OOS CIAL
Imperial War Museum IWM
National Archives (USA) NA
The National Archives Kew (UK) TNA

Prologue

1   David Ramsay, *Blinker Hall Spymaster,* p.18, 'Physically, Hall was...'
2   Ibid, p.7, 'Whilst the fleet...'
3   Donald McLachlan, *Room 39, Naval Intelligence in action 1939–45,* pp.17–18, 'To no one...'
4   Keith Jeffery, *MI6,* p.328, 'The sixty-six year old...'
5   Ibid, p.327, 'Keeping Afloat.'
6   Philip Vickers, *Finding Thoroton,* p.157, 'Stafford goes on...'
7   Ibid, p.160 'There is an...'
8   Jan Morris, *Spain,* p.146, the cross is said to be visible from Madrid.
9   Giles Tremlett, *Ghosts of Spain,* p.34, 'The *Valle de los Caidos...*'

Chapter 1 – The Ideas Man

1   Winston S. Churchill, *The Second World War Volume Two Their Finest Hour,* p.194 'In the closing ...'
2   Patrick Beesly, *Very Special Admiral,* p.158 'He was by ...'
3   John Pearson, *The life of Ian Fleming,* p.108 'As long as Paris ...'
4   Naval Historical Museum, Unpublished papers of Admiral J. Godfrey.
5   Donald McLachlan, *Room39 Naval Intelligence in Action 1939–1945,* p.8 'If not the wisest ...'
6   *The Times,* May 1917.
7   Robert Harling, *Ian Fleming a Personal Memoir,* p.317 'As I have noted ...'
8   Fergus Fleming *The Man with the Golden Typewriter,* p.3 'To put the contents ...
9   Lycett Andrew, *Ian Fleming,* p.10 'As Ian began ...'
10 Pearson, p.27 'Perhaps it was ...'
11 Pearson, p.29 'There was trouble ...'
12 Ian Fleming, *You Only Live Twice.* p.200 'Obit *The Times ...*'

13   Pearson, p.36 'we were all …'
14   Ibid, p.43 'During the first year …'
15   Ian Fleming, *On Her Majesty's Secret Service,* p.162 'The ground shook …'
16   Pearson, p.55 'His Majesty's …'
17   Ibid, p.58 'It was an uneasy …'
18   Lycett, p.57 'Ian's itinerary took him …'
19   Ibid, p.59 'The caviar took its …'
20   Ibid, p.63 'Ian was deeply …'
21   Ben Macintyre, *For Your Eyes Only Ian Fleming & James Bond,* p.40 'Fleming's distinctive …'
22   Pearson, p.77 'In fact …'
23   Lycett, p.97 'After five days …'
24   Beesly, p.99 'The appointment …'
25   Churchill Archive Cambridge, MCBE1/2 J.H.Godfrey p3
26   McLachlan, pp.17–18, 'However, none of …'
27   David Ramsay, *Blinker Hall Spymaster,* p.46 'Hall's other choice …'
28   Pearson, p.98 'A few days after …'
29   McLachlan, p.1 'To pay a call …'
30   Ibid, p.2 'For the man …'
31   Lycett, p.101 'So it was …'
32   McLachlan, p.8 'If not the …'
33   Ibid, p.9 'Fleming suffered not …'
34   Pearson, p.106 'This idea of …'
35   Ian Fleming, *For Your Eyes Only (From a View to a Kill)* ,pp. 32–33 'Now from the direction …'
36   Pearson, p.107 'A lot of …'

Chapter 2 – France 1940

1   Geoffrey Cox, *Countdown to War,* p.186 'Paris had three weeks …'
2   IWM-No 7183 Private Papers Lieutenant-Commander A. F. Whinney, p.2.
3   Ibid, p.4.
4   Ibid, p.24.
5   Ibid, p.60.
6   Ibid, pp.18–19.
7   Auphan Rear Admiral Paul & Mordal Jacques, *The French Navy in World War II,* p.25.
8   IWM-No 23941 Private Papers Commander M. Mackenzie, p.5.
9   Ibid, p.9.
10 IWM Whinney papers, p.47.
11 Jeffery Keith, *MI6 The History of the Secret Intelligence Service 1909–1949,* pp.199–200 'From the mid-1920s …'
12 *Daily Telegraph,* Naval obituaries 10/6/2006.
13 IWM Whinney papers, p.69.
14 IWM Mackenzie papers, p.10.
15 IWM-No 8489 Private Papers Miss R. Andrew, p.1.
16 IWM Whinney papers, p.73.
17 Cox, *Countdown,* p.203 'The rest of the road …'
18 Pearson, p.109 'By the time …'
19 Beesly, p.159 'The terms of …'

20 IWM Whinney papers, p.77.
21 IWM Mackenzie papers, p.10.
22 IWM Whinney papers, p.81.
23 Lycett, p.116 'Having finally accomplished ...'
24 IWM Andrew, p.3 & *Sunday Times.*
25 IWM Whinney papers, pp.90–91.
26 Lochery Neill, *Lisbon,* p.42 'By the middle of June ...'
27 Ibid, p.43 'Initial estimates ...'
28 Hoare Sir Samuel, *Ambassador on Special Mission* p18 'Once again my ...'
29 Pearson, p.112 'It went on ...'
30 IWM Mackenzie, pp.11–12, Whinney p111–113, Andrew, p.5.
31 Beesly, p.143, 'A country which ...'
32 Charles B. Burdick, *Germany's Military Strategy and Spain during World War II,* p.9 'Between five and ...'
33 Churchill, *Finest,* p.197 'The addition of the French ...'
34 Ibid, p.195 'For the rest ...'
35 TNA/Admiralty files 223/463
36 Major-General I. S. O Playfair, *The Mediterranean and Middle East Vol I,* p.136 'At times it seemed ...'
37 Bullock, p.543 'Hitler waited another ...'
38 Count Galeazzo Ciano, *Ciano's Diary 1937–1943,* pp.368–369 'News of the British ...'

Chapter 3 – Naval Attaché

1   Hoare, p.19 'Our anxieties were ...'
2   Sybil & David Eccles, *By Safe Hand,* p.97 'The Embassy agreed ...'
3   Ibid, p.101 'Sir Samuel and Lady ...'
4   Hoare, p.19 'Worse still, it seemed ...'
5   Ibid, p.19 'Flying over ...'
6   Ibid, p.21 'As we drove ...'
7   Ibid, p.22 'As the Embassy ...'
8   Ibid, p.33 'To Lord Halifax ...'
9   The Templewood Papers XIII 'In effect your ...'
10 Ibid, 'I have really ...'
11 TNA/ADM 223/490 Int Part II
12 Duff Hart-Davis, *Man of War,* p.11 'The tradition of ...'
13 Ibid, p.17 'We arrived on board ...'
14 Ibid, p.5 'Three days later ...'
15 TNA/ADM 53/34644 54 The log of the Bacchante.
16 Nigel Steel & Peter Hart, *Defeat at Gallipoli,* pp. 184 185 'A far more serious ...'
17 Hart-Davis, p.42 'The Triumph was struck ...'
18 Ibid, p.46 'Death had become ...'
19 Ibid, p.60 'Far from sounding ...'
20 Ibid, p.53 'I hope you got ...'
21 TNA/ADM 196/147
22 Hart-Davis, p.70 'In the autumn ...'
23 Hillgarth Alan, *The Princess and the Perjurer,* pp 13–14

24 Hart-Davis, p.73 'Given his good looks ...'
25 Ibid, p.79 'He was placed ...'
26 TNA/ADM 196/147
27 Hart-Davis, pp. 77–78 'I, Alan Hugh ...' & *The Times* 3/9/1926.
28 Ibid, p.81 'Alan was no ordinary. ...'
29 Ibid, p.80 'Whatever he did ...'
30 Ibid, p.105 'Sacambaya is a poisonous ...'
31 *The Peruvian Times* 15/1/2017.
32 Hugh Thomas, *The Spanish Civil War,* p.227 'So now there ...'
33 TNA/Foreign Office 371/34147.
34 Jeffery, p.285 'SIS was less ...'
35 TNA/FO 371/20537
36 Ibid, 371/20537
37 Ibid, 371/20551.
38 Stanley G. Payne, *Franco & Hitler,* pp. 32–34 'The Italian and ...'
39 TNA/FO 371/24147.
40 Hart-Davis, p.166 'In April 1937 ...'
41 TNA/FO 371/21391.
42 Hart-Davis, p.169 'Through his strong ...'
43 Ibid, pp.178 179 'As usual, Alan ...'
44 TNA/FO 371/24147.
45 Beesley, p.143 'A country which had ...'
46 Churchill Arch Cam, GDFY/1'5.
47 Eccles, pp. 23–24 'You wouldn't know ...'
48 Alan Hillgarth, *The role of NA,* 2/4 'Disadvantages of ...'

Chapter 4 – The Network

1 TNA/FO 371/245526
2 Ibid, 371/245526
3 Burns, p.70 'He was excellent ...'
4 Thomas, p.238 'The rebel's main victories ...'
5 Burns, p.71 'The landscape ...'
6 Laurie Lee, *As I Walked out one Midsummer Morning,* pp.87–88 'Where should I go ...'
7 Tom Burns, *Here in Spain',* pp.10–11 'Penetrating the Pyrenees ...'
8 Burns, p.72 'A group of ...'
9 Ibid, p.77 'He was happier ...'
10 TNA/ADM 116/416 'Hillgarth is already ...'
11 Philip Vickers, *Finding Thoroton,* p.141 'In Majorca he is ...'
12 Ibid, p.151 'Most importantly March ...'
13 Christopher Andrew, *Secret Service,* p.116 'Mason sometimes ...'
14 Ramsay, p.142 'In January 1917 ...'
15 Vickers, p.126 'The great success ...'
16 Ibid, p.126 'The great success ...'
17 Ibid, p.166 'Finally, I am delighted ...'
18 Ibid, p.159 'It was Hillgarth's ...'
19 Ladislas Farago, *The Game of Foxes,* pp.512–513 'The cordial relations ...'
20 David Kahn, *Hitler's Spies,* p.230 'For the Kos faced ...'

21 Walter Schellenberg, *The Memoirs of Hitler's Spymaster*, p.133 'Madrid was …'
22 Hillgarth, *The Rolke of NA, V Relations.*
23 TNA/ADM 223/490
24 Jeffery, pp. 403–404 'In the spring of …'
25 TNA/ADM 223/490
26 Vickers, p.158 'March's first contact …'
27 TNA/ADM 223/490 'It would be …'
28 Beesly, p.144 'The A1 Spanish …'
29 TNA/ADM 223/490 'This man is …'
30 Vickers, p.191 'We obtained a copy …'
31 Payne, p.56 'The activity …'
32 Ibid, p.57 'The re-supply operation …'
33 Hart-Davis, p.193 'He was to my …'
34 TNA/FO 371/24526
35 Churchill, *Finest*, p.36 'On Monday, May …'
36 Payne, pp.69–70 'British efforts did …'
37 Richard Wigg, *Churchill and Spain*, p.6 'Hillgarth settled the details …'
38 The Templewood Papers, XIII 'When I arrived …'
39 Hoare, p.48 'The other subject …'
40 Sir Alexander Cadogan, *Cadogan Diaries*, p. 282 'I suppose they …'
41 TNA/Prime Minister's Office Records, 4/21/2
42 Ibid.
43 Hart-Davis, p.203 'After flying to …'
44 Ibid, p.203 'One of the brightest …'

Chapter 5 – The Wayward Royals

1   Michael Bloch, *Operation Willi*, p.43 'The Italians were …'
2   Lochery, p.61 'In fleeing the …'
3   Bloch, pp. 23 24 'That day the …'
4   TNA/FO 800/326
5   The Templewood Papers XIII/16/29, 27/6/1940.
6   TNA/FO 800/326
7   Bloch, pp.23–24 'That afternoon …'
8   The Templewood Papers, 'A deep laid plot, p.12.
9   TNA/FO 800/326.
10 Ibid, 25/6/1940.
11 Bloch, p.58 'Having received …'
12 TNA/FO 800/326 'Hoare to FO 1/7/1940.
13 Bloch, p.64 'Zoppi's report would …'
14 The Templewood Papers, Hoare to Churchill 5/7/1940.
15 Bloch. P.66 'At all events …'
16 Lochery, p.68 'Along the Lisbon …'
17 Eccles, p.107 'I saw Salazar …'
18 Ibid, p.105 'Lisbon at first …'
19 Lochery, p.9 'Of greatest significance …'
20 Bloch, p.74 'In the event …'
21 TNA/FO 371/24249.

22 Bloch, p.77 'Eventually the Duke ...'
23 Ibid, pp.77–79 'Eventually the Duke ...'
24 Eccles, pp131–132 'Dearest Angel ...'
25 Ibid, pp. 139–140 'Your description ...'
26 Schellenberg, p.129 'Here I tried ...'
27 Ibid, p.129 'If the British ...'
28 Ibid, p.130 'In the near ...'
29 Ibid, p.131 'I went at once ...'
30 Bundesarchiv R58/572 Schellenberg's Log.
31 Schellenberg, p.136 'In the evening ...'
32 Ibid, p.138 'Within six days ...'
33 Bloch, p.82 'Throughout his stay ...'
34 Ibid, pp.168–169 'On my return to Spain ...'
35 Ibid, p.175 'Monckton on the ...'
36 Bundesarchiv R58/572 Schellenberg's log Monday 29 July.
37 Schellenberg, p.139 'Replies from Berlin ...'
38 Ibid, p.142 'The next day ...'
39 Burdick, p.41 'After his visit ...'
40 Bloch, pp. 155–160 Interview with Angle Alcazar de Velasco.

Chapter 6 – *Felix* and *Sealion*

1   Hart-Davis, pp.203–204 'Having returned ...' & TNA/ADM 233/490
2   Nobel Frankland & Christopher Dowling, *Decisive Battles of the Twentieth Century*, p.121 'The battle of Britain ...'
3   Peter Fleming, *Operation Sealion*, p.15 'On 16 July ...'
4   Burdick, p.12 'Hitler after ...'
5   Payne, p.76 'Hitler had at last ...'
6   Burdick, p.17 'Beyond the immediate ...'
7   Ibid, pp.16–18 'One of the chief ...'
8   Ibid, p.18 'On the following ...'
9   Ciano, pp.367–368 'Mussolini has returned ...'
10 Ibid, p.369 'I arrived in Berlin ...'
11 Burdick p.21 'Subsequently, Keitel spoke ...'
12 John H.Waller, *The Unseen War in Europe*, p.155 'On July 10 ...'
13 Burdick, p.24 'They observed ...'
14 Richard Bassett, *Hitler's Spy Chief*, p.36 'Abshagen relates ...'
15 Ibid, p.67 'On 1st April ...'
16 Ibid, p.42 'As a fluent ...'
17 Ibid, p.42 'As a fluent ...'
18 Ibid, p51 'With the intuitive ...'
19 Ramsay, p.139 'In both World Wars ...'
20 Vickers, p.150 'In 1916 ...'
21 Bassett, pp.55–57 'By March 1916 ...'
22 Gannon Paul, *Inside Room 40*, p.125 'Back in the Admiralty ...'
23 Ibid, p.126 'Another important factor ...'
24 TNA/ADM 223/739
25 Vickers, pp.146 147 'In the context ...'

26 Bassett, p.84 'On 3 October 1924 …'
27 Christer Jorgensen, *Hitler's Espionage Machine*, p.25 'In January 1925 …'
28 Bassett, p.94 'Patzig proved …'
29 Mark Simmons, *The Rebecca Code*, p.27 'In January 1921 …'
30 Burdick, p.25 'Shortly after …'
31 Ibid, pp.25–27 'The next day …'
32 Ibid, p.25 'Shortly after …'
33 Farago, p.559 'The feverish action …'
34 Burdick, pp.27–28 'The fighting would …'
35 Ibid, p.29 'In the midst …'
36 Peter Fleming, p.243 'On 31 July …'
37 Ibid, p.244 'Ostensibly Raeder …'
38 Ibid, p.252 'On 7 August …'
39 Burdick, pp.31–32 'The next day …'
40 Peter Fleming, p.178 'We are divided …'
41 Ibid, p.179 'No one in …'
42 Christopher Andrew, *The Defence of the Realm, the Authorised history of MI5*, p.225 'Anna Wolkoff was …'
43 Farago, pp.202–207 'The secret war …'
44 Ian Colvin, *Canaris Chief of Intelligence*, p.32 'Canaris and his master …'
45 Ian Kershaw, *Hitler: A Biography*, p.520.
46 Bassett, p.185 'It has been said …'
47 Gerard Noel, *Pius XII The Hound of Hitler*, p.63 'In 1921 …'
48 Bassett, pp.188–189 'Was the Pope …'
49 Churchill, *Finest*, p.245 'Even while these …'
50 Colvin, p.118 'The intelligence evidently …'
51 Nicholas Rankin, *Ian Fleming's Commandos*, p.106 'Ian Fleming felt …'
52 TNA/ADM 223/463
53 Nigel West, *GCHQ*, p.169 'Ismay's intervention …'
54 Andrew, pp. 439–440 'While the Germans …'
55 West, p.118 'When Arthur Owens …'
56 Andrew, *MI5*, p.212 'In August 1939 …'
57 BUN/OKW/OTH 644/40 'Felix'.
58 Burdick, pp. 36–37 'Warlimont's staff …'
59 APLG/Yale Library SGA No 4 Hitler and Serrano Suner.
60 Ibid, No 5 Franco and Hitler 'I would like …'
61 Payne, p.83 'The second intervention …'
62 Ciano, p.385 'I had two conversations …'
63 Payne, p.85 'Though perhaps …'
64 Jeffery, p.402 'Once the Germans …'
65 Eccles, p.144 'Dearest Syb I write a note …'
66 Jeffery, p.403 'In the end …'
67 Macintyre, *For your Eyes Only*, pp. 170–171 'In some ways …'

Chapter 7 – Meeting at Hendaye

1 Bullock, p.553 'Like most people …'
2 Ciano, p.387 'Rarely have I seen …'
3 Ibid, p.387 'These are my …'

4   Hoare, pp.66–67 'Perhaps it was ...'
5   Ibid, p.50 'Over this small ...'
6   Payne, p.72 'Beigbeder followed up ...'
7   Bassett, p.198 'The SD then ...'
8   Schellenberg, pp.259–260 'The first thing ...'
9   Colvin, p.125 'The German infantry ...'
10 Ibid, p.129 'Canaris, this fluent ...'
11 Ibid, p.131 'Canaris was discreet ...'
12 Ibid, p.128 'The Admiral asks ...'
13 NA/US Department of state, No8 23/10/1940.
14 Bassett, p.199 'David Schmidt ...'
15 Payne, p.91 'What was unusual ...'
16 Bullock, pp.555–556 'The departure of the ...'
17 NA/USDS, Documents on German Foreign Policy.
18 Payne, p.92 'The Protocol was ...'
19 Bullock, p.555 'The departure of the ...'
20 Payne, pp. 92–93 'Hendaye 23 October 1940 ...'
21 Bullock, p.556 'Although he ...'
22 Ibid, p.556 'By contrast, Hitler's ...'
23 Ciano, pp.390–391 'With General Pricolo ...'
24 Christopher Hibbert, *Benito Mussolini*, p.166 'He had reason ...'
25 Burdick, pp.69–70 'Hitler signed ...'
26 TNA/PMOR, 3 405/1
27 Hoare, pp.98 99 'At the moment ...'
28 TNA/FO 371/19131 25/11/39
29 Wigg, p.21 'The cries that ...'
30 Churchill, *Finest*, p.420 'Former naval person ...'
31 Wigg, pp.24–25 'After Serrano inveigling ...'
32 Eccles, pp.206–207 '6 December 1940 ...'
33 Wigg, p.26 'Chuchill had lunch ...'
34 Ibid, p.22 'In reality, Hoare ...'
35 Ciano, p.396 '18 19 November 1940 ...'
36 Payne, p.101 'At Berchtesgaden ...'
37 Bundesarchiv/OKH No 676/40 20/11/40
38 Colvin, pp.130–131 'When Hitler got over ...'
39 Burdick, p.104 'This time there ...'
40 Ibid, pp.114–115 'These events clouded ...'
41 Payne, p.113 'After seeing Mussolini ...'

Chapter 8 – Operation *Golden Eye*

1   McLachlan, p.8 'If not the wisest ...'
2   TNA/ADM 223/464, p.38
3   Ibid, p.39
4   Ibid, p.39
5   Eduardo Martinez *Alonso, Adventures of a Doctor*, p.70 'To teach us ...'
6   Paul Preston, *The Spanish Holocaust*, p.508 'Franco's rhetoric ...'
7   Patricia Martinez de Vicente, *The Enclave Embassy*', see also *MI6 in Spain: A love story*, Online article, see also Nicholas Coni, *Surgeon who undertook Special Operations*, Online article.

8   TNA/SOE HS 9/26/5
9   Ibid HS 9/61
10 Lycett, p.123 'As Delmar later wrote …'
11 Ibid, p.123 'Ian himself …'
12 Pearson, p.118 'It began in …'
13 Ibid, p.118 (the single page courier's passport was sold at Sotherby's in 2000 for £15,525.)
14 Maurice Harvey, *Gibraltar,* pp.140–141 'Gibraltar was fortunate …'
15 Ian Fleming, *Dr No,* pp.137–138 'Bond answered …'
16 TNA/ADM 223/490
17 Paul Bowles, *Too Far From Home: The selected writings of Paul Bowles,* p.314.
18 Warner Brothers, *Casablanca,* 1942.
19 Hoare, p.82 'As a result …'
20 TNA/ADM 223/490 29/4/41
21 TNA/ADM 223/490 17/4/41
22 McLachlan, p.227 'So Donovan was …'
23 Admiral Andrew Browne Cunningham, *A Sailor's Odyssey,* p.306 'At about this …'
24 Alex Danchev, *Establishing the Anglo-American Alliance,* p.62 'Donovan came around …'
25 Danchev, p.62 'Quare had not …'
26 Hoare, p.110 'Colonel Donovan who …'
27 Ibid, p.110.
28 TNA/ADM 223/490
29 Danchev, p.62 'We dined with …'
30 TNA/ADM 223/480 3/4/41
31 TNA/PMOP 4/21/2
32 Hart-Davis, p.207 'Alan himself …'
33 TNA/ADM 223/490
34 TNA/SOE HS 6/962
35 Hillgarth, *The role of a Naval Attache,* 1946
36 Ibid, relations with SIS & SOE.
37 Jeffery, p.404 'What then happened …'
38 Ibid, p.405 'There was some …'
39 Ibid, pp.404–405 'But it was …'
40 Ibid, pp.406–407 'The second affair …'
41 Hart-Davis, p.221 'He claimed he …'
42 Wigg, p.14 and TNA/PMOR 421/2A 21/6/40
43 Kim Philby, *My Silent War,* p.39 'One day, Cowgill …'
44 TNA/ADM 223/490
45 Ibid.
46 Ibid, 7/4/41
47 Hart-Davis, p.220 'Deeply involved …'
48 TNA/ADM 223/490
49 Lycett, p.125 *'Golden Eye* proved …'

Chapter 9 – Operation *Tracer*

1 Harvey, p.98 'Although his north …'
2 Lawrence Durrell, *Balthazar,* p.213.
3 TNA/ADM 223/463, p.268
4 Ibid.

5 Nigel West, *Historical Dictionary of Naval Intelligence,* p.213

6 Royal Geographical Society, *With Scott to the Pole,* p.62

7 TNA/ADM 223/463, p.269 *'On 25 January a meeting was held…. Cordeaux & Fleming as well as Harder & Levick, were present.'*

8 Ian Fleming, *For Your Eyes Only,* pp.30–34 'It was the pigeons …' (From a View to a Kill).

9 Neill Rush, *Operation Tracer-Stay behind cave* www.aboutourrock.com

10 TNA/ADM 223/463, p.268

11 Rush, *Operation Tracer.*

12 TNA/ADM 223/463, p.269

13 Ibid.

14 McLachlan, p.61 'For 18 months …'

15 *Daily Telegraph,* obituary 3/1/2011

16 Ibid.

17 TNA/ADM 223/463, p.270

18 Bundesarchiv/OKW No 55455/42 8/3/42

19 Burdick, p.130 'The naval authorities …'

20 TNA/ADM 223/463, p.270.

Chapter 10 – Portugal

1 Hoare, p.58 'Beigbeder was then …'

2 Eccles, p.107 'I saw Salazar.'

3 Lochery, p.2 'During the years …'

4 Wigg, p.10 'Economics as a weapon …'

5 Eccles, p.180 'We are getting …'

6 Ibid, p.106 'It needed a …'

7 Ibid, p.111 'Salazar's character …'

8 Idid, p. 110 113 'Selby and I …'

9 Wigg, p.10 'I did …'

10 Hoare, p.48 'The other subject …'

11 Wigg, p.122 'We are faced …'

12 Lochery, p.116 'An unregulated Wolfram …'

13 Ibid, p.117 'Salazar's defense was …'

14 Eccles, pp.311–312 'We have had …'

15 Lochery, p.179 'In order to try …'

16 Hoare, p.257 'For the next …'

17 Payne, p.166 'The first part …'

18 Mark Simmons, *Agent Cicero,* p.102 'It was certainly …'

19 Simmons, *The Rebecca Code,* p.137 'There is no doubt …'

20 Simmons, *Agent Cicero,* p.62 'Having encountered counterfeiting …'

21 Ben Macintyre, *Agent Zig Zag,* pp.101 102.

22 Lochery, p.201 'The origins of …'

23 Pearson, p.24 'Ian Fleming was not …'

24 Ian Fleming, *On Her Majesty's* … p.40 'The Union Corse …'

25 Ian Fleming, *Octopussy,* p.33 'With a last …'

26 Ibid, p.40 'They are German …'

27 Jeffery, pp.408–409 'The intelligence challenge …'

28 Ibid, p.409 'Some of SIS's …'

29   Philby, pp.56–57 'With respect to …'
30   Lochery, p.151 'Kim Philby described …'
31   TNA/ADM 223/490
32   Lochery, p.126 'On May 20 …'
33   Ibid, pp.58–59 'Lourenco's loyalty …'
34   Pearson, p.121 'The reality seems …'
35   Ian Fleming, *Casino Royale*, p.1.
36   Ibid.
37   IWM-No 17063 Private Papers Lieutenant-Commander J. A. C. Hugill.
38   Ibid.
39   Macintyre, *For your eyes …'* pp.54–55 'In May 1941 …'
40   Eccles, p.303 'He came straight. …'
41   Lycett, pp.131–132 'On 18 July …'
42   TNA/ADM 223/490 17/4/41 Greenleaves report.
43   Ibid.
44   Ibid.
45   Ibid.
46   Ibid.
47   Ibid 19/8/41
48   Jack Beevor, *Recollections and Reflections,* p.31.
49   TNA/SOE HS/6/978 Operation Panicle 19/5/41.
50   TNA/SOE HS/6/943
51   TNA/SOE HS/6/987 31/3/42.
52   Ibid.
53   Lochery, p.158 'On the morning …'
54   Ian Colvin, *Flight 777 The Mystery of Leslie Howard,* see chapter 19, *Flight 777,* for a fuller explanation.
55   Lochery, p.161 'On June 7 …'

Chapter 11 – *Isabella-Ilona*

1   Payne, pp.146–147 'The animus toward …'
2   Ibid, p.163 'Franco quickly …'
3   Hoare, pp.138–139 'As evidence …'
4   Payne, p.148 'The official …'
5   Ibid, pp.148–150 'On the first …'
6   Lycett. P.130 'In the wake …'
7   Patrick Dalzel-Job, *From Arctic Snow to Dust of Normandy,* p.115 'Our boss …'
8   Lycett, p.132 'Godfrey, however …'
9   Thomas, pp.140–141 'Francisco Franco …'
10   Hoare, p.47 'My first interview …'
11   Thomas, p.141 'Life at Toledo …'
12   Stanley G. Payne, *Fascism in Spain 1923–1977,* p.347.
13   Payne, *Franco & Hitler,* pp.150–152 'During January …'
14   Bundesarchiv OKW 44672/41 9/5/41.
15   Hoare, p.196 'I cannot claim …'
16   Burdick, pp.150–151 'As part of this …'
17   Ben Macintyre, *Operation Mincemeat,* p.26 'At thirty eight …'

18 Ewen Montagu, *Beyond Top Secret Ultra,* pp.90–91 'That great sailor …'
19 Ibid, p.91 'The question was …'
20 Philby, p.41 'The first step …'
21 Wigg, p.63 'In the spring …'
22 Montagu, p.91 'We were glad …'
23 Bundesarchiv OKW WF 55129/42 29/6/42
24 Payne, pp.176–177 'Franco was greatly …'
25 Hoare, pp.164–165 'On September 3rd …'
26 Payne, p.177 'The most important …'
27 Hoare, p.166 'An interesting sidelight …'
28 Payne, p. 178 'All the while …'
29 Bundesarchiv OKW 55896/42 26/9/42
30 Hoare, p.162 'When I arrived …'

Chapter 12 – *Golden Eye* Activated

1 Danchev, p.224 'Lunched with …'
2 Ibid, p.224 'Sunday 8 November 1942 …'
3 Winston Churchill, *The Second World War, Vol III The Grand Alliance,* p.509 'We must however …'
4 TNA/ADM 223/500 & Nicholas Rankin, *Ian Fleming's Commandos,* p.136.
5 Lycett, p.152 'The run-up …'
6 TNA/ADM 223/500 & Lycett, p.141.
7 Major J. C. Beadle, *The Light Blue Lanyard,* p.20 'The South Saskatchewan Regiment …'
8 Montagu, pp.89–90 'Urgent instructions …'
9 Commander Marc Antonio Bragadin, *The Italian Navy in World War II,* pp.227 228 'On the other hand …'
10 Ibid, pp.282–285 'Even before the attempt …'
11 Ibid, pp.289–295 'In the spring of 1942 …'
12 McLachlan, pp.197–198 'None the less …'
13 Ian Fleming, *Thunderball,* p.143 'Same as you …'
14 Ibid, p.50 'The founder and …' & p.70 'The aircraft was …'
15 Ian Fleming, *Live,* p.220 'Sixty yards to go …'
16 Pearson, p.128 'The training staff …'Lycett, p.149 & Rankin, p.223 cast some doubt on the story Pearson supports it …'
17 Ibid, p.129 'Altogether Fleming …'
18 Beesly, pp.229–230 'Find that …'
19 Ibid, pp.229–230 'Godfrey himself …'
20 Lycett, p.143 'On a personal …'
21 Ian Fleming, *Live,* p.83 'Pennsylvania station …'
22 Ivar Bryce, *You Only Live Once,* pp. 71–72 'Ivar I have …'
23 Beesly, p.240 'It might have …'
24 John Pearson papers interview with Joan Saunders 24/3/65 & Rankin, p.142.
25 Hart-Davis, p.210 'In the event …'
26 TNA/ADM 223/490 Golden Eye experience …'
27 Ibid, 25/4/41.
28 Ibid, 20/11/41.

29 Hoare, p.177 'It was essential …'
30 Payne, p.183 'Despite Anglo-American …'
31 Hoare, p.179 'Franco seemed to …'
32 Payne, p.184 'When Franco replied …'
33 Ibid, p.185 'The new strategic …'
34 Andre Brissaud, *The Biography of Admiral Canaris*, p.284 'Canaris is a fool …'
35 Waller, p.252 'Operation Torch …'
36 Simmons, *Agent Cicero*, p.132 'He awarded …'
37 Ibid, p.98 'Elliot handled …'
38 John Pearson papers, Interview with Dunstan Curtis 16/4/65 & Rankin, pp.152 153 & note p.359.
39 Mavis Batey, *Dilly The man who broke Enigma*, p.189 & David Nutting, *Attain by Surprise*, p.35.
40 Ian Fleming, *From Russia with Love*, p.109 'She had a …'
41 Ibid, p.192 'Bond reached up …'
42 Churchill, *Grand Alliance*, p.572 'I regard these …'
43 Anthony Cave Brown, *'C'*, p.437 'As Giraud came …'
44 Jeffery, pp.495–496 'Algeria was the …'
45 Cave Brown, pp.447–449 'By mid November …'
46 Ibid, p.449 'In what was …'
47 Ibid, p.451 'Whatever the …'
48 Ibid, pp.451–453 'Coon also admitted …'
49 Payne, p.183 'The most impressive …'
50 Bundesarchiv-OKW 552344/42 & Burdick, p.171.
51 Operation Backbone July42–May43 located at TNA/WO 106/2737 & TNA/FO 954/17A/45.

Chapter 13 – The Canaris Factor

1   Bassett, p.133 'On the whole …'
2   Hoare, p.48 'As to the …'
3   Churchill, *Finest*, p.412 'His Majesty's government …'
4   Bassett, p.129 'One of the reasons …'
5   Preston, p.471 'That Franco had …'
6   Ibid, p.521 'Despite the massive …'
7   Gabriel Jackson, *The Spanish Republic and the Civil War 1931–1939*, p.539.
8   Thomas, pp.926–927. He estimates 200,000 died in action or as a result of wounds. Including starvation and executions after the war this could have risen to 500,000, also 300,000 emigrated. Payne, in *The Spanish Republic …'* p.245 puts the total during the war at 300,000.
9   Hoare p.276 'What particularly surprised …'
10 Waller, p.156 'Knowing that Franco …'
11 Colvin, p.128 'The Admiral asks …'
12 Waller, p.262 'Canaris in fact …'
13 Burdick, p.171 'The sudden …'
14 Waller, p.264 'Hitler's reaction …'
15 Bassett, p.236 'The most important …'
16 Ibid, pp.235–236 'The assassination team …'
17 Ibid, p.237 'There is no evidence …'

18   Andrew, *MI5*, p.253 'Through the security service ...'
19   Cave Brown, p.308 'Popov arrived in ...'
20   Ibid, p.310 'On that solemn ...'
21   Bassett, p.22 'Such vignettes suggest ...'
22   Larry Loftus, *Into the Lions Mouth*, pp.283 284.
23   Philip Knightly, *The Master Spy*, p.106 'Away from Hess ...'
24   Schellenberg, p.338 'After the coffin ...'
25   Bassett, p.243 'As Trevor-Roper ...'
26   Ibid, p.243 'According to ...'
27   Hugh Trevor-Roper, *The Philby Affair*, pp.78–79 'Indicated wiliness ...'
28   Bassett, p.255 'Algeciras was at ...'
29   Ibid, p.250 'C's personal assistant ...'
30   Cave Brown, *'C'*, p.452 'This was perhaps ...'
31   TNA/HW GCHQ 1/1659 Turkish Ambassador Tokyo to Turkish PM 2/5/1945.
32   Bassett, p.283 'In May 1944 ...'
33   Colvin, p.158 'Algeciras was one ...'
34   Ibid, p.163 'Canaris reckoned with ...'
35   Schellenberg, pp.409–412 'The inevitable downfall ...'
36   Ibid, p.409 'You know ...'
37   Ibid, p.410 'I went to ...'
38   Colvin, p.210 'By first light ...'
39   CIAL/p.19 & Waller notes, p.413 & text, p.162.

Chapter 14 – Body at Huelva

1   Montagu Papers 13/9/1964 & Ben Macintyre, *Operation Mincemeat*, p.31
2   Macintyre, *Mincemeat*, p.31 'Before placing Montagu ...'
3   Ewen Montagu, *The Man Who Never Was*, p.11 'It all really ...'
4   Montagu, *Ultra*, p.144 'At several meetings ...'
5   TNA/ADM 223/478
6   David Kahn, *Hitler's Spies*, pp.453–454 'A Royal Navy postmaster ...'
7   Ibid, p.454 'But their suspicions ...'
8   TNA/ADM 223/794
9   Montagu, *Ultra*, pp.143–144 'Against that background ...'
10   IWM 97/45/1 folder II2 & Macintyre, *Operation Mincemeat*, p.14
11   Montagu, *Ultra*, p.145 'Charles and I ...'
12   Macintyre, *Operation Mincemeat*, p.77 'Bill would need ...'
13   Montagu, *The Man*, pp.60–61 'I do think ...'
14   Ibid, p.58 'Lloyds Bank ...'
15   Ibid, p.58 'It had been ...'
16   Ibid, p.58.
17   TNA/ADM 223/794, p.444 & Macintyre, *Operation Mincemeat*, p.103.
18   Montagu, *The Man*, pp.66–67 'We had gone ...'
19   Ibid, p.75 'All went well ...'
20   Ibid, p.78 'From Commanding officer ...'
21   TNA/ADM 223/794
22   Ibid.

23 Montagu, *The Man,* pp.83–84 'On the 3rd May ...'
24 Macintyre, *Operation Mincemeat,* p.243 'On 12 May ...'
25 TNA/ADM 223/794
26 IWM 97/45 1.
27 Macintyre, *Operation Mincemeat,* p.306 'Bill Jewel often ...'

Chapter 15 – The Ideas Man and 007

1   Pearson, pp.149–150 'When Commander ...'
2   Ibid, p.116 'For the most part ...'
3   Nutting, p.47 'Curtis seemed rather ...'
4   Ibid, p.80 'We found that ...'
5   Pearson, p.137 'He was summoned ...'
6   Lycett, pp.151–152 'The unreality ...' & Pearson p.137.
7   Harling, pp.83–84 'I left on the ...'
8   Ian Fleming, *From Russia with Love,* pp.98–99 'That morning ...'
9   Ian Fleming, *On Her Majesty's,* pp.258259 'Ten minutes later ...'
10 Nutting, p.160 'Although this formation ...'
11 See Anthony Rogers book *Churchill's Folly*
12 WO 32/11430
13 Nutting, p.59 'This ended ...'
14 Ibid, p.59 'In any event ...' & p.160 'At a meeting ...'
15 Ibid, p.165 'The unit had ...'
16 Harling, p.55 'Pamela nodded ...'
17 Nutting, p.180 'By now the ...'
18 Harling, p.77 'Within an hour ...'
19 Ibid, p.357 'Then came preparations ...'
20 Nutting, p.204 'Shortly after this ...'
21 Ian Fleming, *Moonraker,* p.109 'It was like being ...'
22 Harling, pp.92–93 'Patton received his ...'
23 Ibid, p.97 'In due course ...'
24 Hart-Davis, p.257 'When he left Madrid ...'
25 Lycett, p.155 'He had arrived ...'
26 Nutting, p.249 'The first possible ...'
27 Ibid, p.250 'Dr Walter a rather ...'
28 Ibid, pp.244–252 'One of the most ...'
29 Pearson, p.142 'All the same ...'& Lycett, p.156.
30 Nutting, pp.259–260 'A special party ...'
31 Ibid, pp.261–262 'The library contained ...'
32 Harling, p.188 'In the course ...'
33 Ibid, p.190 'The DNI has ...'
34 Ibid, p.190 'And what happened ...'
35 Lycett, p.159 'By the end of 1945 ...'
36 Ibid, p.165 'Now Ian drew ...' & Matthew Parker, *Goldeneye,* pp.16, 17 & Pearson, p.146.
37 Bryce, p.50 'Extremely uncomfortable ...'
38 Lycett, p.165 'In Jamaica Ian ...' & Parker, p.23.
39 Pearson, p.254 'Then in the ...'

40 Harling, pp.109–110 'In this manner …'
41 Pearson, p.193 'She had first …'
42 Harling, p.128 'Her gift for …'
43 Parker, p.15 'Ann continued her …'
44 Bryce, p.84 'Violet Cummings …'
45 Pearson, p.195 'After this first …'
46 Parker, p.38 'This visit was …'& Mark Amory, *The Letters of Ann Fleming*, p.79.
47 Pearson, p.201 'He entered marriage …'
48 Parker, p.128 'On around 17 February …' & Amory p.108.
49 Pearson, p.203 'James Bond was born …'
50 Lycett, pp.216–217 'In a diary fragment …'
51 Ibid, p.111 'The barges having …'
52 Harling, p.323 'Such claims were …'
53 Patrick Dalzel-Job, *From Arctic Snow to Dust of Normandy,* p.115 'One boss in …'
54 Lycett, p.128 'The event is …'
55 Pearson. P.129 'The trouble …'
56 Andrew Cook, *Ace of Spies,* p.10 'The idea of writing …' He met Leonard Mosley who later wrote spy stories himself.
57 John Le Carre, *Call for the Dead'.* Foreword to the Lamplighter edition 1992 & Adam Sisman *John le Carre the Biography,* p.208.
58 Pearson, p.208 'This was what …'
59 Ian Fleming, *The Man with the Golden Gun,* p.10 'James Bond frowned …'
60 Ian Fleming, *On Her Majesty's …* ' p.190 'These thoughts ran …'
61 Ian Fleming, *For Your Eyes Only,* p.60 'I knew the Havelocks …'
62 Pearson, pp.123–124 'To the young …' & Fleming, *Casino,* p.134 'Well in the last …'
63 Franz von Papen, *Franz von Papen Memoirs,* pp.485–489 'Amid these minor …'
64 Ian Fleming, *Casino,* p.37 'When a ghastly …'
65 Ian Fleming, *Thunderball,* p.153 'The drinks came …'
66 Ian Fleming, *Casino,* p.11 'It does not …'
67 Ibid, p.181 'This is 007 …'
68 Duff Hart-Davis, *Peter Fleming,* p.329 'Once again …'
69 Pearson, p.216.
70 Fergus Fleming, p.23 Letter to Jonathan Cape 29/10/1952.
71 Sisman, p.233 'Leaman's outburst …'
72 Ian Fleming, *Casino,* p.54 'A fine wine …' & p.30 'Bond's car was …'
73 Ibid, p.79 'Bond swallowed …'
74 Miller, p.89 'As Popov arrived …'
75 Pearson, p.215 'In his contact …'
76 Miller, p.252 'Until the publication …'
77 Beesly, pp.335–336 'I had been …'
78 Commonwealth War Graves Commission. Latin inscription from the Roman poet Horace strict translation; *It is sweet and proper to die for the fatherland.*

Bibliography

Ian Fleming's Bond Books, all published by Jonathan Cape

Casino Royale (1953)
Live and Let Die (1954)
Moonraker (1955)
Diamonds are Forever (1956)
From Russia with Love 1957)
Dr No (1958)
Goldfinger (1959)
For Your Eyes Only (1960)
Thunderball (1961)
The Spy who Loved Me (1962)
On Her Majesty's Secret Service (1963)
You Only Live Twice (1964)
The Man with the Golden Gun (1965)
Octopussy and the Living Daylights (1966)

Children's Fiction

Chitty-Chitty-Bang-Bang (1964–65)

Non-Fiction

The Diamond Smugglers (1957)
Thrilling Cities (1963)

Books

Alonso, Eduardo Martinez, *Adventures of a Doctor* (Robert Hale, 1962)
Andrew, Christopher, *Secret Service* (Heinemann, 1985)
_____, *The Defence of the Realm, The Authorised History of MI5* (Allan Lane, 2009)
Ashley, Rod, *Wolfram Wars: Exposing The Secret Battle in Portugal* (Dark River, 2016)
Bassett, Richard, *Hitler's Spy Chief* (Weidenfeld & Nicolson, 2005)
Beadle, Major J. C. *The Light Blue Lanyard* (Square one, 1992)
Beesly, Patrick, *Very Special Admiral* (Hamish Hamilton, 1980)
Beevor, Antony, *The Spanish Civil War* (Cassell, 1999)

Beevor, Jack, *SOE: Recollections and Reflections 1940–45* (Bodley Head, 1981)

Bloch, Michael, *Operation Willi* (Weidenfeld & Nicolson, 1984)

Bragadin, Commander Marc Antonio, *The Italian Navy in World War II* (United States Naval Institute, 1957)

Borghese, J. Valerio, *Italian Naval Commandos in World War II* (United States Naval Institute, 1995)

Bowles Paul, *Too Far from Home; The Selected Writings of Paul Bowles* (Ecco Press 1991)

———, *Points in Time: Tales from Morocco* (Harper Perennial 2006)

Brown, Anthony Cave, *Body Guard of Lies* (Harper & Row, 1975)

———, *'C' The Secret life of Sir Stewart Menzies Spymaster to Winston Churchill* (Macmillan, 1989)

Brissaud, Andre, *The Biography of Admiral Canaris* (Grosset & Dunlap, 1974)

Bryce, Ivar, *You Only Live Once* (Weidenfeld & Nicolson, 1975)

Bullock, Alan, *Hitler a Study in Tyranny* (Oldham Press, 1953)

Burdick, Charles B, *German Military Strategy and Spain* (Syracuse University Press, 1968)

Burns, Jimmy, *Papa Spy* (Bloomsbury, 2009)

Cabell, Craig, *Ian Fleming's Secret War* (Pen & Sword, 2008)

Churchill, Winston. S. *The Second World War Vol 2: Their Finest Hour* (Reprint Society,1949)

———, *The Second World War Vol 3: The Grand Alliance* (Reprint Society, 1950)

Ciano, Count Galeazzo, *Ciano's Diary 1937–1943* (Methuen & Co, 1952)

Colvin, Ian, *Canaris Chief of Intelligence* (George Mann, 1973)

———, *Flight 777: The Mystery of Leslie Howard* (Pen & Sword, 2013)

Cook, Andrew, *Ace of Spies* (The History Press, 2002)

Cox, Geoffrey, *Countdown to War* (William Kiber, 1988)

Cuningham. A. B. *A Sailors Odyssey* (Hutchinson, 1951)

Dalzel-Job, Patrick, *From Arctic Snow to Dust of Normandy* (Nead-An-Eoin, 1992)

Danchev, Alex, *Establishing the Anglo-American Alliance* (Brassey's, 1990)

Day, Peter, *Franco's Friends* (Biteback Publishing, 2011)

Deakin, F. W. *The Brutal Friendship* (Weidenfeld & Nicolson, 1962)

Durrell, Lawrence, *Balthazar* (Faber & Faber, 1958)

Eccles, David & Sybil, *By Safe Hand Letters of David & Sybil Eccles 1939–42* (Bodley Head, 1983)

Farago, Ladislas, *The Game of the Foxes* (David McKay, 1971)

Fleming, Fergus, *The Man with the Golden Typewriter* (Bloomsbury, 2015)

Fleming, Peter, *Operation Sealion* (Pan Books, 2003)

Loftis, Larry, *Into the Lions Mouth* (Berkley, 2016)

Frankland, Noble and Dowling, Christopher, (eds), *Decisive Battles of the Twentieth Century* (Sidgwick & Jackson, 1976)

Gannon, Paul, *Inside Room 40; The Codebreakers of World War I* (Ian Allan, 2010)

Harling, Robert, *Ian Fleming a Personal Memoir* (Robson, 2015)

Hart-Davis, Duff, *Man of War* (Arrow Books, 2013)

———, *Peter Fleming a Biography* (Jonathan Cape, 1974)

Harvey, Maurice, *Gibraltar* (Spellmount, 1996)

Hibbert, Christopher, *Benito Mussolini* (Reprint Society, 1962)

Hinsley. F. H, *British Intelligence in the Second World War* (HMSO, 1993)

Jeffery, Keith, *MI6: The History of the Secret Intelligence Service 1909–1949* (Bloomsbury, 2010)

Jorgensen, Christer, *Hitler's Espionage Machine* (The Lyons Press, 2004)

Kahn, David, *Hitler's Spies* (Hodder & Stoughton, 1978)

———, *The Code Breakers* (Weidenfeld & Nicolson, 1968)

La Carre, John, *The Spy Who Came in from the Cold* (Sceptre edition, 2009)

Lee, Laurie, *As I Walked out one Midsummer Morning* (Andre Deutsch, 1969)

Lochery, Neill, *Lisbon: War in the Shadows of the city of Light 1939–1945* (Public Affairs, 2011)

Lycett, Andrew, *Ian Fleming* (Weidenfeld & Nicolson, 1993)

Macintyre, Ben, *For Your Eyes Only: Ian Fleming and James Bond* (Bloomsbury, 2008)

_____, *Agent ZigZag* (Bloomsbury, 2007)

_____, *Operation Mincemeat* (Bloomsbury, 2010)

Masterman, J. C. *The Double-Cross System* (Folio Society, 2007)

McLachlan, Donald, *Room 39: Naval Intelligence in Action 1939–45* (Weidenfeld & Nicolson, 1968)

Miller, Russell, *Codename Tricycle* (Secker & Warburg, 2004)

Montagu, Ewen, *The Man Who Never Was* (Penguin Books, 1955)

_____, *Beyond Top Secret Ultra* (Coward, McCann & Geoghegan, 1978)

Morris, Jan. *Spain* (Faber & Faber, 1964)

Newby, Eric, *On the Shores of the Mediterranean* (Harvill Press, 1984)

Noel, Gerard, *Pius XII: The Hound of Hitler* (Continuum, 2008)

Nutting, David, (ed), *Attain by Surprise* (David Colver, 2003)

Papen, Franz von, *Memoirs* (Andre Deutsch, 1952)

Parker, Matthew, *Goldeneye: Where Bond was Born: Ian Fleming's Jamaica* (Hutchinson 2014)

Payne, Stanley G. *Franco & Hitler* (Yale University Press, 2008)

_____, *Fascism in Spain 1923–1977* (University of Wisconsin Press, 1999)

Pearson, John, *The Life of Ian Fleming* (Companion Book Club, 1966)

_____, *James Bond Biography* (Century, 2006)

Philby, Kim, *My Silent War* (Macgibbon & Kee, 1968)

Playfair, Major General I. S. O. *The Mediterranean and Middle East, Volume I* (The Naval & Military Press, 2004)

Popov, Duško, *Spy? Counterspy* (Grosset & Dunlap, 1974)

Preston, Paul, *The Spanish Holocaust* (HarperCollins, 2012)

Ramsay, David, *Blinker Hall Spymaster* (Spellmount, 2009)

Rankin, Nicolas, *Ian Flemings Commandos* (Faber & Faber, 2011)

_____, *Churchill's Wizards: The British Genius for Deception 1914–1945* (Faber & Faber 2008)

Rogers, Anthony, *Churchill's Folly* (Cassell, 2003)

Schellenberg, Walter, *The Memoirs of Hitler's spymaster* (Andre Deutsch, 2006)

Simmons, Mark, *The Battle of Matapan 1941* (Spellmount, 2011)

_____, *The Rebecca Code* (Spellmount, 2012)

_____, *Agent Cicero* (Spellmount, 2014)

Smith, Peter C. *Critical Conflict* (Pen & Sword, 2011)

Steel, Nigel & Hart, Peter, *Defeat at Gallipoli* (Macmillan, 1994)

Thomas, Hugh, *The Spanish Civil War* (Penguin, 1979)

Tremlett, Giles, *Ghosts of Spain* (Faber & Faber, 2006)

Vickers, Philip, *Finding Thoroton* (Royal Marines Historical Society, 2013)

Waller, John H. *The Unseen War in Europe* (Random House, 1996)

West, Nigel, *Historical Dictionary of Naval Intelligence* (Scarecrow Press, 2010)

_____, *GCHQ: The Secret Wireless War 1900–1986* (Weidenfeld & Nicolson, 1986)

Wigg, Richard, *Churchill and Spain* (Sussex Academic Press, 2008)

Archives

The Avalon Project, Lillian Goldman Law Library (USA)

Bundesarchiv (Germany)

Central Intelligence Agency Library (USA)

Winston Churchill Archive Cambridge (UK)
Imperial War Museum (UK)
National Archives (USA)
The National Archives KEW (UK)
Royal Navy Historical Museum (UK)
Viscount Templewood Papers Cambridge (UK)

Journals & Newspapers

Daily Telegraph
Dime Detective Magazine
The Guardian
The Peruvian Times
Sunday Times
The Times

Websites

www.commandoveterans.org
www.aboutourrock.com

Index